Oklahoma Populism, the first book-length study of the People's party in Oklahoma, closely examines the origins, character, accomplishments, and demise of the party that, even more than the Socialist party, constituted a major electoral force in Oklahoma's early years.

Because the major sectional groups settling Oklahoma—southern and plains farmers—were the primary source of electoral support for the national Populist movement, this book provides a view of American Populism in microcosm as well as a detailed account of third-party insurgency during Oklahoma's territorial years.

The author's extensive researches provide the basis for lively and detailed accounts of territorial politics and local debates on major national issues of the day. He traces the origins of the Oklahoma People's party to the south-Kansas egalitarian movements of the 1880s and substantiates the Populists' claim that their movement transcended sectionalism (always an important factor in Oklahoma politics) and posed a major threat to mainstream-party control of the territorial government.

Using quantitative methods, the author also identifies a significant political division between cosmopolitan areas of the territory and the hinterlands. Railhead towns and their environs, settled by entrepreneurs, became havens for laissez-faire capitalism, social Darwinism, and mainstream-party support. The hinterlands, meanwhile, were settled by homesteaders more likely to uphold an egalitarian, agrarian tradition rooted in the nation's founding. The exploitative

(*Continued on back flap*)

Oklahoma Populism

Oklahoma Populism:

A History of the People's Party in the Oklahoma Territory

By WORTH ROBERT MILLER

University of Oklahoma Press :
Norman and London

Library of Congress Cataloging-in-Publication Data

Miller, Worth Robert, 1943–
  Oklahoma populism.

  Bibliography: p. 245
  Includes index.
  1. People's Party (Okla.)—History. 2. Populism—
Oklahoma—History. 3. Oklahoma—Politics and
government—To 1907. I. Title.
JK2374.04M54 1987   324.2766'07   87-40214
ISBN 0-8061-2072-X

Publication of this work has been made possible in part by a grant from the
Andrew W. Mellon Foundation.

Contents

Illustrations

Maps

Preface

John Steinbeck's 1939 novel, *The Grapes of Wrath*, imprinted upon the American psyche a vision of Oklahoma as a land of grinding rural poverty and hopelessness. For many observers the region that late-nineteenth-century boosters had labeled the "land of the fair God" became the epitome of how exploitative capitalism had perverted the American dream. Instead of the affluence and independence Boomer elements had promised, privation and tenancy became the lot of most Oklahoma farmers in the first half of the twentieth century. The victims frequently turned to political reform, sometimes even radicalism, in response to their fate.

In recent years historians Garin Burbank and James R. Green have examined the Oklahoma Socialist party in detail, verifying the strength and vitality of this movement where it reached the apex of its electoral support in America. Little, however, has appeared on the Oklahoma Socialists' agrarian predecessor, the People's, or Populist, party. Populists addressed many of the same issues Socialists would later agitate. Socialist solutions sometimes even mirrored those of the Populists, most notably in advocating government ownership of railroads, telephones, and telegraphs. It is doubtful, however, that more than a handful of Oklahoma Populists had even heard of Karl Marx before 1900. Their world view came from a thoroughly American egalitarian tradition that stretched back through the democracy of Jefferson, Jackson, and Lincoln to the ideology of the American Revolution. Because Populism had its intellectual roots in such a time-honored American tradition, its appeal far exceeded that of the Socialists. Only at the very peak of the Socialist party's popularity, in 1914, did it receive a share of the Oklahoma vote comparable to that of the Populist party in its weakest showing.[1]

This is the first book-length treatment of the People's party in the Oklahoma Territory.[2] I undertook this study primarily to fill the near void that exists on the subject of Populism in the literature on Oklahoma reform and radicalism. Previous scholars apparently have shied away from the subject because of the dearth of pertinent manuscript collections. Almost all major studies of American Populism, however, rely heavily on the era's highly partisan press for information. Oklahoma scholars are truly blessed on this account with one of the finest local newspaper collections in the nation. I was able to supplement the information gleaned from this source with materials from several relatively unused manuscript collections and with quantification.

I present this study as both local history and an examination of the national Populist movement in microcosm. Both plains and southern farmers, the two most important sources of the third party's electoral strength, settled the Oklahoma Territory beginning in 1889. I found that Oklahoma Populism more closely resembled that of Kansas than of Texas. Kansans brought the agrarian movement to the territory in 1889, and northerners slightly outnumbered southerners in the territorial years. Yet the relative balance in numbers of natives of these two regions was closer in Oklahoma than in any other state or territory where the People's party had a significant presence. This provided me with the opportunities to test the Populists' contention that their party bridged sectionalism to address more important issues and to examine the controversy over fusion with the Democratic party in a setting where the inhabitants were not overwhelmingly either northern- or southern-born. Additionally, because Oklahoma was a territory, the president appointed its executive officers, making them relatively impervious to local pressures. Antipathy toward remotely wielded power and rejection of the era's insensitive political elite constituted two of Populism's most important themes, regardless of region.

I wish to express my sincere thanks to H. Wayne Morgan for his advice and encouragement during the course this study. John S. Ezell, Paul W. Glad, Arrell M. Gibson, and John W. Wood also provided me with valuable suggestions. Any errors contained in this study, of course, are my sole responsibility.

A number of other people were quite helpful in the development of this book. Jack Haley, formerly of the Western History Collections at the University of Oklahoma, graciously led me to possible sources of information. The cooperation of Barbara Mathis, at the Herbert Priestly Resources Center of the University of Oklahoma School of Journalism and Mass Communications, was particularly important to viewing the relevant Oklahoma newspapers. Newspapers not available there were viewed at the Oklahoma Historical Society in Oklahoma City. A variety of people too numerous to mention at both the Oklahoma Historical Society and the Oklahoma Department of Libraries, also in Oklahoma City, provided valuable assistance. I also made liberal use of the University of Oklahoma Computing Services Office and would particularly like to thank Tanya Stewart for her kind assistance. My special thanks also go to Michael Roark, of Southeast Missouri State University, for sharing his suggestions and birthplace data on Oklahomans. John Womack, Sr., was kind enough to provide a great deal of valuable information on Cleveland County and its people. Last, but certainly not least, I would like to extend my thanks to Merrily Cummings Ford for sharing several valuable family manuscripts concerning her grandfather Henry Vincent and great-uncle Leo Vincent.

WORTH ROBERT MILLER

College Station, Texas

Oklahoma Populism

CHAPTER ONE

Kansas Origins

For nineteenth-century Americans westward expansion was an integral part of what made their nation a land of opportunity. When the prospects for personal advancement in the East or in the old country proved meager, the hope for improvement continually led people westward. The idea of an egalitarian frontier lured those with ambition, and the vast natural resources of the American interior promised independence and even wealth to those willing to seize the opportunity. The chance to participate in building up the great American empire also afforded pioneers a status their allegedly effete eastern cousins could never hope to attain. Traditions stretching back at least to the founding of the nation made westward migration the embodiment of Americanism.

As the nineteenth century neared its end, so did the land available for settlement in America. The 1889 opening to non-Indian settlement of the two-million-acre Unassigned Lands in what is now central Oklahoma committed the federal government to a policy of bringing under cultivation the last truly arable virgin farmland in America. The process was designed to extinguish Indian claims to land set aside, supposedly in perpetuity, for their exclusive use a half century earlier. As expected, the region surrounding the Unassigned Lands quickly fell to the home-seeker's plow, and by 1901 the entire western half of present-day Oklahoma was under non-Indian control (see Map 1 for the date of each opening). Federal authorities completed the process in 1907, when they dissolved the governments of the Five Civilized Tribes in eastern Oklahoma. With the Land Run of 1889, the ten-year-old Oklahoma Boomer movement, an amalgam of

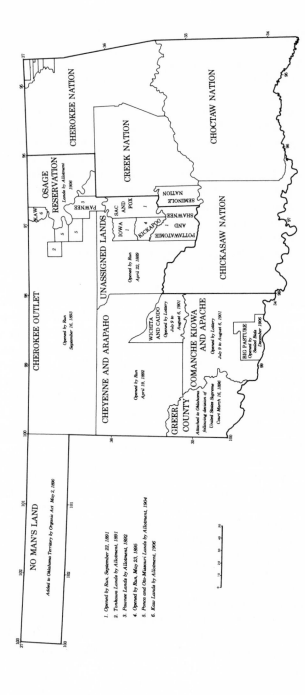

Map 1. Land openings. From *Historical Atlas of Oklahoma*, 3d ed., by John W. Morris, Charles R. Goins, and Edwin C. Mc-Reynolds (Norman: University of Oklahoma Press, 1986), Map 48.

homesteader, mercantile, and railroad interests, finally secured its entering wedge against Indian control of what it called the "Promised Land."[1]

More than any other place in the American West, Oklahoma promised to fulfill the homesteader's dream of free land. The enormous government land grants made to railroads elsewhere would not extend into the new territory. Nor would federal authorities hold back the choicest acres for sale to speculators or the already prosperous. Aside from allotments to extinguish Indian claims and plots set aside for the maintenance of public education, all of the Oklahoma Territory would be open to the homeless. Truly, Oklahoma was to be the land of the homesteader.[2]

Boomers saw Oklahoma as a panacea for all the ills of the late nineteenth century. Most Americans had already accepted the safety-valve concept of westward expansion that Frederick Jackson Turner would soon immortalize. They believed that the westward migration of excess workers would defuse the mounting labor troubles of the East. A new beginning for those ambitious enough to make the trek west would keep social mobility open and undermine the development of economic classes. New markets would boost commerce in the adjoining states and industrial production in the East. For people representing a wide variety of interests, Oklahoma provided the last best chance in America to achieve the economic independence and personal success that traditionally accompanied westward expansion.

Nature provided an idyllic setting for the April 22, 1889, opening of the Unassigned Lands. An early spring furnished the virgin plains with a luxuriant carpet of bluestem grass. The beauty of the physical setting, however, belied the seriousness, even desperation, of the participants. Federal authorities invented the land run especially for this opening. Because potential homesteaders vastly outnumbered the available claim sites, a Darwinistic struggle for the land would ensue. Only the strong and aggressive could hope to succeed. For this reason most of the homeseekers were in the springtime of their lives.

To facilitate passage to the "Promised Land," the government allowed entry to the surrounding Indian lands for a few days before the run. Most of the prospective homeseekers gathered on the northern border. The recent bust in Kansas farming ensured that northerners would constitute a majority of the new territory's population. Rail transport, for those shunning the more traditional horse or wagon, also favored the northerner. Both the Rock Island and the Santa Fe railroads entered Oklahoma from Kansas, although the former did not reach the southern boundary of the Unassigned Lands until after the run.

Settlers coming to Oklahoma in 1889 represented a wide variety of humankind: blacks and whites; northerners, southerners, and foreigners; merchants, farmers, and speculators; honest and dishonest all made the run for free land. Late-nineteenth-century America encompassed many different patterns of life and values. Rail service, which linked more and more people to the cosmopolitan world, encouraged a more uniform culture. Many in the newly settled West and the war-retarded South, however, still resided, both emotionally and physically, on the periphery of this homogenizing civilization. Because of its central location, Oklahoma became a crossroads for the various creeds found in Gilded Age America.

From the very first, observers noted the importance of the settlement patterns that Oklahoma's earliest migrants established in the cultural and political texture of the new territory. Northerners, with their Yankee traditions and Republican party sympathies, entered the territory from Kansas and settled primarily north of the Canadian River.[3] Sons and daughters of the South, with their sectional loyalties and Democratic party affections, entered the new territory from Texas and settled mostly south of the Canadian. Map 2, which shows the birthplace or race of Oklahomans in 1900, reveals this pattern. While significant regional minorities existed in every county, this North-South cleavage has dominated most considerations of partisan politics in Oklahoma since 1889.[4]

Another migration pattern the earliest settlers formed proved equally important to the cultural and political makeup of Oklahoma in the 1890s. The early migrants' choice of transportation to the "Promised Land" also produced sharply divergent culture areas. People with especially commercial orientations—bankers, lawyers, merchants, and speculators—came to Oklahoma by

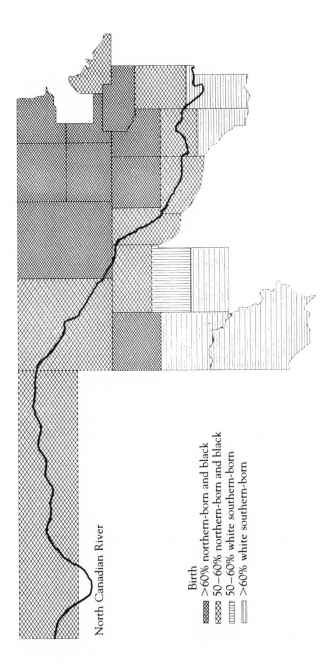

North Canadian River

Birth
▨ >60% northern-born and black
▨ 50–60% northern-born and black
▥ 50–60% white southern-born
▯ >60% white southern-born

Map 2. Birthplace or race, 1900.

rail. The cosmopolitan world's panaceas of laissez-faire capitalism, social Darwinism, and business boosterism constituted their gospel. Once in view of one of the designated townsites, they bolted for the nearest unclaimed town lot. If particularly speculative they might even try for a nearby quarter section in the hope that urban expansion would move in their direction. In these railhead enclaves seekers of the main chance entered into a cutthroat scramble for profits.

Through unrestrained competition, the intellectual spokesmen of the cosmopolitan ethos claimed, the new territory would experience sustained economic and social advance. The resultant manipulations and slick deals naturally produced the carnival atmosphere endemic to all boomtowns. An exceptionally exploitative population emerged in and around the railroad towns. Here the tooth-and-claw version of "Gilded Age enterprise" reached its apex. Because cosmopolitan Oklahoma epitomized the late nineteenth century's ruling ethos, both of the mainstream political parties received a disproportionately large share of their electoral support from the territory's railhead towns and their environs in the 1890s.[5]

One man who took the railroad to Guthrie, the new territorial capital, on opening day was Henry Vincent, the reform-minded editor of the *American Nonconformist and Kansas Industrial Liberator*. Although he went by train, his heart was with those who traveled overland to the new territory. Not only did the young editor denounce the Darwinistic nature of the land run at the time, but more than forty years later he still expressed outrage at the petty exploitations he encountered. It even cost him a nickel for a sip of water from the Cimarron River on the day after the opening.[6]

After visiting Oklahoma City, Vincent returned to Kansas reinforced in his belief that opening the new land would not be enough to solve the nation's problems. His hometown of Winfield had been a center of Boomer activity. While Vincent did not begrudge the homeseeker a new chance, he had personally refrained from the boosterism prevalent among other southern Kansas newspapers in 1889. In his own words, Vincent was an exponent of "the most ultra reform."[7] The frontier safety valve was choked with too many refugees seeking too little land. Americans, he believed, finally would be forced to face the problems that commercial and industrial development had produced.

Because of their slower mode of transportation, those who traveled to Oklahoma by horse or in a wagon filled up the quarter sections away from the railroad towns. Isolated from the cosmopolitan culture, these settlers held fast to the agrarianism of their fathers. Although no longer the self-sufficient yeomen of Jefferson's dream, agrarians still firmly believed that only through a union of equality and liberty could Americans provide for the general welfare.[8]

A variety of sources contributed to and helped define the egalitarian values of late-nineteenth-century agrarianism. Puritan communalism, which placed controls upon rampant individualism to serve community interests, first established a tradition of substantive equality among Europeans in America. Although visions of the community ideal waned with the commercialization of the colonial environment, the Great Awakening of the 1740s revived the emphasis upon human equality. The most succinct and widely recognized exposition of the cherished balance between equality and liberty to affect the nineteenth-century mind, however, came from the republican ideology of the American revolutionary period.[9]

As the intellectual heirs of the English Commonwealth and Radical Whig traditions, America's founding fathers viewed history as a never-ending battle between the forces of governmental power and personal liberty. Whig ideology predicted alternating periods of social advance and decay as the forces of liberty and power vied for dominance. The attempt of eighteenth-century European thinkers to understand the onrushing commercial revolution of their day easily influenced the founding fathers' Whiggish orientation. Enlightenment figures formed the theory that societies evolve from crude simplicity to civilized complexity through several discrete stages. By the late eighteenth century, French and Scottish writers had settled upon four successive stages of social development: hunting, pasturage, agriculture, and commerce. Each level of development occasioned a revolution in society's customs, habits, manners, and morals. The writers came to believe that while the transition from hunting and pasturage to agriculture added values of civilization to the strength and vitality of the previous stages, the advance to commercial complexity appeared to bring only corruption and decay.[10]

Eighteenth-century moralists believed that "luxury," which "left minds stupefied and bodies enervated by wallowing forever in one continual puddle of voluptuousness" corrupted societies. They laid luxury at the doorstep of the greedy and hedonistic new commercial human being. It was an easy step for the founding fathers then to perceive a difference between the virtuous character of the frugal, industrious, and temperate colonial farmer and the social malaise that luxury had brought to a refined England. In the end colonists separated themselves from the spreading cancers of the Old World and in the process institutionalized an egalitarian spirit in the American psyche.[11]

In considering the problem of establishing and maintaining a virtuous republic, the revolutionary generation focused upon the citizens' ability to maintain their liberty against the designs of those wielding power. Jeffersonians especially feared that the commercialization of society would create a mass of poverty-stricken laborers, dangerously dependent upon a privileged class of property-owning employers. For the average citizen to maintain his freedom would require the kind of economic independence that implied an egalitarian society.

Benjamin Franklin, in his "Observations Concerning the Increase of Mankind" (1751), reflected the prevalent eighteenth-century belief that population density was the force that propelled societies through their stages of development. To Franklin, commerce and manufacturing became necessary only when overpopulation drove large segments of the agrarian population off the land. As long as the land was not overcrowded, people would not be forced to give up their independence for subservience to an employer. The vast American wilderness thus provided a means for stabilizing population density and avoiding the degeneration into servile dependence that the undesirable fourth stage of development implied.[12]

Because farmers constituted the rock upon which the Republic stood, Americans developed a freehold concept of land tenure consistent with the advancement of the small farmers' interests. Included were notions that all men had a natural right to land, that contact with nature morally invigorated the farmer, and that freehold tenure was a just source of dignity and status. Agrarians believed that labor, especially in agriculture, was the only legitimate source of wealth.[13]

The concept of a classless, egalitarian society, based upon the virtues of the morally invigorated freeholder, influenced American thought throughout the nineteenth century. The antimonopoly ethos of the Jacksonian period owed much to the Jeffersonian tradition. To abolitionists the slaves' subservience and loss of the fruits of their labor violated the same egalitarian tradition. When the fledgling labor movement of the 1830s transmitted its neo-Jeffersonian ideas to the American frontier, it informed the republicanism of Abraham Lincoln, as well as a number of other late-nineteenth-century egalitarian efforts.[14]

Conflicts between economically and socially developed older sections and a regenerative, egalitarian periphery have a long tradition in America. Movements of the periphery, such as Puritanism, the Great Awakening of the 1740s, the Carolina Regulators, the American Revolution, and Radical Republicanism, each contained egalitarian strains. The long-standing Tidewater-Piedmont rivalry in the American South can be seen in the same vein. Common to the tenets of each peripheral group was a hostility to special privilege, opposition to gross inequalities in wealth, antipathy toward luxury, and a concern for human rights over those of property. The homesteader element of the Oklahoma Boomer movement and the Populist party both operated within the time honored concepts implicit in the agrarian tradition and movements of the periphery.[15]

The Oklahoma Boomer movement originated with railroad attorney Elias C. Boudinot's statement that a thorough examination of the pertinent laws and treaties showed that 14 million acres of land in the western part of the Indian Territory actually belonged in the public domain. Boudinot's announcement suggested that the land was subject to homestead settlement. Railroad interests clearly favored freight-generating farmers to the seminomadic Indians in the questioned territory. Boudinot, himself a Cherokee, favored legal action to open the region. But David L. Payne, a farmer and southern Kansas politico, quickly emerged as the on-the-scene leader of the Boomers through his advocacy of direct action. Payne took his cue from squatters, whom federal troops had earlier ejected forcibly from the Cherokee Nation. In the spring of 1880 the Boomer leader began orchestrating a series of homesteader invasions of the Indian Territory. His plan was to create a court case in which the questioned lands would be ordered open to settlement.[16]

Boomer invasions were only the most flamboyant part of Payne's plan to open Oklahoma to settlement. Ranchers actually occupied the land in question under leases with Indian tribes. To secure their removal, Boomers sent lobbyists to Washington to urge a congressional investigation of the Indian cattle leases. Payne also established a newspaper, the *Oklahoma War Chief*, early in 1883 to arouse support for Boomer efforts. Until his death in November, 1884, however, invasion was Payne's most noteworthy tool.

With Payne's death the Boomer movement gradually developed a new stance. William L. Couch, Payne's successor, led one final invasion of the Indian Territory in December, 1884. Afterward, Couch led the Boomers into a less belligerent phase. Signifying the change, the *Oklahoma War Chief* became the *Oklahoma Chief*, and in place of homesteader intrusions Boomers began lobbyist invasions of the nation's capital. Because the Republican administration of Chester A. Arthur had rebuffed the Oklahoma movement, Boomers placed great hope in the incoming Democratic administration of Grover Cleveland in 1885.[17]

The Boomers' new tactics appeared to bear fruit when the new president signed legislation authorizing government negotiations for the purchase of the questioned lands. Jubilation soon turned to anger, however, when Cleveland showed no haste in fulfilling his commitment. The appointment of Samuel Crocker, an experienced political agitator, as editor of the *Oklahoma Chief* in June, 1885, marked the end of the Boomer honeymoon with Cleveland. The new editor renamed the Oklahoma movement's mouthpiece the *Oklahoma War Chief* two months later. Crocker provides a direct link between the homesteader wing of the Boomer movement and the Oklahoma People's party. He would lead the Oklahoma third-party ticket in 1890.[18]

The Crocker family migrated from their native England to the rustic simplicity of the American frontier shortly after young Samuel's birth in 1845. Eventually the family settled in south-western Iowa, where the elder Crocker took up farming and stock raising. Soon Crocker's father opened a general store, leaving his children to manage the farm. Such responsibilities kept the future Boomer leader's formal schooling to a minimum.[19]

Crocker permanently crippled his left arm as a child. While the injury kept him out of the Civil War, his domineering and sometimes sadistic father found it insufficient reason to train young Samuel in any less arduous profession than farming. These childhood experiences did leave a mark on Crocker's personality. Throughout his adult life he empathized with those he believed to be hard-working but oppressed underdogs.[20]

Samuel Crocker set out on his own in his late teens. He worked at a variety of jobs until he saved enough money to open his own general store. Keenly aware of his lack of education, Crocker also became a voracious reader. Permanent residence, involvement in a relatively secure profession, and exposure to political economy through his reading soon led the young store-keeper into political activism. His favorite works were those of the vehemently anticorporate abolitionist, Amasa Walker. Speechmaking, writing, and eventually editing his own news-paper brought Crocker to the center of Iowa's Antimonopoly and Greenback movements.[21]

Greenback monetary theory fit conveniently into the late-nineteenth-century agrarians' ideology. An integral part of the American freehold concept was the belief that labor was the only valid source of wealth. Agrarians contended that because value rested in production alone, money simply measured how much work one had accomplished. It needed only government fiat, not metal with intrinsic value, to be good. These ideas received spe-cial affection on the debt-ridden frontier of the Great Plains after the panic of 1873 began an accelerated deflation of commodity prices. By the end of the Greenback era, Crocker's attacks on accumulators, speculators, and the pretensions of the wealthy gained him the nickname of "Iowa's Political Agitator."[22]

With the eclipse of the Greenback party in the election of 1884, Samuel Crocker decided to cast his fortunes with a new crusade, the Oklahoma Boomer movement. In the early months of 1885 he organized a small band of homesteaders and joined Payne's Oklahoma Colony in southern Kansas.[23]

Because Boomers focused upon cattlemen's occupation of the questioned territory, Crocker stepped into a farmer-rancher rivalry that was as old as the West. Historian Edward Everett Dale, himself a former cowboy, once drew an analogy between ranching and the feudal society of medieval Europe that presents a revealing insight into the homesteaders' view of ranchers. Like every other man on horseback, Dale contended, the cowboy considered himself superior to the man who walked. He was a knight, a chevalier, a ritter, or a caballero. Those who walked were timid men of limited vision—in short, peasants. By the 1880s, America's greatest ranchmen occupied ranges larger than the fiefdoms of many German princes. Their riders were every bit as numerous as the men-at-arms of a medieval baron. The rancher's brand was the counterpart of the feudal lord's coat of arms. His ranch house frequently served the same purpose as a medieval castle. From it the rancher dispensed rewards, justice, and a gracious hospitality. If the cow country offered the modern knight no tilt or tournament, the rodeo provided an appropriate alternative. In short, the culture of the cattle kingdom was everything the egalitarian farmer feared and hated. The "cattle baron" and his hirelings easily conjured up in the homesteader's mind the vision of swaggering pseudoaristocrats bent upon diverting the advance of American republicanism.[24]

Samuel Crocker's commitment to the Boomer cause required no great shift in his political orientation. The intrigues cattlemen perpetrated upon Indian leaders to secure grazing rights in the Indian Territory frequently resembled those "of various European nations to gain or widen a sphere of influence among the savage peoples of Africa," according to Dale.[25] To secure exclusive use of the Cherokee Outlet, ranchers even formed the restrictionist Cherokee Livestock Association. Boomers charged that the secretary of the interior promoted a beef monopoly by sanctioning the ill-gotten cattle leases in return for lavish political contributions. A corrupted commercial system combined with the hunting (Indians) and pasturage (ranchers) stages of social development to destroy the advances in civilization that agrarians had achieved.[26]

The ascension of Samuel Crocker to the editorship of the *Oklahoma War Chief* marked the beginning of a broader reformist orientation of the paper. The *War Chief's* owner gave his editor a free hand in attacking national banks, government bonds, railroads, and the tariff, in addition to the homesteader's natural enemy, land syndicates. As the outgoing editor, S. J. Zerger, wrote, "Monopoly will be handled with ungloved hands in all of its branches." Crocker promised to "send the poison arrow of death into the heart of Master Monopoly." Included on the *War Chief's* revised masthead were calls for universal suffrage and a federally controlled currency.[27]

In partisan politics the Boomer movement developed a definite preference for the Democratic party early in the 1880s. David L. Payne had served in the Kansas legislature as a Democrat. A Democratic-Greenbacker fusion had elected Sidney Clarke, the Boomer Colony's best-known Washington lobbyist, speaker of the Kansas house. Samuel Crocker had campaigned for the Iowa Democratic-Greenbacker-Antimonopoly fusion in 1884 and promised a return engagement for 1886. Spirits in Payne's Oklahoma Colony were never higher than when Sidney Clarke and pro-Boomer Congressman James B. Weaver of Iowa received an encouraging interview with President Grover Cleveland early in 1885. When the president failed to follow through on legislation authorizing negotiations for Indian lands, however, or on the attorney general's decision that the Indian cattle leases were invalid, the Boomer movement quickly turned against the new administration.[28]

In July, 1885, Cleveland responded to the Oklahoma Colony's criticism by issuing sixty-eight warrants charging Boomer leaders with treason. Samuel Crocker was the most prominent agitator arrested. Rather than post bail, the *War Chief* editor chose to publicize his martyrdom by giving interviews from what he labeled the "American Bastille." From his cell Crocker dramatically charged that a "dangerous aristocracy" controlled government, bringing the time near "when toiling industry would be enslaved, incarcerated, and even shot down for asserting the rights of free men."[29]

Samuel Crocker found it no coincidence that "English and Scotch Dudes" made up a significant part of the robber-baron class. He charged that while such "aristocratic enemies" received privileges that the government refused to grant to "honest, homeseeking American citizens," they would overthrow America's democratic institutions tomorrow if they could. Had not English landlords already legislated Ireland into "starvation's early grave?" Crocker asked.[30]

Jeffersonians feared that the prostration of agriculture would jeopardize American institutions. That farm poverty would bring about a subservient underclass of workers in its wake never seemed truer to late-nineteenth-century egalitarians than in their own time. Government officials who supported cattle barons over homesteaders not only favored an indolent Europe and an effete East over the industrious West but also unfairly discriminated between capital and labor. According to Samuel Crocker, a corrupt government placed accumulators above producers in the battle between those who fought "to hold the fruits of their labor" and those who sought "to steal them by law."[31] Not surprisingly, in addition to his Boomer activities Samuel Crocker also became an organizer for the Knights of Labor, the largest producer-oriented labor organization of the era.

In conjunction with his membership in the Knights of Labor, Samuel Crocker let slip the rumor that he might "organize a people's party, . . . put a full ticket into the field and knock the brains of Democracy out."[32] Knights membership enjoyed an unparalleled growth during the mid-1880s, and Crocker, along with many other members, saw the union as a political organization. The order had supported the Greenback party in 1880.[33]

In an 1886 speech giving the Knights' official "Declaration of Principles," the union's Washington lobbyist, Ralph Beaumont, committed the organization to securing to "the wage worker the

The law condemns the man or woman. Who steals a goose from off the common.

But turns the greater villain loose. Who steals the common from the goose

Populists drew insight from a number of preindustrial traditions. This poem, originally a response to the English enclosure movement, was centuries old by the 1890s. From the *Guthrie Oklahoma Representative*, January 5, 1895.

full enjoyment of the wealth they create." Specifically, the union pledged itself to support health-and-safety legislation; the eight-hour day; the nationalization of railroads, telephones, and telegraphs; the abolition of child and convict labor; greenbacks; silver; a postal-savings system; and preserving the public domain for actual settlers. In January, 1886, the Knights of Labor specifically endorsed the Oklahoma Boomer movement. In a categorization that would be repeated in the Populist Omaha platform of 1892, Beaumont labeled the major issues agitating labor as land, transportation, and finance. Notably, Ralph Beaumont would lead the Oklahoma Populist ticket in 1894.[34]

In a sense the Knights of Labor were a product of the failure of the frontier to act as a safety valve and cure industrial ills. As great accumulations of wealth, with their inevitable corollary of exploitation, emerged, the Knights advocated a "cooperative in-

dustrial system" in which each man would remain independent
by becoming his own employer. In this way Jeffersonian values
were applied to the newly emerging industrial setting. Knights
envisioned a future in which the frontier safety valve was no
longer necessary for the maintenance of an independent citizenry. The exceptionally activist southern Kansas Knights movement drew Henry and Leo Vincent, who would play a crucial role
in founding the Kansas People's party, to the area. From these origins the Oklahoma third-party movement would also take root.[35]

Henry and Leo Vincent's reform heritage stretched back
through the Greenback and Radical Republican movements in
the United States to the Chartist and abolitionist agitation of England in the person of the Vincents' father, James, Sr. The Vincents' grandfather had been the Congregationalist minister of
Deal, Kent County, England, from 1808 until his death in 1848.
James Vincent, Sr., briefly succeeded to his father's pastorate before migrating to America in November, 1848. Of the "strictest
Puritan stock," Vincent came to the United States at the behest
of an English antislavery society to stump the Old Northwest in
the cause of human freedom. He met his wife, Mary Sheldon,
the daughter of a presiding elder of the Methodist church, while
continuing his theological studies at Oberlin College, in Ohio.
In 1855 the Vincent family set out for "Bleeding Kansas" to do its
part to make the territory free. The family ran out of money in
Tabor, a colony of former Oberlin residents in southwestern
Iowa, and decided to settle there. Four of the five Vincent children who survived infancy were born in Tabor. Growing up in a
religiously oriented college town on John Brown's Underground
Railroad, the Vincent boys naturally became engrossed in the
nineteenth-century reform tradition.[36]

In their midteens, Henry and Leo acquired a small printing
press which served as a diversion from the routine of farm life. At
first they printed calling cards for local college boys. Their father,
a longtime contributor to various reform journals, soon talked
the boys into publishing a weekly newspaper. The first edition of
the *American Nonconformist*, with James Vincent, Sr., as editor
and Henry and Leo Vincent as publishers and proprietors, appeared in July, 1879. The elder Vincent identified his paper as "a

weekly Anti-slavery Journal devoted to the cause of emancipation from slavery to bond-holders and railroad corporations." The *Nonconformist* would be passionately Antimonopoly and Greenbacker in its political orientation.[37]

As the "traveling missionary," or solicitor, Leo built up a list of about sixteen hundred subscribers in Iowa and its surrounding states before the move to Kansas in 1886. Much of the paper's growth resulted from young Leo's facility for charming railroad officers into giving him free passes in spite of the paper's stridently antirailroad orientation. This enabled Leo to attend reform gatherings throughout the region.[38]

As the Iowa economy turned downward in the mid-1880s, Leo raised the issue of relocating to the booming economy of south-central Kansas. He had discovered Winfield as a hotbed of Knights of Labor sentiment on one of his trips. With the move, James, Sr., who remained in Iowa, gave up his editorship to Henry, and Leo became the firm's business manager. A year later brother Cuthbert joined the staff as "traveling missionary." Despite his retirement from the editorship, the elder Vincent continued to supply a steady stream of articles on what he called his "third anti-slavery struggle." Prophetically, he feared this one would be "the most hopeless of all."[39]

It was in their maiden edition from Winfield that the Vincent brothers announced that their policy would be to advocate "the most ultra reform." Their first great journalistic cause after moving to Winfield was to defend the "Haymarket Riot Anarchists." The *Nonconformist's* sharp tone soon led the local courthouse elite to label the newcomers anarchists themselves.[40]

The Vincents' stridence almost certainly emanated from their devoutly religious upbringing. Bible reading and prayer services were daily affairs in the Vincent household when Henry and Leo were children. As former schoolteachers, the Vincent parents educated their own sons largely without recourse to public facilities. Because their father's life "was not given over to the one purpose of making money," the Vincent brothers easily accepted a strong moralism. Labeled an "idealistic country saver," Henry Vincent explained that "we never learned even to try to curry favor."[41] They were not, however, typical Bible thumpers. In

Henry's words they were "working-class, shirt-sleeve, non-church-going men . . . but without vices." Even their bitterest enemies conceded that the Vincents led morally upright personal lives.[42]

In Winfield the Vincents expanded their operations to include a speaker's bureau and the printing of patent insides, which reprinted political editorials, for smaller papers in Kansas and its adjoining states. This expansion paralleled the shift by the Knights of Labor toward direct political action in the wake of the Great Southwest Railroad Strike of 1886. Grover Cleveland's use of the militia to break this strike caused a spectacular rise in political activity among laborers. In 1886 local labor parties polled 68,000 votes in New York City, 25,000 in Chicago, and a clear majority of the vote in a three-way race in Milwaukee. The next year the National Industrial Union Conference met in Cincinnati and organized the Union Labor party. In Kansas the Vincents embraced the new party, which placed them at the center of the maelstrom. The Union Labor party succeeded in electing its candidate for sheriff in Cowley County (Winfield) in 1887.[43]

As the *Nonconformist* became recognized as a propagator of the political change sweeping Kansas, the Vincents "became targets for all manner of Tory propaganda," in the words of Leo Vincent.[44] Two events hindered the reform effort's 1888 Kansas campaign. First, the Republican party exposed the constitution, oaths of office, and rituals of a mysterious organization called the National Order of Videttes. This apparently was a secret Union Labor party auxiliary formed to prevent fusion with other parties. GOP spokesmen labeled the group anarchist because its oath pledged members "to sacrifice their bodies to the just vengeance of their comrades should they fail to obey the commands or keep the secrets of the order."[45] The Vincents' defense of the Haymarket bombing anarchists lent credence to Republican charges.[46]

The second damaging event of the 1888 Kansas campaign was the explosion of a bomb in the home of a Coffeyville express agent. After receiving the package containing the bomb, the agent carried it home, planning to drop it off at the railway station on his way to work the next day. As Henry Vincent later explained: "Anarchists and bombs were sometimes associated.

What better than to find an infernal machine on our premises! But it didn't get as far as Winfield."[47] In 1891 the Kansas House of Representatives, which the People's party controlled, forced a congressional investigation of the incident, but it proved inconclusive. The person who sent the package was never identified.[48] The Vincents' arch rival, Edwin P. Greer, editor of the Republican *Winfield Courier*, charged the bombing to the Videttes.

The GOP buried the Union Labor party at the polls in the 1888 Kansas election. Still, the Vincents had reason for hope. Thirty-one percent of the party's national vote came from Kansas alone.[49] A major part of its success must be credited to the downturn of farming on the Great Plains in the late 1880s. Unusually abundant rains in the middle years of the decade caused farmers to move too far west. During the boom times speculators ran up the price of farmland exorbitantly. Then, in 1887, drought struck. Kansans, who had raised 31 million bushels of wheat in 1882, managed only 10 million in 1888. Reduced production should have raised farm prices, but a bumper crop on the other side of the world caused just the opposite effect. Between 1888 and 1892 half the population of western Kansas was forced to move. Many of these refugees migrated to Oklahoma, providing a ready clientele for agrarian insurgency in the new territory.

Debt was the crucial issue on the high plains in the late 1880s. In the four years after the drought began, unpaid debts caused eleven thousand foreclosures in Kansas. Meanwhile, interest rates for debt-plagued settlers soared. The farmers' anger naturally turned toward bankers and the "money conspiracy" they represented. Union Laborites lost no opportunity to tell farmers that corrupt legislation caused the deflation that made their chances of getting out of debt remote.

In an address before the Kansas State Historical Society in 1904, William F. Rightmire, an associate editor of the *Nonconformist* in the late 1880s, gave his version of how the People's party in Kansas was founded. In December, 1888, Vidette leaders met in Wichita to form the State Reform Association and "select some existing organization, or to organize a new one, into whose ranks the reformers and farmers and laborers of Kansas could be enlisted as members." They chose the Southern Farmers' Alli-

ance, which Rightmire claimed "embodied every tenet of the
platform on which the Union Labor party had waged its campaign." Believing that the word "labor" in the existing party's
name posed too great an obstacle in recruiting farmers, the Vincents readily agreed to the strategy. Rightmire claimed that he,
Cuthbert Vincent, and John R. Rogers (later the Populist governor of Washington state) traveled to Texas for initiation into the
alliance and brought it back to Kansas. Rightmire was incorrect,
at least on the date of the Vidette meeting. That same month
more than one hundred alliancemen, representing five thousand
members in nine counties of Kansas, met to organize the state
organization of the Southern Alliance.[50] It is clear, however, that
Union Labor leaders latched on to the alliance for overtly political purposes at a very early date. In Kansas the Southern Alliance always emphasized both economic cooperation and direct
political action.[51]

Benjamin H. Clover, a former Greenbacker and Union Labor
man, became the first president of the Southern Farmers' Alliance in Kansas. As a third-party sympathizer he worked closely
with the State Reform Association. In an Independence Day,
1889, article entitled "Objects of the Alliance," Clover made
clear the political orientation of his order. He called upon alliance members to "close up the ranks, stand shoulder to shoulder,
and clear the decks of all old hindering prejudices, party strifes,
or sectional animosities . . . [to save] the America given into our
keeping by the Revolutionary Fathers, with the admonition that
'eternal vigilance is the price of liberty.'"[52] Farmers and laborers,
he continued, were all that stood between the "monarchy of
wealth, on the one hand, and the anarchy of poverty, on the
other."[53]

Clover and the Vincents believed that the "educational program" of the Farmers' Alliance was its most valuable function.
Henry and Leo Vincent contended that "a people united by agitation could not be depended upon to remain united long. . . .
agitation puts in motion a force which once started can not be
controlled, and in its energy destroys all." Education, on the
other hand, created an "intelligent cohesibility." If the educator's
lessons were correct, uniformity of belief among producers would

WASHINGTON'S PROPHECY FULFILLED.

THRONE OF PLUTOCRACY.
INJUNCTION. JENKINISM. TRUST

SHAM DEMOCRACY.		SHAM REPUBLICANISM.
SPECIAL PRIVILEGES.	TAX THE POOR.	INTEREST.
FOREIGN GOLD — AT 14%.	NO TAX ON THE RICH.	LAND MONOPOLY.
WALL STREET.	TAX ON NECESSITIES.	RENT.
MONOPOLIST.	NO TAX ON LUXURIES.	
AMENDMENTS TO CONSTITUTION.		BALLOT FRAUDS.
LAND GRANTS TO ALIENS.		PUBLIC PLUNDER.

Populists considered great wealth a threat to America's republican institutions. This cartoon suggests the intellectual tradition from which they drew such notions. From the *Norman Peoples Voice*, March 31, 1894.

create a concert of action that could "be depended upon to resist the diverting effects of both prejudice and passion." Alliance leaders believed that once farmers began rationally inquiring into their collective situation their thoughts would begin "boring holes into the ship of corruption."[54] As the *Populist Handbook for Kansas* for 1891 read, "A thoroughly informed people cannot be enslaved, nor kept in slavery long after they become educated."[55]

In line with the Vincents' views on "education" they also claimed that only those whose principles or interests inclined them to work on behalf of the producer class should be trusted. In an article on political farming, alliance leaders told their members that "it is just as essential for you to send men of your own kind to represent you as it is for you to go out and cultivate your own crops." Politicians swayed only by fear of losing office were especially to be distrusted.[56]

The growth of the Vincents' new reform vehicle eventually led them to challenge the Union Labor party's national leadership for the direction of the party. While farm organization membership claims in the late nineteenth and early twentieth centuries were notoriously unreliable, there clearly was a vast expansion of the Kansas alliance between its December, 1888, organizational meeting and the 1890 election. Alliance sources claimed 21,000 Kansas farmers in April, 1889, 100,000 a year later, and 145,000 just before the general election of 1890.[57]

In apparent ignorance of the Kansas phenomenon, the Union Labor party's national leadership proposed to advance the cause of labor through a fusion with the Prohibition party. This was obviously a desperation move, which Kansas party members believed was not only unnecessary but "a compromise with the narrowest kind of fanaticism." Such an obnoxious connection could ruin efforts to bring alliancemen into the third party.[58]

The Vincents' terminology in denouncing the proposed merger revealed the strong political orientation of the Kansas alliance in its infancy as well as their commitment to the alliance as a reform vehicle in early 1889. Although the new farm order offered an advanced organizational technique, the Vincents would always consider the alliance and the People's party to be simply union laborism under another name.[59]

The immediate catalyst for founding the People's party in Kansas occurred in the alliance's home county of Cowley in 1889. In the Republican county convention that year, courthouse clique leaders Ed Greer and William P. Hackney directed the proceedings in such a heavy-handed manner that leading farmer representatives walked out. That night the rebellious Republican delegates met and decided to suggest a "People's Ticket" to Democratic and Union Labor party leadership.

Two weeks later Democratic and Union Labor executive committees met in separate conferences to plan strategy. The Democrats suggested a division of the ticket. When Union Laborites declined, the two parties decided to appoint special committees to come up with an acceptable plan. The committee for the Union Labor party consisted of former Republican Ed Green, former Greenbacker Ben Clover, and former Democrat George Gardenhire. This group came up with the plan that was finally accepted. Neither party would make nominations. All elements of the anticourthouse ring would unite in a separate "People's Convention." In this way the new movement avoided the stigma of an overt fusion simply for offices. Throughout the early years of the movement, the People's party in Kansas drew supporters in relatively equal proportions from of each of the three parties of 1888.[60]

On election day, 1889, the People's party in Cowley County turned what was normally a 500-vote Republican margin into an 800-vote majority for the new party. The Cowley County "People's Movement" platform "favored such legislation as would give the producing class a just reward for their labor, favored the reduction of salaries of county officials, opposed trusts and monopoly and ring rule in politics." As news of the People's victory swept the state, inquiries on the new party's plan of action flooded the local chairman's mailbox.[61]

Two weeks after the new third party's victory, alliancemen assembled in their second state convention and reelected Ben Clover as their president. At this meeting the alliance resolved to submit its platform to the Kansas congressional delegation for delegates' approval or rejection. Only U.S. Senator Preston B. Plumb gave his unqualified approval. Alliance county presidents met in March, 1890, to adopt direct political action. Three months later members of the Southern Farmers' Alliance, the Grange, the Knights of Labor, the Farmers' Mutual Benefit Association, and single-tax clubs founded the People's party of Kansas. U.S. Senator John J. Ingalls, the third party's primary target in 1890, had stated that "the purification of politics is an iridescent dream." The new party set out to prove him wrong. On election day, 1890, the People's party carried five of the state's seven congressional races and elected 91 men to the 125-member Kansas House of Representatives. When the state legislature convened in 1891 it selected farm journal editor William A. Peffer to succeed Ingalls in the U.S. Senate.[62]

George Gardenhire, a member of the Union Labor party committee that called the original People's Convention in Cowley County, provides the direct link between the Oklahoma Populist movement and its Kansas origins. At the time he helped found the third party in Kansas, Gardenhire was the official alliance organizer for the Oklahoma Territory.[63]

Gardenhire was born eighteen miles south of Chattanooga, Tennessee, in 1841, and moved to Arkansas with his parents as a child. Serving with the Confederate cavalry during the Civil War, the future alliance leader then moved on to southern Kansas in 1869. After some hardship Gardenhire eventually built up a successful farming and stock-raising business. In April, 1889, he left his Kansas farm in the care of a son and made the run to Oklahoma. Along with many other Cowley County emigrants, Gardenhire settled in Payne County, which became the earliest stronghold of Oklahoma Populism.[64] Following the pattern set in Kansas, he organized alliances throughout the northern section of the new territory. By April, 1890, the alliance claimed one hundred local chapters in Oklahoma. At this point Gardenhire began holding "People's" conventions.

The People's party in the Oklahoma Territory originated in the southern Kansas egalitarian movements of the 1880s. Throughout the Gilded Age successive waves of reform ferment kept alive a long-standing dissenter tradition with roots that went back at least to the founding of the United States. This tradition, as later refined and synthesized in the democracy of Jefferson, Jackson, and Lincoln, provided late-nineteenth-century agrarians with a value system they believed was valid for all times and situations.

With the materialization of standards that came with Gilded Age development, this egalitarian tradition came under severe attack. But the newer cosmopolitan ethos did not engross all Americans by the 1890s. In fact, the downturn of the farm economy in the late 1880s brought the newer ideology itself under criticism and caused many to reaffirm their faith in the old verities.

The Southern Farmers' Alliance in Kansas and Oklahoma provided a vehicle for mobilizing both third-party veterans and old-party farmers who were losing faith in the panaceas of the Gilded Age's cosmopolitan spokesmen. By reaffirming the values of the Jeffersonian tradition, while at the same time introducing those concerned about the direction of American civilization to the possibilities of independent political action, the alliance provided a valuable stepping stone from old party to new. The process was not one of persuading angry farmers to accept a strange, new ideology but rather one of persuading men and women to accept the verities of the agrarian tradition and embrace Populism as its most logical next expression.

CHAPTER TWO

Organizing the
Oklahoma Territory

The beauty and immensity of the two-million-acre Unassigned Lands district that black and white migrants began to settle on the afternoon of April 22, 1889, lent credence to the Boomers' claim that this was the "Promised Land." Climate combined with terrain to reinforce the impression that infinite possibilities were at hand. Because the Oklahoma District lay almost totally within the rich grasslands of the redbed plains, a luxurious mantle of bluestem grass stretched as far as the eye could see, justly fascinating the early settlers with its height and density and frequently obscuring from sight all but the tops of their wagons. Since it was springtime, the grass appeared as an ocean of light green when viewed from upwind, darker when one faced the breeze. As the seasons changed, the grass would turn reddish brown and then purple and copper. Small trees and shrubs broke the vastness of the rolling prairie only along creek beds.

Nature seemed to do everything on a grand scale in the new territory. When the newcomer asked a veteran of the plains if the wind blew this way all of the time, the reply might well have been, "Hell no! It blows the other way about half the time."[1]

With few topographical features to slow it, the wind always seemed strong on the plains. When cold fronts from the continental climate of the interior collided with humid, semitropical air masses moving north from the Gulf of Mexico, gentle breezes could suddenly become violent cyclones. At such times shallow streams would turn into raging torrents, sweeping away everything in their path. Immigrants from the wooded East found Oklahoma both invigorating and frightening at the same time.

Oklahoma pioneers found little natural growth that was of use in building their new homes. The small trees and shrubs native to the area were suitable only for brush arbors and firewood. For the first few days after the run, tents littered the landscape. Industrious lumber and hardware merchants, however, booked every available space on the trains serving the new territory. Small frame buildings sprang up in and around railhead towns. In the hinterland, dugouts and sod houses sufficed until the products of civilization arrived, a process that took several years in some places.

Throughout the 1890s newspaper editors, land company agents, and other assorted boosters promoted Oklahoma as an agricultural paradise. According to one paper the new territory was "the greatest wheat country in the world . . . with corn bigger than saw logs and watermelons bigger than whales."[2] Best of all, virtually the entire district was open to homestead entry. By the end of July, 1889, 5,764 settlers had filed claims on 903,962 acres of land. Within the next year, 7,033 more would file on another million.[3]

Not all of the filings immediately resulted in farms. The prospect of 160 free acres attracted adventurers as well as homeseekers. While as many as 125,000 people made the Run of 1889, the territorial census of June, 1890, counted only 60,416 residents. A claimant had five years to build a dwelling and plant a crop. For some the opportunity to make a quick profit by selling a relinquishment or to hold a plot for speculative gain proved more appealing than the hard work involved in building a farm.[4]

Most of the Oklahoma District's early settlers endured significant hardships during their first two years in the territory. The April land run put them on the land too late to plant crops for 1889. Having little capital, they existed on stocked provisions of coffee, dried beans, and flour. Most were able to supplement this sparse diet with wild fruits and game. Farmers passed their time building houses, digging wells, and breaking ground for the 1890 planting. Unfortunately, a severe drought in 1890 caused farmers to spend their second year in the territory without income from their crops. Some decided to return to older sections of the country. Most, however, were determined to stick with this last chance to own their own farm. Eventually Congress and the territorial legislature, when it finally met in late 1890, provided aid to the destitute. To develop their new markets, railroads also provided wheat seed at cost to settlers in 1890.[5]

Because the land run caused men to begin as competitors, the choicest quarter sections frequently went to bullies. Some rightful claimants dared not even set foot on their own land until the courts had ordered an interloper to leave. Recourse to litigation, however, could be expensive and time consuming. Frequently adventurers filed on lands to which they clearly had no legal claim in the hope of extorting a few dollars from the rightful homesteader. Almost certainly, lawyers reaped the greatest harvest of 1889. One settler found "more of them to the acre than anything else" in Oklahoma. Many of Oklahoma's pioneers lost their farms for want of legal fees to defend them.[6]

If claim jumpers and drought plagued hinterland Oklahomans, town dwellers faced problems of their own. Perhaps one-third of the migrants to the new territory tied their fortunes to one of the numerous townsites that sprang up in 1889. Companies organized in Kansas before the run founded the cities of El Reno, Oklahoma City, and Stillwater. At Oklahoma City the Seminole Townsite Company counted many of the Payne Colony leaders among its number.[7] The Santa Fe Railroad provided them with surveying jobs near the townsite on the day of the opening. At noon they quit their jobs, stepped off the right of way, and claimed every important town lot and quarter section in sight. Before legitimate claimants could arrive on the scene, the "Sooners" had even filed patents on their claims in Guthrie. They then proceeded to rush municipal elections and called in the army to safeguard their "rights." Other townsites suffered similar, although less outrageous, manipulations. By the end of 1889 even Republican papers were denouncing speculation in town lots as hindering material progress.[8]

A territorial government capable of harnessing such exploitations was clearly the remedy that early Oklahomans needed. Because legislation opening the new lands had been a rider to an Indian appropriations bill, it had failed to provide for such institutions. Oklahomans were forced to live for more than a year

TWILIGHT AMUSEMENT IN OKLAHOMA

A Populist's view of the Darwinistic land run that opened Oklahoma to non-Indian settlement on April 22, 1889. From the *American Nonconformist* (Winfield, Kansas), May 2, 1889.

with no legally constituted government. For this reason a large backlog of problems would face the first legislature.

The experiences of pioneers in Oklahoma's first year of settlement seemed to validate the pessimistic attitude of Henry and Leo Vincent's *American Nonconformist*. As they had predicted, hardship and privation were the lot of many. Even before the opening the *Nonconformist* had asked, "What difference does it make how fine a country is . . . if it requires money [to meet] expenses while raising a crop." Only a few Oklahomans had enough money to be called capitalists. Financiers in adjoining states, of course, were quite eager to establish banking facilities in the new territory. The Vincents noted that "the shorter route to possession [of the land] is that of loaning money, while the poor fellows who do the work, develop the farms, will be in five years just where thousands of Kansas farmers are—not in the ring, but 'in the soup.'"[9] Opening the Oklahoma Territory to non-Indian settlement, the Vincents claimed, would benefit railroad stockholders more than the producers who worked the land under the present system. To meet expenses, homesteaders would be forced to mortgage their household furniture at rates of interest that would be considered usurious elsewhere. As destitute farmers defaulted, a disproportionate number of secondhand shops would emerge. One 1898 estimate valued the household furniture of the average Oklahoma family at $7.50.[10]

To impose familiar patterns upon the unsettled situation in 1889, provisional grass-roots institutions sprang up in every locality. Municipal officers were elected, and in many cases franchises were even let, without legal sanction. As prospects for early congressional action waned, the city of Guthrie even called a convention to establish a provisional territorial government. Once the government was in operation, Congress might recognize it, the organizers calculated. Oklahoma City refused to participate and, in a fit of jealousy, called its own convention at Frisco. This town rivalry destroyed hopes for a provisional government and foreboded a town conflict that continued throughout the territorial period.[11]

Finally, on May 2, 1890, Congress passed the Organic Act for Oklahoma. It gave legal sanction to the provisional municipal governments and established a territorial government. As with previous territories, the act was based on the Ordinance of 1787. It provided for six counties, with seats of government set at Guthrie, Oklahoma City, Norman, El Reno, Kingfisher, and Stillwater. The Public Land Strip (the present-day Panhandle) was attached as a seventh county. Legislative power was vested in an appointed governor and an elected two-house legislature. After the governor commissioned a census and apportioned the territory, the newly elected legislators would draw up a legal code and locate territorial institutions. In addition to the governor, the president would also appoint a territorial secretary, the judiciary, an attorney general, and a marshal. Each would serve for four years. Because homesteads were not taxed until claims were proved (usually after five years), Congress would appropriate general expenses for the territory. In the early years only railroads and personal property were taxed.[12]

Most descriptions of Oklahoma politics in the 1890s emphasize the primacy of factionalism over an interest in ideology or issues. Such factionalism was endemic to all western territories in their early years. Local concerns, particularly the placement of townsites, territorial institutions, and railroads, overshadowed other considerations. Because most settlers were concerned primarily with the mundane chores of building a house or starting a farm, those who had tangible interests to promote normally emerged as the earliest political activists. Town boosters, newspaper editors, lawyers, and other professionals, whose careers depended upon the growth of their communities, took the lead. Frontier businessmen, eager to speed local development, also became prominent. Each realized that control of government would bestow economic privileges. Only with time would enduring combinations emerge and stable political alignments dominate.[13]

While early Oklahoma politics was primarily factional, there are two caveats. First, because the land was opened to white settlement later than other western territories, the rise of the People's party in Oklahoma coincided with the earliest years of settlement. This lent a more ideological orientation to territorial politics. Second, because of its geographic location, the balance between northerners and southerners was closer in the Oklahoma Territory than it was in most of the West. Their respective regions, for instance, would be known as "Jayhawker Country" and "Little Dixie."

The presence of significant sectional minorities in each of the Oklahoma Territory's counties tended to transform conflicting views about education, materialism, race, and a hundred other cultural values into party commitment. While internal squabbles plagued both the Democratic and Republican parties in the 1890s, those who cooperated with the opposition risked being labeled sectional traitors. Less than a generation after Reconstruction, such a tag could devastate a politician's career. Although Democrats and Republicans might work arm in arm to promote community development, partisan feelings in the Gilded Age were far too strong to be sidetracked for long.

In the late nineteenth century, politics constituted one of the average American's favorite pastimes. Men prided themselves on participating in the great democratic experiment that others in the most advanced nations of Europe could only dream about.[14]

Politics also provided a regular source of entertainment, featuring some of the era's most popular heroes and villains. Between 1856 and 1896 no race for the presidency polled less than 70 percent of the eligible voters. Although the Civil War was a quarter century in the past, and Reconstruction had ended thirteen years before, issues of race and the proper role of the government were still far from settled by 1890. Industrialization raised the question of the government's role in a democratic society to an even higher level in the late nineteenth century.

As the party of union during the Civil War, the inheritor of the Hamilton-Clay economic tradition, and the repository of white Anglo-Saxon Protestant cultural values, the Republican party identified itself as the purveyor of nationalism and morality in the Gilded Age. Although the period from 1876 to 1896 was actually one of party equilibrium, Republicans seemed to be in control most of the time. Their national orientation caused the GOP to develop far more leaders of national standing than their opponents.

The Republican party was the party of "big government" in the Gilded Age. The Hamilton-Clay tradition of government intervention to promote development defined the party's economic program in this era. As northerners tired of Reconstruction in the 1870s, GOP leaders embraced the protective tariff as the party's premier issue. Spokesmen successfully identified it with patriotism and prosperity. They claimed the tariff would sever the bonds of English economic domination and help bind the various sections of the United States into a fully integrated national economy. Appropriations for internal improvements in the tradition of Hamilton and Clay also formed a prominent part of the Republican program for national growth in the late nineteenth century.

In addition to its economic program, the party could also use its big-government orientation to promote pietistic cultural values. Party professionals generally, however, understood the perils of moral authoritarianism in a culturally heterogeneous nation and rarely went beyond paying lip service to the slogans of prohibition and blue laws. To face the problems arising from industrialization, the GOP promoted moderate doses of railroad regulation, civil service, and currency reform. The tariff, however, remained the party's most effective and most unifying issue in the Gilded Age.[15]

While the GOP was the party of nationalism and WASP culture in Gilded Age America, the Democratic party firmly committed itself to decentralization, limited government, and racism. More a loose coalition of out-groups than a national party, Democrats failed to develop national leaders or policies in the late nineteenth century. Theirs was primarily a party of negativism.[16] As inheritors of the Jefferson-Jackson tradition of small government and antipathy toward privilege, Democrats appealed most to those who were ill at ease with the course of national development. Republican policies seemed to subvert the immutable laws of nature or impede the right to cultural heterogeneity. In contrast to the Republican's nationalistic orientation, Democrats focused on the individual or, at best, on the ethnic-sectional group.

In their common opposition to Republican policies, Democrats and third-party advocates frequently found an affinity for each other. They generally stood together on little more than their opposition to a common foe during the Populist era. Many Democrats, to a greater degree than they cared to believe, actually betrayed much of their Jeffersonian past by accepting large portions of the late-nineteenth-century panaceas of laissez-faire capitalism and social Darwinism.[17] Once engaged in fusion, Democratic foot-dragging on positive reforms inevitably led to recriminations within the Populist movement over affiliation with the older party. While the phrase "keep in the middle of the road," meaning no fusion with either of the old parties, is most closely associated with the Populist infighting of the mid- and late-1890s, it actually appeared in the recriminations surrounding the defeat of the Union Labor party in 1888 and may be older than that.[18]

If Gilded Age Americans believed politics was important, they also perceived a significant difference between parties. Ticket splitting in this period was rare. For this reason, weaning Democrats and Republicans away from their old party loyalties was not easy for third-party organizers. Third-party leaders found the Southern Farmers' Alliance to be an ingenious vehicle for mobilizing support behind the People's party. It provided political education in an outwardly nonpartisan setting which served as a halfway station between old party and new.

Beginning in the autumn of 1889, George Gardenhire, the alliance organizer for the Oklahoma Territory, traveled across the new land preaching the gospel of economic and political cooperation to farmers. Alliance organizers met with greatest success wherever former Kansans were numerous and established more than one hundred locals by April, 1890. Some migrants had probably joined the farm order before locating in the new territory.[19]

Contact with Kansas was a prime factor in the political development of the Oklahoma Territory. George Gardenhire constantly traveled back and forth between his new home and "the state" in his official capacity as an alliance organizer. Most Oklahoma newspapers, whatever their political affiliation, received most of their national and regional news from Kansas sources.[20] To provide a brief summary of territorial news, many papers simply reprinted the *Wichita Eagle*'s Oklahoma column. Patent insides, which supplied national news and party propaganda, normally were printed in Kansas and then mailed to editors in Oklahoma. The *American Nonconformist* and the *Industrial Free Press*, both of Winfield, Kansas, provided such services for alliance, and later for People's party, organs in the Oklahoma Territory.

Even where southerners predominated, Oklahomans received their alliance news from Kansas, not Texas. The first newspaper to serve alliance members in the southern part of Oklahoma, for instance, was the *Territorial Topic*, of Purcell. Actually located across the South Canadian River, in the Chickasaw Nation, the *Topic* began publication in August, 1889, and became the official alliance paper of the Indian Territory in May, 1890. In March, 1890, the *Topic* began carrying the alliance column of the *Industrial Free Press*.

While it is impossible to determine exactly what proportions of economic and political appeal Gardenhire and his alliance subordinates used in organizing the Oklahoma Territory, their efforts probably mirrored those of Kansas organizers.[21] Alliance sources claimed that trusts, pools, rings, and other unnatural amalgamations subverted the natural laws of commerce and thus robbed the laborers of their due. To gain their favored position, the rich and powerful enthroned themselves behind a network of "vicious" legislation. This, alliance leaders stated, forced the masses to combine in self-defense. Although alliancemen might find the drawing of class lines distasteful, those with similar interests to protect were told they must join hands to ward off the avarice of exploiters. Cooperation among producers, they claimed, was only "business upon Christian principles."[22]

Fundamental to the alliance appeal was the belief that the rich and powerful had not attained their positions legitimately. Agrarians forever considered immense fortunes suspect. They believed that no one person could accumulate vast fortunes solely through individual labor. Exploitation or manipulation must come into play. The injustices of the rich, not the envy of the poor, caused such cataclysms as the French Revolution, third-party agitators proclaimed.[23] Alliance organizers portrayed the concentration of wealth in apocalyptic terms. According to one, the greed of the "Robber Kings" brought about an underclass of the poverty-stricken that was "contrary to the germs of our republican institutions and contrary to the laws of God." God had created all men equal, and only man could impoverish man.[24]

Because concentration of wealth created economic classes, alliance leaders advised their followers to "do more voting for the right men and less petitioning to the wrong men."[25] Even the era's patriot statesmen seemed to "believe in that ridiculous and utterly absurd doctrine that made some to be poor and some to be rich, thereby justifying the robbery of the people by the money kings."[26] Lawyers, bankers, and millionaires could be trusted to legislate only in their own interests. Rather than focus only upon the symptoms of their distress, alliance leaders challenged producers to go to the heart of their problems and overthrow their rulers. This pattern of antielitism is common to all so-called "populistic" movements.

Dissatisfaction among alliance members with the Republican party in Kansas and Oklahoma gave Democrats much cause for jubilation in the early years of territorial government. They

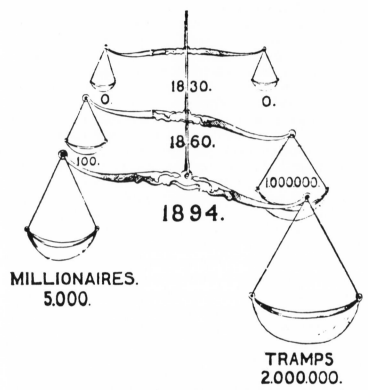

TRAMPS AND MILLIONAIRES.

Some Figures Which go to Prove that Created Millionaires Create Poverty

Manipulation caused America's degeneration from its egalitarian past, according to this cartoon. From the *Kingfisher Reformer*, May 3, 1894.

hoped for a permanent realignment in favor of their party. According to the Democratic *Oklahoma City Evening Gazette*, the alliance seemed to "amalgamate with Democracy" quite naturally. Alliance resolutions calling for tax reduction and open markets seemed to be drawn directly from Democratic platforms.[27] Indian Territory alliance leader H. C. Randolph, who influenced alliancemen in Cleveland and Oklahoma counties in the early territorial years, acknowledged that farmers must seek relief through legislation but proclaimed the order strictly nonpartisan. As in other southern states, Randolph advised pushing the dominant party to nominate alliance representatives for office. This attitude, plus fear of breaking with the white-man's party and the late organization of the Farmers' Alliance in southern-dominated sections of the territory, retarded the growth of the People's party in southern Oklahoma.[28]

According to popular legend the People's party was the first to organize in the Oklahoma Territory. This is true only if the Farmers' Alliance is considered a political party from its inception. In a literal sense the People's party was the last to organize in the new land. Republicans took the lead in formally organizing a political party in Oklahoma. Guthrie Republicans formed a local GOP club in mid-November, 1889. In anticipation of formal territorial government, and thus patronage appointments, Republicans met in Oklahoma City on January 17, 1890, to establish a territorial organization. Democrats followed with their own territorial convention, held in Oklahoma City on March 11, 1890. Alliance members, under the guidance of George Gardenhire, organized the first third-party local at Stillwater on March 29, 1890, after both of the older parties had perfected territorial organizations.[29]

Representatives of the Farmers' Alliance, Knights of Labor, and Union Labor party met in Oklahoma City on June 21, 1890, to found the territorial organization of the People's party. They subsequently set August 13, 1890, as the date of the third party's first territorial convention. They were caught by surprise a week after their June meeting, when Governor George W. Steele proclaimed August 5, 1890, a full week before the third party's proposed convention, as election day for the territorial legislature.[30]

George W. Steele was born on December 13, 1839, near Connorsville, Indiana. After graduating from Ohio Wesleyan University, Steele served as a lieutenant colonel under General William Tecumseh Sherman during the Civil War. In 1865 he returned to Indiana to take up banking and the practice of law. Steele's appointment as governor of Oklahoma resulted from his personal friendship with President Benjamin Harrison.[31]

Steele proved to be a highly partisan Republican during his

tenure as governor of the Oklahoma Territory. To reduce minority representation he made each county an at-large election district.[32] At first Republican party slates did not extend into the countryside. It looked to third-party activists as though the GOP planned to pack the legislature with urbanites. Steele, however, intervened and forced fellow Republicans to include some rural representation on GOP tickets. Still, Populists were not amused. Without at-large districts they would almost certainly carry some rural districts in Kingfisher and Logan counties, where former Kansans were numerous (see map 3 for county names). As it stood, they would carry only Payne County. At one point Steele even attempted to have Payne County annexed to Logan County.[33] In addition Steele denied the third party representation on election boards. Populist leaders believed the governor's early election date was designed to "steal a march on the labor movement."[34] The third party founded its official territorial newspaper, the *Oklahoma State Journal*, of Guthrie, only in the wake of the governor's election proclamation.[35]

Considering its lack of preparation, the People's party fared quite well in Oklahoma's first territorial election. Populists swept Payne County, electing a councillor (senator) and three representatives. Not wishing to give the GOP the opportunity to win a plurality, local Democrats declined to field candidates. Their newspaper, the *Payne Hawk*, warmly supported the Populist ticket.[36] The third party came in second behind the Republican ticket in Logan and Kingfisher counties. Because the People's party made its nominations only a week before the election in the latter county, its showing was remarkable.[37] In Canadian County the three parties ran so close that names scratched from party ballots proved decisive. Each of the three parties elected a representative. The two council seats, however, went to the Democrats.[38] The People's party was not on the ticket in Beaver County (the Panhandle), and it polled only minuscule totals in Cleveland and Oklahoma counties. Although Democrats and Republicans made separate nominations in Oklahoma County, cleavages emanating from the Seminole Townsite Company scandal obliterated party lines. Their opponents printed a mixed ticket, which carried the election. Democrats elected two coun-

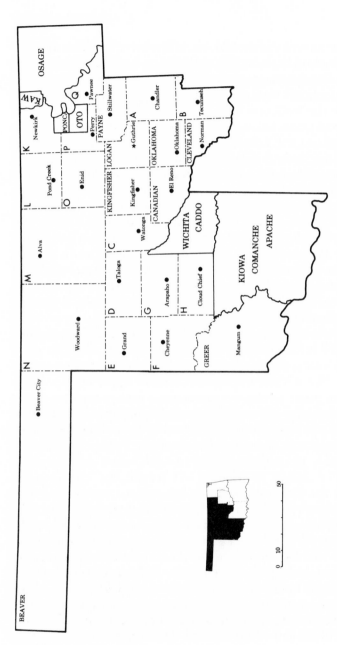

Map 3. Oklahoma Territory, 1890–1899. From *Historical Atlas of Oklahoma*, 3d ed., by John W. Morris, Charles R. Goins, and Edwin C. McReynolds (Norman: University of Oklahoma Press, 1986), Map 54.

cillors and three representatives, while Republicans elected one councillor and two representatives.[39]

Unfortunately, territorywide returns for the August 5 election do not survive. On August 23, 1890, however, Oklahomans returned to the polls to replace an at-large representative who had died. Returns from this election are available and presumably resemble the first poll.[40]

An analysis of the August, 1890, vote shows that Populists drew overwhelmingly from northern-born Oklahomans, especially those born in the Midwest (see appendix A, table 1). Democrats, on the other hand, drew overwhelmingly from white, southern voters. While Democrats frequently carried such northern states as Indiana and New York in the Gilded Age, few northern Democrats appear to have made the trek to Oklahoma. Republicans split the northern vote with Populists, showing more strength among northeastern-born voters than among midwesterners. Northeasterners were more likely to live in urban areas, to have commercial skills, and to have connections back East. The GOP also received strong support from the Oklahoma Territory's black and European-born settlers, who also were more likely to reside in or near urban areas. Most foreign-born voters came to the new territory by way of the North.[41]

As suggested in the Populist party's protest over Governor Steele's decision to hold at-large elections in each county, there appears to have been a significant rural-urban cleavage between third- and old-party voters in northern-dominated counties. Unfortunately, no precinct-level returns for the legislative races could be found. Township (precinct) returns for the November race for delegate to the U.S. Congress, however, are available (see appendix A, table A-2). Although turnout dropped because of voter fatigue and the actions of the territorial legislature then in session, these returns are still useful. Populists show a strong rural vote in northern-dominated Kingfisher and Logan counties, while the mainstream parties in this region are quite urban. The third-party vote in southern-dominated Cleveland County was minuscule and came primarily from northerners who settled in the railhead towns of Moore and Norman.

Oklahoma voters in 1890 largely remained loyal to the party with which they had affiliated before coming to the new land. Although economic conditions in the Oklahoma Territory were reputedly conducive to the growth of Populism, the third party came in last on election day. At-large districts and early elections were only part of the reason. Economic conditions only caused voters to consider their plight. It would take time to educate and organize non-Kansans before they would become an integral part of the People's party in the Oklahoma Territory.

CHAPTER THREE

The First Legislature, 1890

At 2 p.m. on Wednesday, August 27, 1890, the first legislature of the Oklahoma Territory convened in the McKennon Opera House in Guthrie. The 1890 assembly was certainly the most exciting, and probably the most outrageous, legislature to sit during territorial days. In employing all of the fine and confusing points of parliamentary strategy, the first assembly was unexcelled.[1] The quality of representation ran the full spectrum of possibilities. Some men were seasoned legislators. Others were novices but earnest in their endeavors. The suggestion of one editor that "a vast horde of political fiends who have been run through the political fanning mills of other states, dumped with the chaff, and by adverse winds settled quite promiscuously over Oklahoma" also held much credence.[2]

Nominally, Republicans held a majority in both houses of the 1890 legislature. The council (senate) consisted of six Republicans, five Democrats, one People's party representative, and an Independent, who generally voted with the GOP. In the house of representatives there were fourteen Republicans, eight Democrats, and four Populists. Local considerations, however, split the GOP from the very beginning. Before the legislature adjourned on Christmas Eve, a variety of combines had developed, some reputedly held together only by the cohesive qualities of hard cash. Mobs even sought vengeance upon unpopular solons, and conspiracy theories proliferated without end. At one point a legislator even drew his revolver to obtain recognition from the speaker of the house. By the end of the session the suggestion of Representative Samuel Clark of Payne County that the legislature deserved a spanking met with general acclaim.[3]

Two primary tasks faced legislators in August, 1890: drafting a legal code and placing the territorial institutions, particularly the permanent capital. Placement of the capital quickly emerged as the prime concern. The Guthrie–Oklahoma City rivalry that had emerged in 1889 was aggravated when Congress designated Guthrie as the site of the first legislature. Located thirty-one miles north of Oklahoma City, in Logan County, Guthrie was overwhelmingly Republican. Northerners, blacks, and European-born Oklahomans constituted more than 80 percent of its population. Logan County had the largest concentration of blacks in the territory.[4] It was the only county in the territory to return a GOP majority in each of the territorial elections.[5] Although northerners constituted a modest plurality in Oklahoma City, its black population was only half that of Guthrie. Democrats (the Free Silver party in 1896) carried Oklahoma County in five of the eight territorial elections. Both cities were on the Santa Fe rail line and claimed populations of approximately ten thousand in 1890.[6]

Although the People's party contingent constituted the smallest group in the assembly, the Guthrie–Oklahoma City rivalry offered third-party legislators an opportunity to exercise far more influence than the size of their delegation warranted. Because Governor Steele's at-large districts had caused Populists to be grossly underrepresented in the legislature, they found a certain poetic justice in their situation.[7]

George Gardenhire, the Southern Farmers' Alliance organizer for Oklahoma, became the pivotal figure in forming the coalition that would control the legislature. Payne County voters elected him to the council, and he arrived in Guthrie on the afternoon before the assembly was scheduled to convene. Republican legislators from Logan and Kingfisher counties had already formed a coalition committed to keeping the capital in Guthrie and distributing the remaining public institutions among the other counties. Because Payne County did not have rail service in 1890, the coalition considered it ineligible for the location of public facilities and assumed that the Payne County delegation would acquiesce in the arrangement because of Guthrie's proximity to its constituents.

Upon his arrival in Guthrie, Gardenhire called upon Republican leaders and demanded the agricultural college for his county. He threatened to deal with the Democrats if not appeased. GOP leaders counted on popular opinion in Payne County to keep Gardenhire and company in line and called his bluff.[8] Democrats, on the other hand, were most eager to treat with the People's party. They conceded the agricultural college, organization of both houses of the legislature, and some patronage in the assembly to the third-party contingent.[9]

Even with the fusion of Democratic and Populist legislators, Oklahoma City forces still constituted a minority in both houses. To control the assembly, Oklahoma County's two Republican representatives and one Republican councillor also had to be won over to the combine. When the legislature convened, the council elected Gardenhire temporary president and elevated Republican Joseph Post to the temporary speaker's position. Both houses then immediately adjourned. That evening the Oklahoma County delegation traveled to Oklahoma City to confer with local Republicans. They returned to Guthrie the next day with orders to vote with the Democrats if necessary to obtain the capital for Oklahoma City. To secure the vote of Councillor James L. Brown, who hailed from Edmond, located in Oklahoma County halfway between Guthrie and Oklahoma City, Democrats promised his town the Oklahoma Normal College.[10]

Two days after the assembly first convened, legislators permanently organized both houses. The names of George Gardenhire and William A. McCartney were placed in nomination for president of the council. McCartney, a native of Pennsylvania who had moved to Kansas in 1882, was a lawyer and an experienced parliamentarian. Because he was also a former employee of southern Kansas political boss Bill Hackney, Populists could rejoice doubly in Gardenhire's seven-to-six victory.

In the house the names of Arthur N. Daniels, the Industrial Union (Populist) representative from Canadian County, and William H. Merten of Guthrie were put forward for the post of speaker. Daniels was born in Galesberg, Illinois, in 1860. A graduate of Knox College, he had read law and was admitted to the Illinois bar in 1883. He served two terms in the Illinois legislature before immigrating to Minnesota and then Oklahoma. Merten, a Guthrie merchant of Prussian heritage, was born in Delaware County, Iowa, in 1845. A veteran of the Union army, he spent a year in college and served twice in the Iowa legislature. Daniels won the speaker's chair by a fourteen-to-twelve margin. Although both Gardenhire and Daniels proved adequate in their posts, both acknowledged the better qualifications of their opponents in their acceptance speeches. Qualifications, of course, had nothing to do with the issues.[11]

James L. Brown of Edmond introduced the bill that would move the capital to Oklahoma City. Council Bill no. 7 breezed through committee and passed the upper chamber in mid-September. It then sailed through the house committee. When it reached the floor of the house, however, trouble struck. Republicans successfully rammed through an amendment delaying the date for moving the capital by a week. Although seemingly innocuous, this action required a new vote on the bill in the council. Democrat William Adair of Cleveland County and third-party legislators Ira N. Terrill and Samuel Clark, both of Payne County, deserted the Oklahoma City combine to vote for the amendment. Suspecting a plot, Democrats sought out Councillor Charles Grimmer of Beaver County (the Panhandle) and promised to build a railroad from Oklahoma City to Beaver City if he would join their ranks. When the council met the next morning, Gardenhire also deserted the Oklahoma City ranks and voted with the Republicans to reject the new amendment and thus kill the bill. Grimmer, as Oklahoma City forces had planned, made up the difference, and the amendment passed.

In defending his actions, Terrill cited both the belief that Democrats could not deliver the promised agricultural college and the sentiment among his constituents against locating the capital in Oklahoma City.[12] The eccentricity and sometimes outrageous behavior of Representative Terrill accounted for a good part of the first legislature's notoriety as a circus sideshow. Ira N. Terrill was born in Clark County, Illinois, in 1843. He moved to Kansas in 1874 and joined the Oklahoma Boomer movement in the early 1880s. He accompanied William Couch on the Boomers' last raid into Oklahoma in 1883.[13] Terrill professed to be a lawyer and certainly created general aggravation with his litigious interruptions in the house. It was Terrill who demanded recognition from the speaker at gunpoint in the most colorful event of the first legislature.[14]

When Council Bill no. 7 passed the council as amended, Terrill moved to reconsider the measure in the house. As with the original amendment, the motion carried, fifteen to eleven. Democrats, however, considered this illegal, since the bill had been reconsidered earlier.[15] Representative Peery of Oklahoma County enrolled the bill and presented it to the speaker for his signature. Daniels signed the bill and sent it to the council for Gardenhire's signature. The council had adjourned, leaving Peery in possession of the bill. He then narrowly escaped an angry Guthrie mob bent upon destroying the bill and perhaps its bearer as well.[16]

The next morning Daniels asked the council to return the bill, stating that he had signed it under a misapprehension. In the end the Oklahoma City crowd concluded a deal with the Kingfisher County delegation to secure passage of the bill. If the governor vetoed it, Democrats promised that they would support a measure placing the capital in Kingfisher. In the council, Republicans secured Gardenhire's signature by threatening impeachment. After all of the plots, counterplots, and midnight conferences, Governor Steele vetoed the Oklahoma City capital bill, stating that he saw no compelling reason to move the capital. Democrats fulfilled their promise to support a Kingfisher capital bill, but the governor vetoed it as well.[17]

With the exception of James L. Mathews, third-party representatives deserted the Oklahoma City combine on the capital issue. Rumors of bribery naturally emerged. One Democratic paper even labeled the council president "Guthrie-hire." While Gardenhire showed no signs of sudden wealth then or later, he did express doubt at the time about the ability, and perhaps the commitment, of Democrats to deliver the agricultural college to Payne County. Without Republican support, the governor might simply veto the college bill.[18]

In late September, as the capital issue raged, Councillor Charles Brown of Guthrie offered a substitute to the Oklahoma

City capital bill that would locate the capital in Guthrie and the agricultural college in Stillwater. The entire Guthrie coalition voted for it. Although Gardenhire remained loyal in his commitment to the Oklahoma City crowd at that time, it appears to have influenced Populists in their later actions. The Oklahoma City–sponsored House Bill no. 30, which located the agricultural college in Stillwater, passed the house on a partisan vote on September 24. To ensure the loyalty of the People's party on the capital issue, however, the Oklahoma City contingent then refused to bring the measure up for consideration in the council. Because public opinion in Payne County favored Guthrie, legislators Gardenhire, Terrill, and Clark went over to the Guthrie combine. Democrats recognized the third-party defection when Terrill and Clark voted for the Republican amendment to the capital bill in the house. Before the council acted upon the house amendment, Councillor James Brown of Oklahoma County quickly brought the agricultural college bill up for consideration in an attempt to revive the splintering Democratic-People's coalition. The bill passed unanimously as the Guthrie partisans fulfilled their new commitment and the Oklahoma City supporters attempted to retrieve their old one. Gardenhire, however, changed sides and voted with his new allies on the capital bill.[19]

Governor Steele later vetoed both Council Bill no. 7 and House Bill no. 30. While he cited political reasons in vetoing the capital bill, the governor mentioned only technical problems with the college bill. He had previously informed the legislature that federal legislation on agricultural colleges applied to territories. The assistant commissioner of the U.S. Land Office had notified him otherwise. Because the bill had been passed under false pretenses, he could not let it become law.

James L. Mathews later introduced the legislation that located the agricultural college in Payne County. Oklahoma City partisans drafted an open letter inaccurately giving Mathews sole credit for obtaining the college for Stillwater. Sixteen of the seventeen members of the Oklahoma City contingent signed it. Democratic sources contended that the governor vetoed the original bill because Populists had betrayed their colleagues in the legislature, while the Oklahoma City partisans bailed out Mathews, the only third-party legislator to remain loyal to them. George W. Steele, however, was not averse to stating partisan reasons for vetoing legislation, as he had with the capital bill. He stated no such reasons in his veto of the college bill. Of the sixteen Oklahoma City partisans who signed the open letter for Mathews, only six actually voted for the successful agricultural college bill on final passage.[20] The fact is, Guthrie supporters provided most of the votes necessary in the council, and Oklahoma City supporters did so in the house. Other than third-party representatives, no combine or party voted as a unit to place the agricultural college in Payne County.[21]

Oklahoma legislators accomplished little of substance while the capital controversy raged. At the time the governor vetoed the Oklahoma City capital bill, only two other measures had passed his desk. The first provided for the incarceration of felons and the second for badly needed aid to the destitute. Governor Steele had estimated in August that one-third of the population living away from the larger towns was in dire need of assistance. Republicans and third-party legislators supplied the votes to provide relief. As exponents of retrenchment and self-reliance, Democrats labeled the measure "federal aid to the niggers" and abstained.[22]

Because Oklahoma constituted a meeting place for northerners and southerners, race emerged early as a hot issue. Council Bill no. 2, which established the public school system, provided for segregation. It passed the upper house on a partisan vote, with the Oklahoma City combine (five Democrats, Republican Brown of Oklahoma County, and former Confederate Gardenhire) supporting it. In the house, three of the four Populists opposed segregation.[23] Eventually, Speaker Daniels came up with a compromise allowing local option on segregation. Both Daniels and the governor believed segregation to be unconstitutional but were forced to support local option as a means of securing a public school system. Green I. Currin, the only black to sit in the first legislature and a vocal exponent of integration, accepted the measure.[24]

A North-South split also emerged on the issue of adopting a legal code. Northerners generally favored the Dakota territorial statutes. Southerners, on the other hand, favored the Arkansas code, which had been tested in court and presented no problems of unconstitutionality. In addition it was the code that Congress had put into effect in the adjacent Indian lands and, thus, would present no confusion when the Oklahoma Territory annexed them. Northerners, however, had the votes. The fact that lawyers might find the simpler Dakota statutes less rewarding was particularly appealing to Populist legislators.[25]

Council Bill no. 2 allowed women the right to vote on school matters. Third-party representatives desperately attempted to get woman suffrage into the general election bill as well, but to no avail. Representative McCartney introduced the Women's Christian Temperance Union's antiliquor bill into the house, and woman suffrage became unalterably tied to it. Because there was little sympathy for prohibition in the legislature, woman suffrage also went down to defeat.[26]

The third party's attempts to secure economic legislation in the 1890 assembly generally proved ineffective. The Populist platform had denounced usury, high public salaries, and bonding for railroads and corporations. The Organic Act prohibited the latter measure. In fact, third-party legislators generally opposed all bonding. According to Representative Terrill, "The interest bearing bonds of debt-ridden Kansas [stand] as a lighthouse . . . to be heeded by wise men." He later attempted to retitle a bonding bill the "Rob the Many at the Expense of the Few Bill." Although Populist legislators in the house were able to get the legal rate of interest on bonds set at 5 percent, Speaker Daniels moved to agree with the council figure of 6 percent. As for salaries, the People's party contingent constituted the entire opposition to the general appropriations bill on final passage.[27]

Populists' only real legislative victory in the first assembly, other than securing the agricultural college for Payne County, was to sabotage the militia bill. Congress had appropriated $2,000 for the territorial militia. Populist legislators believed that the new land needed no "standing army" and successfully proposed that the appropriation be returned to the federal government.[28]

In the final weeks of the legislature, James Brown of Oklahoma County introduced and pushed through to passage a libel act that journalists generally viewed as an attempt to silence criticism of the legislature. Although most of the legislators supporting the measure were Republicans, some Democrats and Populists went along. In response to press criticism, Representative Campbell of Guthrie claimed the course of the legislature so scandalous as to make the body libel proof.[29]

Four-fifths of the legislation that the assembly passed was pushed through during the final week of the session. Lawmakers literally ripped whole sections from the statute books of other states and introduced them into the assembly in order to finish before adjournment. While most of the legislation proved applicable, sections relating to the rights, duties, and responsibilities of shipmasters, pilots, mates, and seamen proved embarrassing in a territory where the deepest body of water could be traversed on foot much of the year.[30]

Although the People's party had won unusual power considering their small numbers in the legislature, securing the agricultural college and sabotaging the militia bill were its only real victories in 1890. The circumstances surrounding the Populist legislators' course, especially on the capital issue, brought general opprobrium upon the party. People's party voters vented their disapproval in the election for delegate to the U.S. Congress, which took place while the legislature was in session.

Two delegate positions were up for election, one to finish out the current session of Congress and another for the term to begin the next January. As a peacemaking effort, Governor Steele forced Republicans to nominate David A. Harvey of Oklahoma City over Dennis Flynn of Guthrie for both terms. If Guthrie kept the capital, it was only fair for Oklahoma City to get the delegate positions, Steele reasoned. Democrats nominated real estate man Joseph G. McCoy of Kingfisher County for the long term and, realizing that coalition with the People's party was necessary to win, Populist Representative James L. Mathews for the short one. Democrats were far from united in their choice of McCoy. It took fifty-four ballots for him to obtain the nomination. For their part, People's party spokesmen found Mathews's actions in accepting the nomination disreputable.[31] The third party nominated Hiram C. Diehl and Samuel Crocker, both of Oklahoma County, for the short and long terms, respectively. Diehl was an Oklahoma City hardware merchant, and Crocker was engaged in farming and real estate at the time.

Although weak from a bout with blood poisoning, Crocker made a two-month canvass of the territory. He traveled by wagon and spoke in every county except Beaver. He repeated much of the Greenback-Labor ideology he had used in previous campaigns. His speeches were well received in most instances, but the third party's legislative scandals and the fact that Crocker was a Sooner eventually destroyed his candidacy.[32]

On election day Harvey carried every county in the territory except Cleveland. The People's party vote dropped nearly 30 percent from its showing on the August legislative ballot. In Payne County a majority of the third-party voters simply declined to participate. At their 1892 county convention, Payne County Populists even refused to seat the 1890 legislators. Thus the movement that had swept Kansas in 1890 and threatened to prove significant in the Oklahoma Territory was blunted, largely because of the failures of its leaders. The moral appeal of third-party spokesmen simply sounded hollow coming from men who made secret deals and then broke them or who were Sooners.[33]

In 1890 problems of destitution, lot jumping, and other exploitations seemed conducive to the rapid spread of a moralistic reform movement such as the People's party. Governor Steele's at-large districts and early election were designed specifically to avoid this prospect. Still, the People's party obtained power and notoriety through legislative fusion with the Democrats. If Populist legislators had acquitted themselves more nobly, the third-party movement might have spread beyond Kansas refugees more rapidly. In betraying their commitments, Populist leaders opened themselves to charges of manipulation reminiscent of the exploitations they condemned. Until new leaders and new opportunities appeared, the third party's growth in the new land would be slow and painful. In contrast to its Kansas counterpart, the People's party got off to a rocky start in the Oklahoma Territory.

CHAPTER FOUR

The Populist Response to Gilded Age Development

Late-nineteenth-century Americans lived in a world of revolutionary economic and social change. Ambitious entrepreneurs traversed the continent in search of opportunities. Railroads transported the bounty of a virgin continent to the burgeoning industrial centers of the Northeast and then returned to the hinterland with the finished products of America's growing industrial empire. Manufacturing expanded at a fantastic rate. Laborers from Europe and rural America swarmed into the growing industrial centers to tend the machines responsible for this transformation, while others settled the Great Plains and turned the region into the breadbasket of the world.

Rapid economic development brought forth a truly new America in the late nineteenth century. Between 1860 and 1890 the nation's rail network expanded five fold. Its appearance swept quiet pockets of economic and social distinctiveness out of their placid isolation. The fruits of outdated techniques, no longer secure in their isolated local markets, rapidly gave way to the products of more efficient producers elsewhere. Specialization became endemic, and life in general became more complicated. A younger, more aggressive class of entrepreneurs seized the opportunities provided by the new order and built up what seemed to be vast fortunes, thus dramatically widening the gap between rich and poor. Although the numbers of this economic elite were rather small, the press placed them in the limelight and made them appear more numerous than they actually were.[1]

Rail lines became the purveyors of homogenization in Gilded Age America. They transported the inexpensive, standardized products that replaced the more crudely fashioned creations of home industries. To purchase such treasures, of course, the consumer had to enter the money economy. Diversified family farmers, with their mules and single-blade plows, began to give way to specialized agribusinessmen, with their machinery and fertilizers. As mechanization expanded the acreage a farmer could till, land hunger became acute. The government dutifully swept the Great Plains clean of such impediments to material progress as buffalo and Indians. But as American farmers became an integral part of the world economy, the vagaries of feast or famine in Australia or the Ukraine began to affect their everyday life. While the new national economy expanded opportunities, it also limited independence.[2]

Both the South and the West retained vestiges of colonial debtor economies well into the twentieth century. In the 1890s industry in both regions remained largely extractive. The regions furnished the industrialized Northeast primarily with agricultural goods and other raw materials. Low-paid, unskilled laborers completed only the initial processing of crops and resources in these outlying regions. Finished products emanated almost exclusively from the Northeast or from abroad. The value added through manufacturing, which normally constituted the largest portion of a finished product's worth, accrued to the industrialized sections of the nation or to Europe. Declining prices for raw materials, on the other hand, prevented significant capital accumulation in the South and West. Lack of capital, poor regional markets, and few laborers skilled in the industrial arts hindered development in these regions. When investment capital from outside did materialize, it came with foreign controls, and, usually, reinvestment of profits elsewhere.[3]

As the national economy expanded, its chaotic upswings and slumps affected increasing numbers of people. Two of industrial America's three worst depressions occurred during this era.[4] Widening disparities of wealth, multiplication of economic interests within a community, impersonalization of relationships, religious differences, and ethnic heterogeneity changed the world in which Americans lived. The social results of this new industrial world emerged in bold relief. Fabulous wealth existed in the presence of abject poverty, beauty stood next to squalor, and sophistication encountered the most profound vulgarity. The new national economy brought people closer together, yet divided them as never before.

Despite the problems emerging from late-nineteenth-century development, much that was creative and welcome appeared during the Gilded Age. Industrialization provided jobs for a population that more than doubled between 1860 and 1900. Isolation and rustic crudity gave way to more varied and refined patterns of life, and a bustling inventiveness created products that eased and enriched many lives. Such positive factors, however, could not completely overshadow the dislocations caused by modernization. Emotions of hope and despair coexisted in the minds of many late-nineteenth-century Americans. Because the government opened Oklahoma to settlement in 1889, the excitement and trauma of the period were telescoped into a very few years in the new land. This concentration of development would magnify the responses of optimism and gloom, making Oklahoma a land of cultural, intellectual, and social extremes.

As a territory, Oklahoma was a ward of the nation, and residents in the new land naturally had a strong interest in national affairs. The president appointed the executive and judicial officers for the territory, and Congress would decide when and under what circumstances Oklahoma would be admitted to statehood. Government aid for building new rail lines to service the new land was desired, and territory residents also looked to Washington for fiscal support because land was tax-exempt during the early years of settlement. Oklahoma's territorial status and the fact that southerners and northerners rivaled each other for dominance in the new land gave the press reason to carry a substantial portion of national and regional news in the 1890s.

In partisan politics, the Gilded Age was a period of party equilibrium on the national level. Between 1876 and 1892 no president received a majority of the popular votes. Only twice were chief executives favored with party majorities in both houses of Congress (Republicans from 1889 to 1891 and Democrats from 1893 to 1895). Both times the mandate was sharply reversed in the next congressional race. National campaigns centered pri-

marily on the tariff, with demagogic appeals to Civil War and Reconstruction loyalties adding to the flavor of the times. Public
opinion on both of these issues favored the GOP. Democratic opposition to the tariff centered on a laissez-faire orientation toward economic policy. To win national elections, however, they
had to carry several states in the Northeast, where protection
meant prosperity. Although "waving the bloody shirt of rebellion"
proved less effective as time passed, the tactic could still turn
elections as late as the 1890s.

Because banking and currency reform, civil-service measures,
and railroad regulation divided the two closely matched parties,
professional politicians avoided them when possible. Currency
and railroad issues particularly inflamed the voters of the South
and West. The Civil War had left the South in serious financial
difficulty. The capital that had been invested in slaves before the
war had evaporated with emancipation. As late as 1900 the
South had only one bank for every 58,130 people. The national
average was one for every 16,000 people.[5] Because the Northeast, which was the more lucrative field for industrial investment, engrossed most of the nation's private capital, credit stringency and higher interest rates characterized the South and
West. These regions, which had lower purchasing power, also
suffered higher railroad rates, because railroads moved empty
freight cars into them at harvest time. They naturally passed the
added expense on to the user. With less competition in these outlying regions, long-short haul differentials also emerged. This
practice only mirrored the cosmopolitan policy of charging what
the traffic would bear.

Presaging, and most likely informing, Progressive historians'
interpretation of partisan politics in the Gilded Age as a sham
battle over insignificant or false issues, many in the South and
West charged that the dominant parties refused to address the
real problems facing the nation.[6] In a series of meetings beginning with the Ocala convention of the Southern Farmers' Alliance in December, 1890, and including the Cincinnati convention of May, 1891, and the Saint Louis convention of February,
1892, third-party advocates sought to unite all the egalitarian-
oriented reform groups of late-nineteenth-century America. The

By the National Reform Press Association

Money the Only Issue That Can Unite the North and South.

The People's party symbolically transcends sectionalism to address the money issue. From the *Kingfisher Reformer*, May 17, 1894.

new national party would address the issues that Democratic and Republican leaders avoided.[7]

More than thirteen hundred accredited delegates met in Omaha, Nebraska, in July, 1892, to nominate a national ticket and write a platform for the newly formed People's party of America. Leonidas L. Polk of North Carolina, the president of the Southern Farmers' Alliance, was expected to receive the convention's highest honor. Unfortunately, he passed away a few weeks before the convention. Federal Judge Walter Q. Gresham of Indiana, who had flirted with Populist doctrines, seemed to be the next best choice, but he declined shortly before the convention.

In the end, the presidential nomination devolved upon General James B. Weaver of Iowa, the 1880 presidential candidate of the Greenback party. As Weaver's running mate the convention chose former Confederate General James G. Field of Virginia. This blue-gray ticket of Civil War veterans symbolized the new party's attempt at rapprochement between West and South.

The presentation of the platform, rather than the nomination of candidates, provided the focal point of the Populists' 1892 national convention. As the bible of Populism, the Omaha platform fully revealed the frame of reference that third-party spokesmen used in their critique of Gilded Age America. The preamble, which Ignatius Donnelly drafted, was a catalog of late-nineteenth-century corruption and social decay. The nation, Donnelly contended, had been "brought to the verge of moral, political, and material ruin." He claimed that "corruption dominates" and that the nation was "rapidly degenerating into European conditions." According to the author, "Governmental injustice [bred] two great classes—tramps and millionaires." Donnelly ascribed this degeneration from the egalitarian past to "a vast conspiracy against mankind . . . and if not met and overthrown at once it forebodes terrible social convulsions, the destruction of civilization, or the establishment of an absolute despotism." The great issue, he proclaimed, was "whether we are to have a republic to administer." Notably, convention managers scheduled the presentation of the platform for the Fourth of July, the anniversary of the Declaration of Independence.[8]

Visions of catastrophe if contemporary relations persisted, and utopia if people would only take hold of their own destinies, were not left as uncharted territories of the mind in the literature of the 1890s. From 1888, when Edward Bellamy published *Looking Backward*, until the turn of the century, nearly two hundred novels of the cataclysmic and utopian variety flooded the American market. They represented a tidal wave of speculation about the Republic's future. Of the authors whose politics are known, more than 80 percent supported the People's party. Ignatius Donnelly's *Caesar's Column* (1890), a fictional account of the downfall of civilization, was one of the most dramatic and popular works of this genre. Next to the preamble to the Omaha platform it was his most noted work, and appearing only two years before the 1892 Populist convention, Donnelly's novel underscored the social critique found in the Omaha platform as a desperate plea for civic regeneration reminiscent of the American revolutionary period.[9]

The vision of a nationalized economy, with an army of producers equally sharing the fruits of their collective toil, provided late-nineteenth-century egalitarians with a blueprint for creating a fair society. In Kansas, the Vincent brothers vigorously promoted Bellamy's socialistic novel, offering copies for fifty cents with a year's subscription to the *American Nonconformist*. Samuel Crocker published his own utopian novel, *That Island*, in 1892, specifically for an Oklahoma readership. The work incorporated many of Bellamy's ideas.[10]

Although the Omaha platform of the People's party appeared to be a crazy quilt of unrelated, crackpot proposals, it was not a hastily assembled document. The platform was the accumulation of a half century of proposals that late-nineteenth-century egalitarians had promoted in their quest to save the America of the revolutionary fathers.[11]

Like the Union Labor party platform of 1888, the body of the Omaha platform called for reform in three major areas: land, transportation, and finance. It called for an end to land monopolization for speculative purposes and for prohibition of alien land ownership. This wording was a euphemism for suppressing the English land syndicates that Oklahoma Boomers had fought in the 1880s. Concerning transportation, the People's party adopted Bellamy's solution of nationalization. The sentiment of the convention, however, stopped short of a call for nationalizing all industries. For Populists the railroad issue was a matter of both economics and power. For a railroad to carry a ton of produce one mile in Kansas and Oklahoma cost 27.8 percent above the national average. As the platform's authors explained, "The railroad corporations will either own the people or the people must own the railroads." On finance, the Omaha platform called for the free and unlimited coinage of silver and gold at the ratio of 16 to 1, greenbacks, and a graduated income tax to redistribute wealth. It also endorsed the Subtreasury Plan, a proposal for government-sponsored farm credit originated by the Southern Farmers' Alliance. Credit stringency in the South and West, especially in Oklahoma, where most settlers were cash poor and had little to mortgage, made the finance plank the third party's most popular proposal. [12]

While reformers busied themselves founding a new national party, the political landscape of Oklahoma underwent a major transformation. George W. Steele, finding his office difficult and unrewarding, resigned as governor of Oklahoma in November, 1891, and returned to his native Indiana. Territorial Secretary Robert Martin took over as interim governor until February, 1892, when President Harrison appointed District Court Judge Abraham Jefferson Seay as Steele's permanent replacement.

Seay's appointment as governor of the Oklahoma Territory could hardly have been calculated to undermine Populist organizing efforts. He was obese, a poor speaker, and possessed an antilabor background. Seay was born in Virginia in 1832. Three years later his family moved to south central Missouri, where Seay grew to manhood. Politically, he moved from the Whig to the Know-Nothing to the Republican parties before the Civil War. During the war he served in the Union army, rising to the rank of lieutenant colonel by 1865.

After the Civil War, Seay returned to Missouri to take up banking and law. He unsuccessfully contested Richard ("Silver Dick") Bland for Congress as a pro-gold Republican in the 1870s and then found his calling as a district judge. During the Great Southwest Railroad Strike of 1886, Seay gained notoriety as the first judge to issue an injunction against the Knights of Labor. After twelve years on the bench, union men effected his removal in the election of 1886. When President Harrison opened the Oklahoma Territory to non-Indian settlement in 1889, Seay migrated to the new land with a district court judge's commission in his pocket. [13]

Seay's first responsibility as governor was to organize local governments for the soon-to-be-opened Cheyenne and Arapaho reservation west of the original Unassigned Lands district (see map 1). The federal government also had opened to settlement the Iowa, Sac and Fox, Pottawatomie, and Shawnee lands, east of Old Oklahoma, the previous September.[14]

Although federal authorities had promised the Indians possession of their lands for "as long as the sun rises . . . as long as the waters run . . . as long as the grass grows," settlers looked forward to the day when Indians individually would be allotted enough land to establish a farm, with their remaining tribal possessions opened to white settlement.[15] The Republican *Norman Transcript* claimed that "millions of acres of Indian lands [are] now lying absolutely unused" and demanded that Indians "yield to the demands of civilization."[16] Populists, including Samuel Crocker, drew upon the Enlightenment theory of stages of social development in analyzing the Indian situation. Because Native Americans represented a more primitive level, such Populists believed, they were easy dupes of monied interests, such as the cattle barons.[17] The obvious solution was to bring Indians into the agricultural world and make them independent yeomen. Settled life on an allotted homestead was in their own best interests, and conveniently it would open up more land for white settlement at the same time.[18]

Non-Indians of all political outlooks found the outlawry, corruption, and political instability of the Indian nations a threat to their own society. According to Republican editor Frank Greer, the Indians were "unfit for self-government." Tribal lands, he claimed, were "absorbed by a few enterprising half-breeds . . . [without] attention to the great majority of the people." In addition, whites were not properly protected in the Indian Territory. Greer, of course, failed to mention that they had no business trespassing on Indian lands in the first place.[19]

Populist spokesmen were more likely than their mainstream party rivals to express sympathy for the Indians' plight. Indians were, after all, prime victims of Gilded Age exploitation. Land speculators directed their entire energies toward the destruction of the Indian governments. According to one Populist source, hapless Indians were "slaves of their surroundings and circumstances, dupes of the tricky politicians who abound, [and] gouged

and cheated by the white shylocks of the land." Some even acknowledged that "broken treaties and massacre" were the white
man's usual tools. [20]

Although a few Populists acknowledged that the Indians
wished to retain their tribal relations, most settlers, regardless of
party, claimed that the greatest impediments to individual allotments for the Indians were half bloods and whites who realized
that they would no longer be able to exploit Indians with im-
punity. This logic, of course, provided the justification for a
white takeover. White control, when it did come in 1907, hardly
stopped the exploitation of Indians. [21]

Populists agreed that Indians should become yeoman farmers
so that they would be able to defend themselves. They differed
significantly from mainstream-party spokesmen in their belief
that Indians could rapidly make the transition to "civilized" life.
Populists, such as Samuel Crocker, believed that the Indians'
lack of exposure to "civilization" made them "savages." A homestead and an education would quickly make Indians thrifty and
industrious citizens. According to one Populist editor, "The Cher-
okees, Seminoles, Creeks and many Chickasaws and Choctaws
can cast as intelligent a ballot as the average white man." [22]

Because the Democracy was the party of racism in the Gilded
Age, it is not surprising that one Democratic source found the
Indian "more immoral than the English nobility." Worse yet, another claimed, there was "a natural affinity between the Negroes
and the Indians." He believed that Oklahoma was "lost in the
heart of an African continent." To civilize such barbarians, another explained, would be "one of the most difficult undertakings
ever attempted." [23]

Frank Greer penned the typical Republican response when he
contended that "the Indian youth is more slow to profit by the
ethical or aesthetic learning of the school than the white boy,
. . . no amount of purely book information will do the work." In
short, Greer Darwinistically explained, "The past centuries must
be bred out of him." For this reason such "foreignism and non-
progress" as keeping whites out of the Indian Territory was
counterproductive. [24]

Prospects for statehood also quickly became entangled with

the Indian land issue. As the Five Civilized Tribes area rapidly filled up with southerners in the 1890s, Democrats pushed for a union of the Indian and Oklahoma territories, confident that they could control the new state politically. Republicans, who were equally pragmatic on the subject, favored two states. Populists denounced both parties as interested only in the spoils of office and frequently expressed indifference on the issue. Although a virtual parade of nonpartisan statehood conventions, ostensibly representing men of all political faiths, appeared during the Populist era, lists of officers and those attending such meetings show that few Populists participated in such overt attempts to take the Indians' lands.[25]

As time passed, it became evident that the "the eternal vigilance of the East in their [sic] determination not to yield any more senatorial power to the West," as one Populist stated, would eventually dictate single statehood. Populists, by and large, supported single statehood because the duplication of political offices implicit in establishing two states would cause higher taxation. Another Populist reasoned that "with double statehood we might as well turn everything over to the politicians and tax-gatherers." Populists wanted Oklahoma to be combined with the Indian Territory, however, only if land was allotted to Indians and made taxable.[26]

The land openings of 1891 and 1892 necessitated a redistricting of legislative districts for the 1893 legislature. While the Oklahoma Organic Act had established biennial sessions for the territorial assembly, the 1890 Oklahoma legislature, in its rush to finish business, had neglected to provide for a general election in 1892. Governor Seay considered calling the 1890 legislature into special session to rectify the oversight, but this would require a special territorywide election to fill vacated seats.[27] As the most expedient course, Seay asked Oklahoma's delegate to Congress, David A. Harvey, to secure the appropriate legislation from Washington.[28]

At this point Henry E. Asp, the Oklahoma solicitor for the Santa Fe Railroad and a major Republican politico, intervened to kill any prospective election bill. He argued that it was untimely for Oklahoma to hold a general election before the Cherokee Outlet, located between the older sections of Oklahoma and Kansas, was opened to settlement. According to Asp, "Into it will pass a great body of Republicans and . . . [this will] settle the political complexion of this territory." Not wishing to be labeled the man who derailed free elections in Oklahoma, Seay eventually traveled to Washington, D.C., himself to obtain the required legislation.[29]

Congress appointed a three-man commission, consisting of Governor Seay, Democrat Leslie P. Ross, and Populist Samuel Crocker, to conduct a census and lay out new legislative districts for the territory. The three men canvassed the territory by rail and in a mule-drawn army ambulance. They estimated the June, 1892, population of Oklahoma at 122,000, or approximately double that of 1890. When the commission met to redistrict the territory, Governor Seay found himself in a distinct minority. Ross and Crocker, the governor claimed, had gerrymandered the territory in favor of their own parties. Republicans, however, would still carry the council and twelve of the twenty-six house seats, even though they carried less than 50 percent of the vote in the fall elections.[30]

While the elections of 1890 had centered on issues of local importance, such as the capital fight, the 1892 campaign marked a change toward agitating broader questions. Foremost among the new issues was the fight for "free homes." To secure a patent to land in the Unassigned Lands region a homesteader had to pay only a $14.00 fee to the federal land office. In the newly opened lands east and west of Old Oklahoma, however, an additional charge of $1.25 to $2.50 per acre was added to reimburse the federal government for payments to dispossessed Indians. Although the fees could be paid over a five-year period, many Oklahoma pioneers could not raise the $200 to $400 necessary to secure a title to their homesteads during the depression of the mid-1890s.

As a longtime advocate of homesteaders' interests, Samuel Crocker originated the issue of free homes for settlers in the newly opened regions. While traveling with the census commission in the Cheyenne and Arapaho lands, Crocker organized Oklahoma's first "Free Homes Club," at Cloud Chief, in Washita County. Settlers warmed to Crocker's logic that free land for the poor was necessary to maintaining an independent yeomanry, the bulwark of republican institutions. Crocker organized several other clubs in the western territory and then carried his campaign east as he traveled with the census commission.[31]

In the struggle for political supremacy, territorial politicians were quite eager to recruit followers in the newly opened sections. When the Cherokee Outlet opened in 1893, the free-homes issue directly affected more than half of the territory's population. Men of all political creeds readily embraced it, and the real issue became which party could best secure the needed legislation from Congress.

The most successful politician to ride the free-homes issue to greater glory in the 1890s was the personable Republican postmaster of Guthrie, Dennis T. Flynn. Flynn had been favored for the GOP nomination for delegate to Congress in 1890, before Governor Steele forced the nomination of David A. Harvey. With the capital fight largely in the past and Steele retired from the governor's post, Flynn easily displaced Harvey as the GOP standard-bearer in 1892 and rode the free-homes issue to election in November.

Flynn, the son of Irish immigrants, was born in Phoenixville, Pennsylvania, in 1861. Three years later when his father died, Flynn's mother placed him in a Catholic orphanage near Buffalo, New York. She died shortly thereafter. At the age of twenty-one, Flynn moved west to seek his fortune and edited a small newspaper in Iowa before moving to southern Kansas. In the Sunflower State he read law, was admitted to the bar, and served as the city attorney of Medicine Lodge for three years. In his spare time Flynn involved himself in townsite speculation, the loan business, and editing another newspaper. He secured the Guthrie postmastership through his Kansas connections in 1889. As a Republican, Flynn represented the party that had opened Oklahoma to non-Indian settlement and the party of active government in the Gilded Age. Thus, he contended, the GOP was far more likely to pass a free-homes bill than the Democrats were.[32]

Flynn's ability to seize the free-homes issue came not only through his own attributes as a capable politician but also through infighting and incompetence within the Populist camp. With the inclusion of southern-born Oklahomans in Populist ranks, fusion with the Democratic party became a significant point of contention among third-party supporters. In a sense, the Oklahoma People's party had been founded through fusion. The original Cowley County, Kansas, People's movement owed its first victory largely to the fact that local Democratic leaders declined to nominate candidates in 1889. The 1890 Payne County victory resulted from similar circumstances. The People's party had also organized Oklahoma's first legislature through fusion with the Democratic party.

In the eyes of many potential supporters, the Oklahoma People's party was in danger of becoming a Democratic party annex by 1892. In the February, 1891, elections for county officers, Populists fused with Democrats in all but heavily southern-populated Cleveland County. Democrats carried Cleveland County in a three-way race, and fusion tickets were elected in all of the remaining counties except Logan. There, Republicans came closer to defeat in this election than at any other time in the territorial period. Populist Ira N. Terrill's murder of a witness against him in a land-claim case in Guthrie two weeks before the election discredited the third party and accounted for the GOP's 1891 victory in Logan County. Terrill's actions so outraged local citizens that marshals had to rush him out of the county in the dark of the night to prevent his lynching.[33]

Some Democrats viewed fusion with the People's party as more than simply an expedient for securing county offices. Oklahoma City Democrats, for instance, wanted to mobilize rural support for their town both as a commercial center and as a prospective capital city. To "cement mutual interests for future need," as the Democratic *Oklahoma City Evening Gazette* stated, they were willing to tender a large portion of the county offices to third-party candidates in exchange for later considerations.[34]

Most Oklahoma Democrats viewed the Populist revolt as a prime opportunity to build an anti-Republican majority in a northern-dominated territory. They shrewdly downplayed their own pragmatic motivations and couched their appeals in ideological terms. Both parties, Democrats claimed, stood together in their opposition to "Wall Street, with her thousands-billions

drawn from the sweat of millions of honest toilers." If all parties
with a bias against northeastern capitalists would unite in 1892,
Democrats predicted, "the mammoth corporations, the syndicate
trusts, the high tariff laws, the iron kings, and the plutocrats of
the East will be swept from place and power."[35]

Oklahoma Democrats made an appeal for Populist support
similar to that of their compatriots in the South in 1890. Southern Democrats had contended that adequate reform would be
possible through the dominant party, and they encouraged alliance members to support progressives within the Democratic
party. Southern Alliancemen subsequently helped elect four governors, eight state legislatures, and forty-two congressmen formally committed to their principles. Their support, for instance,
was crucial to the election of James Stephen Hogg in Texas.
When Oklahomans went to the polls to elect county officers in
February, 1891, the Hogg-alliance coalition was still intact.[36]
Adopting the strategy of their Texas cousins, Oklahoma Democrats would include a call for establishing a regulatory railroad
commission in their 1892 platform.[37] For southern-born Populists, however, Democrats constituted an integral part of the elite
from which they had rebelled in joining the People's party.

Throughout its existence the Oklahoma People's party struggled
with the issue of whether to fuse with Democrats or chart an independent course. Midwesterners, who controlled the party machinery, scheduled the third party's territorial convention to co-
incide with that of the Democratic party in 1892. Prospective
fusion was the obvious motive. At the convention, however,
antifusion forces succeeded in nominating one of their own to
lead the third-party ticket. The Populist nomination for delegate
to Congress in 1892 fell upon a little-known editor and part-time
preacher from Dover, in Kingfisher County, N. H. Ward.

In accordance with their choice to run a separate ticket, Oklahoma Populists adopted a strictly middle-of-the-road, or antifusion, platform in 1892. They endorsed the Omaha platform as
"the most profound declaration of rights . . . since the memo-
rable 4th day of July, 1776," specifically denounced fusion, called
for free homes, and asked that Congress open the remaining Indian lands to white settlement. While Oklahoma Populists spe-

cifically endorsed the actions of the third party's U.S. congressional delegation, they remained notably silent on their 1890
territorial representatives. Out of jail on appeal for his murder
conviction, Ira N. Terrill attended the convention as a spectator,
throwing a pall of despair over the entire proceedings.[38]

Little was known, either at the time or later, about N. H.
Ward, the Populist candidate for delegate to Congress in 1892.
He had served with General James B. Weaver, the Populist 1892
nominee for president, during the Civil War. Because Oklahoma
was a land of strangers, this distinction was enough to secure him
the nomination. As a candidate, however, Ward proved woefully
inadequate. His rambling speeches sometimes even bordered
upon profanity. Populists of all shades soon recognized his ignorance of the issues. As a wave of disillusionment spread over the
Populist effort, many party activists turned their attentions to
the legislative races in an attempt to salvage something from the
campaign.[39]

Democrats nominated Oklahoma City attorney Oliver H.
Travers·for the delegate race. A good speaker and an experienced
campaigner, the Democratic nominee proved far superior to his
Populist counterpart. Travers's only weakness was in being a relative newcomer to the territory. He had moved to Oklahoma from
his native Missouri in November, 1891. This forced the Democrats to disregard their traditional "carpetbag-rule" campaign and
focus instead upon the issue of statehood for Oklahoma. The
Democratic platform endorsed free homes, called for uniting
Oklahoma and the increasingly southern-populated Indian Territory into a single state, demanded establishment of a railroad
commission, ratified their party's national ticket, opposed racially
mixed schools, and charged the GOP with importing black
voters to the territory for overtly political purposes.[40]

Because theirs was the party of localism, Democrats found the
rule of officials appointed in Washington "subversive of free born
American Institutions." According to one Democratic spokesman, Oklahomans "instinctively rebelled against being in the
position of an outlying province, governed by foreign rulers."
With the McKinley Tariff a major national issue, Democrats also
stressed the notion that the next Congress would likely have a

Democratic majority and therefore be more favorable to solicitations from a representative of their own party on the free-homes issue.[41]

To secure as much Populist support as possible, Travers's campaign manager asked Sidney Clarke to canvass the territory for the Democratic nominee. Clarke, whose close ties to third-party leaders were well known, went so far as to endorse a large portion of the Populists' Omaha platform in his Oklahoma City address. The newly founded *Norman Peoples Voice*, which quickly became the mouthpiece of southern Populism in the Oklahoma Territory, denounced Clarke's appeal as the same "old thread-bare promises" Democrats in the South had used before.[42]

Although their party was formally committed to a nonfusion course, Populists in Kingfisher, Logan, and Payne counties concluded election arrangements with local Democratic organizations.[43] On election day Populists won three house seats in districts where Democrats failed to field candidates and elected their fusion candidate to the council. Payne County voters also elected a Democrat and a Populist in three-way races. Otherwise, Republicans carried the northern sections of the territory and Democrats secured the southern districts. In Oklahoma County, Samuel Crocker ran for the house seat held by vehemently anti-Populist incumbent James L. Brown, thus throwing the election to a Democrat.[44]

In the race for delegate, Dennis Flynn won a plurality victory over Travers, with Ward finishing a distant third. Populist organizing efforts among southern-born Oklahomans and the establishment of a third-party paper in Norman should have expanded the Populist party's electoral base far more than the three percentage points that Ward gained over Crocker's 1890 total. Ward failed to carry a single county and came in second in only Cleveland and Payne counties. Democrat Travers even ousted the People's party from second place in Ward's home county of Kingfisher.[45]

Despite Ward's poor showing in the delegate race, Populists rejoiced in expanding their constituency beyond its former Kansas base. White border-state natives, the second-largest sectional group in the Oklahoma Territory, were particularly strong prospects for conversion to Populism.[46] Because settlers from the upper South originated from a region with a decentralized trade structure, few exhibited aggressive commercial orientations. They frequently migrated in kin-related groups or in congregations reminiscent of peasant groups and tended to practice a method of agriculture that placed subsistence and production for local markets first and commercial crops for the larger world second. Most had lived in north Texas, a hotbed of Farmers' Alliance agitation, before coming to the Oklahoma Territory.[47]

In line with the tardy organization of the People's party in the former Confederacy, southern-born Oklahomans did not enter the territorial Populist movement until after the election of 1890. White border-state natives found the third party's denunciation of rampant exploitation quite appealing and, in 1892, replaced midwesterners as the most Populistic sectional group (see appendix A, table 1). After 1890, however, the People's party drew from such a regionally diverse population as to validate its claim that Populism bridged sectionalism to address more relevant issues. The Democratic and Republican parties, on the other hand, continued to rely substantially on sectional loyalties for their support.[48]

Economic patterns were established well enough in 1892 to allow some generalizations about partisan support. As in 1890, the People's party drew most of its support from hinterland areas, away from the cosmopolitan railhead enclaves (see appendix A, table A-2). Their negative correlation with the value of manufactured goods confirms this statement. Populists did not, however, draw equally from all rural elements. Ranchers, as might be expected, were strongly anti-Populist. This attitude was a holdover from the Boomer–cattle baron struggle of the 1880s. There also was a partisan skew associated with raising Oklahoma's major commercial crops (see appendix A, table A-4). Republican voters were associated most strongly with wheat acreage, while Populists did best in areas where corn and hogs were the primary agricultural products. Democrats and Populists drew equally from areas where cotton production dominated in 1892.[49]

To turn a consistent profit, both corn and cotton farmers need thirty inches of rainfall a year. The wheat belt, on the other hand, traditionally lies between the twenty- and thirty-inch rain-fall lines on the Great Plains.[50] David Trask has shown that Populism in Nebraska was strongest among farmers who attempted to raise corn in the drier wheat belt. He suggests that their conversion to wheat in the late 1890s, when wheat prices were rising, accounts for the demise of the People's party.[51] Map 4, however, shows that the wheat belt in the Oklahoma Territory straddled the thirty-inch rainfall line. Map 5 helps explain this seeming aberration. The wheat belt in Oklahoma followed the paths of the two main north-south railroads. Wheat was the crop of the cosmopolitan culture in the Oklahoma Territory.

The Republican wheat farmer readily entered the cosmopolitan world of agribusiness, where he expected a larger commercial operation, with substantial investment in fertilizer and machinery, to provide him with a considerable margin of profit. The investment necessary to mount such mechanized operations normally required significant debt by newly settled farmers. Unfortunately, farm-debt figures from the 1890 census are not usable for Oklahoma, which opened to non-Indian settlement only the year before, and are not repeated in the 1900 census. In Kansas, however, Republican farmers tended to accumulate far greater debts than Populists on such commercialized ventures.[52]

In contrast to the agribusiness orientation of Republican wheat farmers, Populists generally engaged in more traditional family operations. Corn farmers invested far less in fencing and livestock than wheat farmers did in machinery. Because family farmers' homesteads constituted both their business and their legacy, they were far less likely to mortgage them in an attempt to mechanize. Most important, rather than pin their hopes on the market value of a single crop, Populist corn farmers engaged in diversified operations. It is an axiom of agricultural economics that 10 bushels of corn will put 100 pounds on a hog. Corn-hog farmers could either feed their corn to their hogs or place both commodities on the market separately. Between 1865 and 1897 corn and pork prices fluctuated so that one of these options was profitable in all but three years. As wheat and cotton prices plummeted in the early and mid-1890s, the vagaries of the marketplace affected the Populist corn-hog farmer far less than they affected his mainstream-party cousins.[53]

Although less affected by the depression of the 1890s, Populist farmers were not prosperous (see appendix A, table A-5). In fact, they appear to have been considerably poorer than Democrats or Republicans. They were not, however, bad farmers. They simply lacked the machinery necessary to bring as much land under cultivation as their competitors. For this reason, Populists correlated more strongly with the value of agriculture per acre than per farm in 1892.

Multiple regression analysis offers the opportunity to calculate the combined effect of several factors on a dependent variable, such as votes for the People's party. The value of manufactured goods (an urban variable), the value of farm implements and machinery (an agribusiness variable), and hogs per farm (a family-farming variable) account for 89.4 percent of the variation in the 1892 Populist delegate vote. In other words, Populists did so poorly in urban and agribusiness farming areas and so well among family farmers that these factors alone explain almost all of the 1892 third-party vote.[54]

Although the 1892 election occurred little more than three years after settlement, farm tenancy appears to have made some headway by this time. It was common for speculators to claim farmland near towns and rent the land out to the less fortunate while values increased.[55] This accounts for the swift rise of cash tenancy. Blacks were the only racial or sectional group to have a significant association with share tenancy.[56] This suggests a direct importation of the southern institution into the Oklahoma Territory. Although both correlated strongly with Populism in 1892, cash and share tenancy were associated with the cosmopolitan regions of Oklahoma. Except for support among tenant farmers, the People's party fared quite poorly among residents of cosmopolitan Oklahoma in 1892. For hinterland family farmers and cosmopolitan-area tenant farmers the Populist accusation that Gilded Age development unjustly widened the gap between rich and poor had great appeal.

As the date for the second territorial legislature neared, Gov-

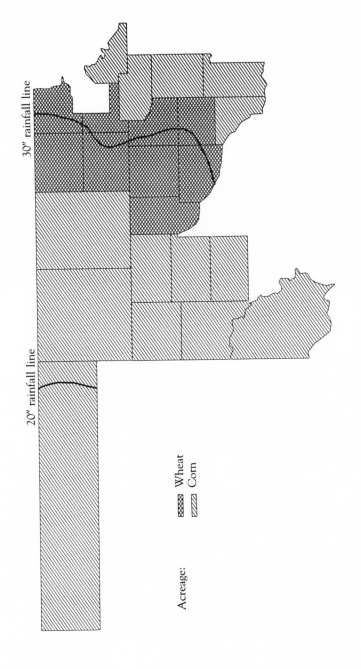

Map 4. Rainfall and dominant crop, 1900.

Acreage:

Wheat

Corn

30" rainfall line

20" rainfall line

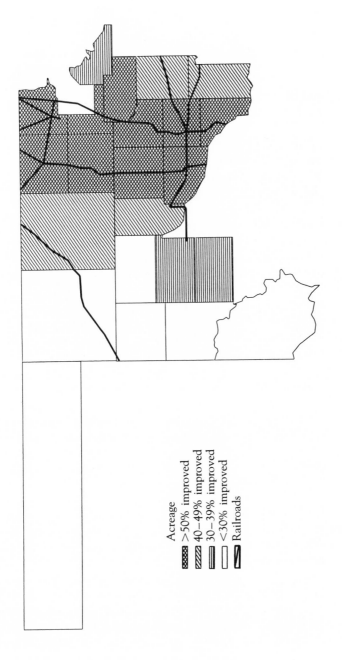

Map 5. Rail lines and percent improved acres, 1900.

Acreage
>50% improved
40–49% improved
30–39% improved
<30% improved
Railroads

ernor Seay informed Samuel Crocker that, while he had learned much about how to redistrict the legislature, he intended to teach his Populist adversary even more on how to organize the assembly. Not one to shrink from a challenge, Crocker traveled to Guthrie for the opening of Oklahoma's second legislature in January, 1893. While Republicans constituted a majority in the council, they held only twelve of twenty-six seats in the house. A Populist challenge to Democratic Representative James L. Stovall, however, sent the Cleveland County rancher into the Republican camp. He feared that Democrats might sacrifice his seat as the price of fusion.[57]

Before the legislature met, the Democratic *Oklahoma City Evening Gazette* predicted that "the hermorphadite [sic] body of two years ago will probably be the coming model." It took the fusionists eight days and 149 ballots to organize the house in 1893. When it became evident that their caucus nominee for speaker could not win, they finally turned to Thomas R. Waggoner of Cleveland County. For Waggoner, a member of the first legislature, selection as speaker was a personal victory. Democrats had passed over his name at their nominating convention, forcing him to run as an Independent. Because he was a party renegade, they also ignored his bid for the speaker's nomination until it became clear that they could not control the house without his support. A coalition of eight Democrats, four Populists, and Republican M. L. Stanley elected Waggoner as the speaker of the house in the second legislature. Stanley was a business partner of Democratic Representative Dan Peery. As their slice of the pie Populists secured the chief clerkship for Pat O. Cassidy, the editor of the third party's new territorial newspaper, the *Guthrie West and South*. James L. Mathews, the Democratic-Populist legislator and candidate for delegate to Congress in 1890, became the messenger of the house. With Republican support, Stovall retained his seat.[58]

Democrats and Populists faced an even greater challenge in the council. Republicans controlled seven of the thirteen seats. In their caucus, however, four eastside Republicans, representing Lincoln, Logan, and Payne counties, voted themselves all of the plums, leaving their westside colleagues with the role of loyal supporters. William A. McCartney of Kingfisher County, also a member of the first legislature, declined this subordinate role and refused to support the eastside nominee for council president, O. R. Fegan of Guthrie. Because Fegan was a follower of former Senator John J. Ingalls, a Republican of Kansas, Crocker and Leslie P. Ross, the Democratic council leader, readily volunteered their support to McCartney. Adding his own vote to that of the fusionists, McCartney became the president of the second Oklahoma council.[59]

The fusionist victory greatly embarrassed Governor Seay, who was present in the council chamber at the time of the vote, and he abruptly stormed out of the chamber. When Crocker encountered the governor later that evening, he teased Seay unmercifully about his promise to organize the legislature. After the passions of the era had subsided, however, Crocker admitted that Seay was "a pretty good old man."[60]

A major factor in Crocker's assessment of Seay was the fact that the governor presided over the most economical legislature in territorial history. Populists had two reasons to favor economy in government. First, their neorepublican mind-set associated governmental extravagance with corruption, and, second, Oklahoma farmers, their main constituency, were cash poor in the 1890s. Large governmental expenditures could bankrupt homesteaders just establishing themselves in the new land.

Although Populist legislators opposed extravagance in government, they did prove willing to support worthy programs. Populist legislators, for instance, supported Governor Seay's proposal to raise revenue for education through a license tax on liquor dealers. The prospective taxpayers may have accounted for some of their ardor. Populists also introduced and secured passage of a revised liquor code in line with the governor's opening message to the legislature. Likewise, they supported Democrat James K. Allen's local-option bill, although the house quickly killed the measure. In addition to the third-party contingent, Allen could muster the support of only three Republicans.[61]

The first expenditure to arouse passions in the second legislature was Republican O. R. Fegan's proposal to increase the salaries and number of legislative clerks. Republicans pushed the bill through the council, while party lines were obliterated on the measure in the house. Seay immediately vetoed the bill, and while legislators quickly overturned the governor's veto, the house finally succumbed to his wishes and failed to appoint the extra help.[62]

For Populists the most obnoxious legislation of the second legislature was clearly the general appropriations bill. Third-party legislators delayed the measure until the final day of the session. Included in the Republican-sponsored bill was a $15,000 appropriation for a territorial exhibit at the Columbian Exposition of 1893. That poverty-stricken Oklahoma farmers should help finance "capitalism's showpiece" outraged third-party legislators. In the end, however, only four Democrats and one Republican joined the Populists in their opposition to the bill. Populist Councillor Pulliam voted to pass the bill, protesting the choice of supporting "unwarranted extravagance or voting against needed appropriations."[63]

Populist legislators in the second assembly proved no more successful in securing Populistic economic legislation than had their predecessors in 1890. They introduced bills on bonding, usury, taxes, contracts, minimum wages, and regulating mercantile agencies, railroads, telephones, and telegraphs. Most of the proposals were killed quickly in committee. A Populist bill to control corporations, which did reach the floor of the house, lost by a single vote. Republicans constituted most of the opposition, while Democrats split on the issue.[64]

Morality and race legislation also appeared in the second legislature. Perhaps the most notable act of the assembly was the passage of Democrat Charles Wrightsman's antigambling bill. Populists, Republicans, and two other Democrats supported the bill in the house. Only two legislators (a Democrat and a Republican) opposed it in the council. On the race issue, Leslie P. Ross introduced a bill segregating railroad facilities. Republicans defeated it by a single vote. Populist Councillor Pulliam, a former Democrat, voted with the forces of racism on this issue. He was absent, however, when a vote on establishing a black college at Langston likewise met defeat. No votes on the race issue emerged from the house in the 1893 legislature.[65]

Although the fusion strategy proved more successful at the polls than that of the middle-of-the-roaders in 1892, Populist legislative accomplishments were almost nonexistent in the territory's second assembly. Third-party legislators introduced only 28 of the 304 bills that appeared in the legislature. Only 3 became law, and none could be considered pertinent to major Populist issues. While fusionists within the third party had good reason to ridicule the midroad strategy in the delegate race, their own lack of accomplishment in the second legislature gave midroaders ammunition for future debates.[66]

CHAPTER FIVE

Democrats at
the Helm

As Oklahoma Populists prepared for another intraparty battle over fusion in the wake of the 1893 legislature, territorial Democrats looked forward to the inauguration of Oklahoma's first non-Republican governor. On the national level, fortuitous circumstances elevated Grover Cleveland to the presidency for a second time in 1893. Defeated for reelection because of his stand on the tariff issue in 1888, he doggedly rode antiprotectionism back to the White House four years later. Democrats captured the presidency and both houses of Congress in 1892 for the first time since the 1850s.

During the Harrison years Republicans at both the national and the local levels had conveniently provided a series of policy excesses for Democrats to capitalize on in 1892. The McKinley Tariff of 1890 seemed to favor the Northeast and raised protectionism to its highest level in the nineteenth century. The GOP's "Billion Dollar Congress" of 1890 provided Democrats with another issue. Henry Cabot Lodge's "force bill," which threatened to reestablish federal oversight where black voting rights were abridged, aroused both white southerners and northern urban bosses, who feared the measure could also be applied to them. In the electorally crucial Midwest, GOP pietists pushed prohibition, blue laws, and measures requiring the use of English in schools with such zeal that a backlash became inevitable.

Grover Cleveland considered the landslide victory of 1892 a personal triumph. Few candidates defeated for the presidency had later secured renomination from their party. Fortunately for Cleveland, the Democratic party of the Gilded Age was such a diffuse coalition of local interests that it produced few men who could effectively challenge an already established national leader for party honors.

Cleveland composed his second administration with personal, rather than party, rule in mind. The new president condemned the office seeking of party regulars as a "demoralizing madness for spoils," and looking elsewhere for administrative talent, he filled his cabinet with friends and men who had little popular following. For postmaster general he chose a former law partner, Wilson Bisell. As secretary of state he appointed renegade Republican Walter Q. Gresham. For attorney general the president chose a less-than-personable railroad lawyer, Richard Olney. The appointments revealed a definite dislike, perhaps fear, of forceful men with independent power bases.[1]

To ensure the victory of 1892, Democrats fused with Populists in a number of western states. For western Democrats fusion was a pragmatic decision to keep the presidential electors from this normally Republican region out of the GOP column. Fusion-oriented Oklahoma Democrats hoped that President Cleveland would foster this winning strategy by appointing a man acceptable to Populists as their new territorial governor in 1893. Their hopes centered upon the candidacy of Sidney Clarke, whose close ties to third-party leaders were well known to most Oklahomans.[2]

Sidney Clarke secured a wide range of support in his 1893 bid for the Oklahoma governorship. Local Democratic executive-committee members from heavily northern-populated Kingfisher and heavily southern-populated Pottawatomie counties promoted his appointment. So did Democratic editors Frank McMaster, of the *Oklahoma City Evening Gazette*, and Mort Bixler, of the *Norman State Democrat*. As a former abolitionist, Clarke also received the warm support of black politico E. P. McCabe, "in the name of the colored people." Outgoing Republican Delegate David A. Harvey and his replacement, Dennis T. Flynn, also sent unsolicited recommendations for Clarke to the president.[3]

From Populist sources Clarke secured the endorsement of James B. Weaver, the party's recent presidential nominee, Kansas Senator William A. Peffer, and a number of minor third-party notables. The most noteworthy Populist recommendations, however, came from former speaker of the Oklahoma house Arthur N.

Daniels and from Clarke's old Boomer colleague, Samuel Crocker. Both men were fusionists. Daniels specifically mentioned the ease with which "a union of our people with the Democratic party" could be arranged with Clarke as governor. Although Crocker's letter of endorsement was respectful and laudatory of Clarke, he unthinkingly listed his return address as "'Agitator Place,' Oklahoma, O.T." Whether Crocker, whom the Cleveland administration had served with a treason warrant in 1885, played a role in the president's final decision is impossible to determine. Administration sources did recognize Crocker, because their list of Clarke's endorsements identified him as "Col. Samuel Crocker." The Populist leader had picked up the honorary military title in his Boomer days, but no such reference appeared in his letter to the president.[4]

Through either obstinance or obtuseness, Grover Cleveland followed the precedent he had set in selecting his cabinet and rejected the qualifications of all who applied for the position of governor of Oklahoma. He asked territorial Democratic Chairman Leslie P. Ross to suggest a nonpolitical candidate. Ross named Norman banker William Cary Renfrow, the man credited with having Oklahoma's third county named after the Democratic president. Cleveland immediately tendered Renfrow the appointment. Fusionists in both Democratic and Populist camps were sorely disappointed. For third-party leaders, Cleveland's choice of a banker for governor would dictate a middle-of-the-road course for 1894.[5]

William Cary Renfrow was born in Smithville, North Carolina, on May 15, 1845. The son of a moderately prosperous planter, Renfrow attended school until 1862, when he enlisted in the Confederate army. After the war Renfrow relocated to Russellville, Arkansas, halfway between Fort Smith and Little Rock. He soon developed a successful mercantile business and married a native of his adopted state.[6]

Throughout his life Renfrow exhibited an exceptional talent for the commercial entrepreneurship that cosmopolitan America exalted in the late nineteenth century. By the time he died, in 1922, Renfrow was one of the wealthiest men in Oklahoma. His business career revealed a physical mobility common to many small entrepreneurs in the Gilded Age. He achieved success through a series of new starts related to previous endeavors only by reinvestment of capital from earlier undertakings.[7]

In the fall of 1889 the lure of fresh prospects in the newly opened Oklahoma Territory brought Renfrow to Norman, the only railroad town in the Unassigned Lands that had a southern-born majority. Because he arrived in the territory after the April 22 land run, Renfrow staked no claim. Instead he opened a lucrative livery business with the capital he had brought from Arkansas. He invested the profits from this enterprise in bank stock, and by 1891 he controlled a majority share in the Norman State Bank. Renfrow also speculated freely in town lots, quickly gaining title to approximately 4 percent of the property in Norman.[8]

Renfrow's rapid business success secured him the presidency of the Norman Board of Trade in 1890. He also served as a delegate to the founding convention of the territorial Democratic party and to the Democratic National Convention of 1892. Renfrow was the epitome of the self-made man that Grover Cleveland so admired. When the president offered Renfrow the governor's appointment in 1893, Renfrow, as he had in the past, freely pulled up stakes and relocated for his new endeavor. Although Norman would claim him, Renfrow resided in Guthrie for the entire four years he served as governor of Oklahoma.[9]

As a banker, urbanite, and speculator, Renfrow would receive little sympathy from the rising forces of Populism in the Oklahoma Territory. Essentially an entrepreneur, the new governor, sworn in only four days after his appointment, also had to learn the business of politics on the job. His native intelligence led him to appoint Roy V. Hoffman, the editor of the Democratic party's territorial newspaper, the *Guthrie Oklahoma Leader*, as his personal secretary and advisor. Frank Greer, Hoffman's Republican counterpart at the *Guthrie Oklahoma State Capital*, lost no time in labeling his rival "Governor Roy" and suggesting that Hoffman was the real power behind the throne in Oklahoma.[10]

One of Governor Renfrow's first acts was to appoint county officials for lands soon to be opened to non-Indian settlement. The run for the Cherokee Outlet, located between the previously

opened sections of Oklahoma and the state of Kansas, was scheduled for September 16, 1893. When Hoffman's publishing company received the printing contracts for the new county governments, charges of official malfeasance emerged. Editor Greer
accused Renfrow of forcing the new county officers to order sup-
plies from Hoffman before receiving their commissions. Rumors
that Renfrow owned half interest in the *Oklahoma Leader* also
circulated freely but were never proved. The governor weathered
the storm in relative complacency, and his offensive link with
Hoffman was severed in October, 1894, when President Cleveland appointed the Democratic editor to the position of assistant
U.S. attorney for Oklahoma.[11]

Although Renfrow pledged in his inaugural address to appoint
men strictly on the basis of merit, he proved to be highly partisan
in his subsequent actions. Once in office Renfrow called for the
resignation of three leading Republican officeholders: Attorney
General Charles Brown, Treasurer Samuel Murphy, and Superin-
tendent of Education Joseph Parker. Acknowledging the governor's right to a Democratic administration, Brown resigned immediately. Murphy promised to leave at the end of the month,
but because of GOP pressure he lingered on for seven more
months before resigning. Renfrow finally secured a court order
evicting Parker from office.[12]

While battling Murphy and Parker, Renfrow also turned his
attention to the Republican administration of the agricultural
college. Charging extravagance and misappropriation of territorial funds, the governor discharged the entire board of regents.
When he subsequently appointed the director of his own bank as
treasurer of the college, his enemies howled conspiracy. As the
panic of 1893 spread to Oklahoma, rumors emerged that the First
National Bank of Oklahoma City might fail. If it had, Renfrow's
Norman State Bank would likely have followed. The governor
later admitted that the agricultural college's new treasurer divided
the institution's reserve funds between the two ailing banks in a
timely fashion. The scandal subsided, however, when an inves-
tigating committee from the Republican controlled 1895 legislature amazingly substantiated the governor's charges against the
school's former regents.[13]

The panic of 1893 and the depression that followed were clearly the worst economic events of America's early industrial period. At its nadir, economic activity declined about 25 percent. The railroad expansion that took place in the late nineteenth century meant that few Americans remained isolated from the effects of business stagnation. By the end of 1893 some five hundred banks and sixteen thousand business firms had closed, and between 15 and 20 percent of the work force was unemployed. Although recovery began in 1897, most industries did not return to full capacity until after the turn of the century.[14]

As early as mid-1892 signs of declining investment that could lead to economic stagnation began to emerge. From a twentieth-century viewpoint it is possible to see a number of serious defects in the American economy of the Gilded Age. Many industries expanded far beyond the market demands for their products and services. Between 1880 and 1890, for instance, railroad companies laid more than 74,000 miles of track. Many lines were hastily constructed to secure regional markets from penetration by competitors. Track laid where future traffic never materialized, however, brought debt-ridden railroads to their knees in the 1890s. Industries closely linked to the fortunes of rail expansion, such as steel, soon found their own operations overextended as well.[15]

Because New York was the center of American banking activity, it attracted a large portion of the nation's reserve capital. In the frenzy of economic expansion that occurred in the 1880s, such resources were used freely for speculative purposes in both the industrial Northeast and the boom areas of the trans-Mississippi West. The opening of vast tracts of virgin farmland in the prairie states and the penetration of rail lines into the piedmont areas of the South brought a flood of agricultural products to both American and European markets. Although wages rose slightly in the Gilded Age, agricultural production vastly outstripped consumption. This sent agricultural prices downward, and many western and southern farms fell into the hands of mortgage-holders. Between 1880 and 1890 farmers' share of the wealth produced in the United States dropped from 26 to 21 percent. Industries dependent upon farmers' prosperity, such as railroads and farm-

machinery manufacturing, likewise suffered reverses as the purchasing power of American farmers declined.[16]

Perhaps the most immediate precipitant of the panic of 1893
was the considerable liquidation of European investment in the
United States that began when the London banking house of
Baring Brothers collapsed in 1890. The withdrawal of badly
needed capital at a time when American investment was overextended caused a substantial call on collateral that by 1893 could
not be met. The result was a curtailment of credit, a decline in
the value of stocks, numerous bank failures, and finally economic
collapse.[17]

As economic stagnation spread throughout the nation in the
spring of 1893, business interests in the East convinced President
Cleveland that a crisis of confidence had triggered the growing
depression. The Sherman Silver Purchase Act of 1890, they
claimed, had caused investors to doubt the government's commitment to maintaining the gold standard. Between 1890 and
1893 the redemption of treasury certificates caused federal gold
reserves to decline by nearly $132 million. As the value of re-
serves neared $100 million, entrepreneurs questioned the sound-
ness of the currency and became timid in their investments.
Cleveland's advisers convinced him that only through dramatic
action to save the gold standard could the administration restore
investors' confidence and rejuvenate the economy.

Men of all parties in the South and West expressed the opinion
that something more fundamental than lack of investor confidence had caused the panic of 1893. Since the Civil War the
American population had doubled, and the volume of business
had tripled. The amount of money in circulation to accommo-
date this increased activity, however, had actually declined. The
resulting deflation, observers noted, had caused economic hardship in the cash-poor outlying regions of the nation long before
1893. Prices for agricultural products had dropped steadily in the
previous two decades. Mortgage payments, on the other hand,
had not. As credit stringency increased, so did interest rates. The
reduced purchasing power of southern and western farmers, critics of deflation contended, also translated into unemployment in
industrial America. According to such men, the American econ-

According to Populists, man-made deflation caused most of the ills of late-nineteenth-century America. Carnegie, Rothschild, and John Bull peer out from behind the gate. From the *El Reno Populist Platform*, October 12, 1894.

omy simply ran out of money in 1893. Further reducing the volume of money by repealing the Sherman Silver Purchase Act, they claimed, would only aggravate the already desperate situation.

By national standards Oklahomans were poor and newly settled on the land when the depression of 1893 struck. Obtaining credit to erect buildings, build fences, and buy fertilizer, farm implements, and seed was particularly important. Settlers could not mortgage their land until they had proved their claims, a process that included a five-year residency requirement. For most settlers in the Unassigned Lands this occurred in 1894. Credit was difficult to obtain, however, even with a land title for collateral. Land ownership also meant inclusion on the tax rolls. Money and credit were prime issues in the early years of the Oklahoma Territory.[18]

Adding to the problems of Oklahoma farmers in the 1890s

were declining prices for agricultural products. Oklahoma cotton prices bottomed out at 4.6 cents a pound in December, 1893, while wheat reached its nadir at 48 cents a bushel a year later. Blaming the nation's problems on paternalism, the Cleveland administration suspended the free distribution of seed to the needy in 1893. Low commodity prices, credit stringency, and the new migrants' inherent poverty made the depression of the 1890s a particularly desperate period for many Oklahoma farmers.[19]

Although a series of radical political movements can be associated with areas of agricultural distress in the late nineteenth century, the relationship between poverty and the rise of the People's party is more sophisticated than simple economic determinism. Hard times have been the lot of the vast majority of men and women throughout recorded history. Still, most have lived out their lives resigned to the fact that they would always be poor. The decision of Kansas and Oklahoma farmers to cast their lot with the People's party as the rural economy turned sour in the late 1880s and early 1890s was the exception rather than the rule. If rural poverty alone was the cause of the Populist Revolt, the Oklahoma Territory would have experienced a much stronger third-party movement.

In good times, most people are content to accept the explanation of the nation's opinion-making elite on how their society should operate. Such explanations are integral to the basic assumptions that define the nation. Frequently they devolve into the kind of unthinking patriotic shibboleths that justify proscription of all who question the accepted verities. As long as people believe that the basic assumptions of society provide a just order, few question them. Economic dislocations that victimize honest, hard working men and women, however, can promote a reexamination of the precepts upon which society's supposedly just order are based.[20]

When the gap between idealized and real conditions becomes noticeable, those who find the dominant explanations unrewarding are likely to convert to an alternative value system if one is available in the society. These rival "truths" can trigger, and then direct, action in formerly complacent individuals. In the case of western Populism, plains farmers did not join the People's party

PROSPERITY.

TWO INDUSTRIES THAT SHOW ABUNDANT SIGNS OF REVIVAL.

Populists ridiculed the panaceas advocated by the cosmopolitan world. From the *Norman Peoples Voice*, July 22, 1898.

simply because they were going broke. Economic stress raised in their minds the possibility that the contemporary economic system might not be just. In a society based upon proper principles, hard-working, honest men succeeded. Because their economic failures were clearly unjust, farmers began to reexamine their fundamental beliefs about society, economics, and politics. In Populism they discovered an essentially preindustrial critique of commercial society that had been adapted to the conditions of the late nineteenth century and seemed to address their innermost concerns. The egalitarian spokesmen of the Gilded Age, who had presented essentially the same explanation of the na-

tion's ills for decades, finally mobilized an unprecedented following among those who found the mainstream tenets of laissez-
faire, social Darwinism, and business boosterism unrewarding in
the face of economic upheaval and government indifference.

The coalescence of the elements necessary for producing the
Populist movement—economic distress, a rethinking of society's
accepted verities, and contact with what might be called the Old
Radicalism of Gilded Age egalitarian propagandists—occurred at
slightly different times in various localities. The strength of the
Union Labor party in Kansas in 1888 suggested that the Sunflower State was ready for political revolt at that time. Third-
party spokesmen organized potential supporters into the nominally nonpartisan Southern Farmers' Alliance, which provided
its members with liberal doses of egalitarian indoctrination; they
then changed their party's name (because the word "labor" had
urban connotations) and watched the agrarian revolt in the
Sunflower State burst into full bloom. The Oklahoma third-
party movement in 1890 was largely a derivative of its Kansas
predecessor.

Not all economically depressed plains farmers joined the
People's party in the 1890s. Many of those who settled in the Oklahoma Territory revealed a lingering commitment to the newer
cosmopolitan ethos by relocating. They contended that the system was just and that starting over would ensure their prosperity.
Those who believed that a faulty economic system was the cause
of their problems moved only when circumstances left them no
choice. These settlers realized that moving was only a temporary
palliative. Most migrants, however, believed that a new start was
all they needed to achieve success. Not surprisingly, the People's
party was the weakest of the three major parties in newly settled
Oklahoma, while its Kansas parent was the strongest.[21]

As the panic of 1893 developed into a prolonged depression,
bread lines, unemployment, and vagrancy spread throughout the
nation. The dispossessed quickly depleted the resources of private charity. Some cities dispensed aid, but state and federal authorities acted on the principle that Americans should support
the government, and not vice versa. Millions came to know
genuine and prolonged privation. There were even reports of

starvation. As unemployment spread, "tramps" became a familiar sight. Wandering aimlessly in search of work, they frightened and irritated respectable society. Tramps were tangible examples of what their more fortunate cousins might become. To some people they were a sign of the nation's general degeneration into social collapse.

In 1892, Jacob S. Coxey, a well-to-do Massillon, Ohio, businessman, put forward a scheme designed to create jobs, expand the currency, and improve transportation in America. The plan called for the federal government to issue $500 million in non-interest-bearing government bonds (a euphemism for greenbacks) to state and local governments, "upon exactly the same terms that it loans to national bankers," for the construction of roads. In the spring of 1894, Coxey decided to "send a petition to Washington with boots on" to prod the timeserving Democratic Congress into action. Coxey named his delegation the Commonweal Army to emphasize the public good he claimed his scheme would accomplish.[22]

Populists generally sympathized with Coxey. Local Commonweal armies, committed to the cause of "General" Coxey, sprang up throughout the nation, especially in the West. In most places the movement was met with fear, ridicule, and hostility. Many Populists were concerned that the movement might further taint their party with charges of anarchism. Lurid tales of outrage and pillage preceded Coxey's Army on its march to Washington. Borrowed trains and pilfered chicken coops, however, proved to be the movement's most egregious offenses. Speculation on the meaning of it all quickly led to overreaction. Mainstream papers freely suggested the simplistic solution of repression. When Coxey and his pathetic band of marchers attempted to deliver their petition to the president on May 1, 1894, authorities arrested the leaders for walking on the White House lawn. Instead of producing legislative action, Coxey's march on Washington strengthened the establishment's determination not to yield to "mob rule."[23]

Coxey's Army provided third-party editors in Oklahoma with the material they needed to dramatize their apocalyptic view of late-nineteenth-century development. Some controversy arose among Populists in Oklahoma, as elsewhere, about the advisability of associating with the Coxey movement. National committeeman Pat Cassidy endorsed the objectives, but not the methods, and proclaimed the order "not a Populist movement." Third-party editors, on the other hand, vigorously promoted Coxey's Army.[24] John Allan, of the *Norman Peoples Voice*, asked whether Congress "will dare deny petitions, if petitioners go in person." Patent insides, which most Populist newspapers carried, labeled Coxey's Army "the first lobby the honest peasantry of this country ever sent to Washington." J. C. Tousley, editor of the *Kingfisher Reformer*, proclaimed, "Coxey's cause is the people's cause," and Mont Howard, of the *El Reno Industrial Headlight*, asked Populists "to vote as you would shoot."[25]

Oklahoma Commonwealers claimed a membership of more than 2,200 by mid-1894. For their own general, territorial Commonwealers chose John R. Furlong, a mysterious faith healer who frequently advertised his services in the Populistic *Guthrie Oklahoma Representative*. In this era when the fields of education, law, and medicine were being professionalized, Furlong represented the epitome of the Populist denial that the cosmopolitan culture had discovered any ultimate truths.

A native of Ireland who had studied for the priesthood as a youth, Furlong had parted company with the Catholic church years before coming to Oklahoma. He did, however, retain a strongly religious moral bent. His greatest notoriety came from leading the territorial fight against capital punishment in 1895. Politically, Furlong was a Bellamy nationalist and served as secretary of the Populist territorial executive committee in the mid-1890s.[26] To cut expenses, Oklahoma Commonwealers tried to make a deal with the Santa Fe Railroad to carry them to Washington in boxcars. The trek apparently never took place. In the wake of Coxey's arrest in Washington, John Allan printed the "suppressed speech" that Coxey had planned to deliver from the steps of the White House. The *Kingfisher Reformer* warned that, while Coxey had gone to Washington in peace, if relief was not forthcoming, "the next army will go with their war paint on."[27]

Oklahoma's mainstream-party editors responded to the Commonweal movement with predictable vilification. Frank Greer claimed that Coxeyites simply wanted "something for nothing, in order to go on a pleasure tramp, while the workingmen of the country are putting in spring crops." He claimed that "every man that wants work in Oklahoma can get it." Greer believed the Commonweal movement was "useless and dangerous to the public good." Personally, he preferred the "less villainous traitors of thirty-four years ago." In the same vein the Republican editor of the *Mulhall Chief* suggested that those Commonwealers stranded in the nation's capital after Coxey's arrest "may even be forced to the extremity of going to work if contributions are not forthcoming." Democratic editors exhibited an equally strong disapproval of the Coxey movement, although with less originality. The main thrusts of their critique centered around Coxey's army as the product of protectionism and prayers that all vagrants would soon be sent to the rock pile.[28]

The Coxey movement also provided Populist editors with a dramatic opportunity to vaporize upon what ailed the nation in the spring of 1894. Western farmers, suffering from declining commodity prices, and silver miners thrown out of work when President Cleveland secured repeal of the Sherman Silver Purchase Act proved to be the strongest supporters of the Commonweal movement. Coxey's popularity in Oklahoma was verified in August, 1895, when he spoke in Guthrie. He was the Populist nominee for governor of Ohio at the time. According to the *State Capital*, "The tail boards of the wagons of the enthusiastic farmers who gathered here to greet General Coxey stuck over the corporation lines [of the city] in every direction." Editor Greer proclaimed enthusiasm for the "great itinerant windbag . . . one of the queerest phases of public life." Rumors that Coxey might move to Oklahoma and run for Congress spread rapidly.[29]

As the excitement over Coxey began to subside, new storm clouds spread over the national political scene. George M. Pullman, builder of the famed railroad sleeping car, operated a company town next to his factory on the outskirts of Chicago. Pullman considered his company town a showcase for a stable industrial order. Rules in the town, on the other hand, were said to be more rigid than the laws of Russia. Pullman's seeming paternalism did not divert him from making a profit, even during the

He don't seem to enjoy it, but on election day
he votes for a continuance of the National Game.

Populists looked forward to the day when labor would rise against monopoly's
abuses and join their cause. From the *Guthrie Oklahoma Representative*, April
25, 1895.

depths of the depression of the 1890s. Between July, 1893, and
May, 1894, Pullman laid off 40 percent of his work force and cut
the wages of those he retained by more than 25 percent. Meanwhile, the cost of rent, utilities, and services at the company
town remained unaltered. By late 1893 there were rumors of starvation at Pullman, Illinois.[30]

On May 11, 1894, Pullman's employees finally went on strike.

In the midst of depression, management easily found strike-breakers to replace them. The strikers turned to the American Railway Union, the nation's largest trade union, for help. Union president Eugene V. Debs sympathized with the strikers and asked Pullman officials to arbitrate. When Pullman stated that there was "nothing to arbitrate," American Railway Union members immediately voted a boycott. When it went into effect on June 26, 1894, union members were careful to move mail trains on schedule to avoid legal difficulties with federal authorities, but they sidetracked all Pullman cars. Railroad companies proclaimed their contracts with Pullman inviolate and refused to let their trains move without Pullman cars. This action stalled most rail traffic west of Chicago. Railroad companies pooled their resources in the General Managers' Association, which provided guards for railroad property, blacklisted workers, and influenced authorities.[31]

On July 2, Attorney General Richard Olney secured an injunction against the strikers, one of the most far-reaching injunctions issued in American history. President Cleveland then ordered federal troops into Chicago to break the strike. The violence, which had been slight up to that point, became spectacular. Mobs destroyed railroad cars, razed the central roundhouse at the switching yard, and put part of the nearby Columbian Exposition to the torch. Although men not associated with the American Railway Union did most of the damage, strikers got the blame. The strike was broken quickly, participants were blacklisted, and Debs was packed away to prison for conspiracy. Attorney General Olney appointed a railroad lawyer as the special federal attorney for cases arising out of the strike.[32]

In Oklahoma, as elsewhere, Populists and Coxeyites immediately took Debs's side in the struggle. Third-party supporters believed that they were witnessing the cataclysm predicted in such Populist tracts as Ignatius Donnelly's *Caesar's Column*. The Coxey and Debs movements were associated with Populism in the popular mind of the South and West. Oklahoma Populist spokesmen embraced the movements as their own. This provided them with a sense of participation in events of national importance.

As general of the local Commonweal Army, John Furlong tele-

graphed words of encouragement to Debs. Allusions to the "slavery" of Pullman workers and the "bastille in Pullman," along
with charges of "an increase of the standing army . . . to crush all
resistance to further encroachments on our liberties" adorned
Populist newspapers. John Allan proclaimed Debs's prosecutors
"the lineal descendants, in spirit, of the men who dragged Garrison through the streets of Boston with a rope around his neck,
mobbed Wendell Phillips, and executed John Brown." Populist
editors were quick to claim that government ownership of the
railroads would have prevented the entire disaster.[33]

Oklahoma's Democratic and Republican leaders were almost a
unit in support of Cleveland's actions in the Pullman strike.
While admitting the justice of labor's grievances, Frank Greer
proclaimed that the fight was between "Debs and the people, not
Debs and Pullman." He also charged that "red-mouthed foreigners" were behind the turbulence and suggested that the "anarchy should be stopped instanter by government orders to 'shoot
to kill.'" All mainstream-party spokesmen seemed to agree with
the editor of the *Alva Pioneer* when he noted that while "every
Populist was not an anarchist, every anarchist was a Populist."
Revealing a growing ambivalence within Oklahoma Democratic
ranks, Mort Bixler of the *Norman State Democrat*, praised Cleveland for his backbone in suppressing anarchy only to congratulate
Oklahoma County Democrats two weeks later for refusing to
commend him for sending troops to Chicago.[34]

Populist farmers had identified unjust laws and insensitive legislators as the primary cause of the nation's problems. They easily
accepted the proposition that a union of interests existed between Populist farmers, Coxeyites, and union members. Articles
and cartoons playing on this proposed union of the oppressed appeared frequently in Populist sheets. Most third-party editors had
also supported labor at the Homestead Strike in 1892.

In principle, Oklahoma Populists did not accept strikes as
useful tools to secure demands. The laws of the nation, they
claimed, were slanted too much in the interests of capital. They
were not surprised when Cleveland successfully broke the Pullman strike. Meaningful and lasting change, they claimed, could
be achieved only at the ballot box.[35]

Populists held high hopes that the events of 1894 would bring a massive influx of urban workers to their ranks. Debs therefore became a major third-party spokesman overnight. The National Reform Press Association covered his speeches and provided third-party papers with articles and letters he had written. Embracing the rhetoric of his newly adopted party, Debs charged that both of the old parties "are controlled by the money power and both are equally debauched by its influence," to the uniform accord of Populist spokesmen. He claimed to prefer the GOP because it "does not hesitate to boldly champion every measure calculated to enlarge the power of plutocracy, where the Democratic party makes professions of loyalty to the people and then turns traitor in the supreme hour of trial." Charging that the "money power now exerts barbaric sway" over America, Debs asked the truly patriotic to "defy public opinion and take your stand with men like Jackson." Along with Jacob Coxey and former abolitionist Lyman Trumball, who had participated in founding the Republican party in the 1850s and converted to Populism on the labor issue in 1894, Eugene V. Debs came to symbolize the rapidly growing fortunes of the People's party both in Oklahoma and in the nation.[36]

CHAPTER SIX

Populism at Floodtide

Oklahoma Populism entered a new phase of development in the mid-1890s. The slow growth of the third party in its early years gave way to spectacular accessions after 1892. A major factor in this growth was the Cleveland administration's response to the panic of 1893. Repeal of the Sherman Silver Purchase Act elevated the silver issue to a position of prime importance in debtor regions. Cleveland's overreaction to Coxey's Army and the Pullman strike also alienated many who sympathized with the unemployed or who opposed railroad transgressions.

As the depression of the 1890s deepened, many who had committed themselves to the dominant ethos of the Gilded Age began to have second thoughts about the economic and social orthodoxies of the period. The cosmopolitan spokesmen of the Gilded Age had predicted uninterrupted material progress. Instead, tight credit, high interest rates, low commodity prices, and high shipping costs led many to question whether the cyclical hinterland ideology of agrarians actually was more valid. By 1894 many Oklahomans had encountered enough disappointment and hardship to become prime candidates for conversion to Populism.

New leaders also helped boost the fortunes of the Oklahoma People's party in the mid-1890s. Vigorous, talented men, untainted by scandal, had been in short supply in the early years of Oklahoma Populism. Samuel Crocker was an admitted Sooner, and although an experienced editor, he never engaged in the newspaper trade in Oklahoma. George Gardenhire, who had obvious organizational talents, forever disqualified himself as a major spokesman for the moral imperatives of Populism by his slick dealing in the first legislature. N. H. Ward simply lacked the talent necessary to mobilize potential supporters. For Oklahoma Populism to become more than a petty nuisance to the GOP or an annex to the Democratic party, new leaders had to emerge with the moral authority and requisite talents to disseminate effectively the doctrines of Populism to those searching for new answers. Between 1891 and 1894 a significant number of third-party newspaper editors arrived in Oklahoma and quickly provided this vital leadership cadre. John S. Allan, Leo Vincent, and Ralph Beaumont were the ablest and most important of these new editors.

John Sterling Allan, the son of Scottish immigrants, was born in Sparta, Illinois, about forty miles southeast of Saint Louis, Missouri, in January, 1866. He cast his first vote for the Union Labor party in 1888. After receiving a law degree from Park College, in Missouri, he moved to Norman, Oklahoma, in 1891, established a law office, and became active in real estate. He also helped organize the town's first Presbyterian church. Along with other local Populists, Allan took part in founding the *Norman Peoples Voice* in mid-1892. He assumed editorship of the paper in early 1893 and made journalism his primary calling for the next seventeen years.[1]

To emphasize his commitment to the natural-rights philosophy of the founding fathers, Allan added the following poem to the masthead of his paper upon assuming the editorship:

> Before the law was written down with parchment or with pen,
> Before the law made citizens, the moral law made men.
> Law stands for human rights, but when it fails those rights to give,
> Then let the law die, my brother, but let human beings live.[2]

Although he was a northerner in an overwhelmingly southern-populated county, Allan quickly became a leader of the middle-of-the-road faction of the Oklahoma People's party.

In September, 1891, Henry and Leo Vincent moved the *American Nonconformist* from the southern Kansas birthplace of the Oklahoma Populist movement to Indianapolis, Indiana, where they hoped to establish the paper as a national People's

John S. Allan (right foreground) in the office of the *Norman Peoples Voice* (ca.
1900). Courtesy of Marjorie Lenore Allan Garrett, of El Reno, Oklahoma.

party organ. Overexpansion and a bank failure associated with
the panic of 1893 eventually forced the Vincents to sell the paper
that they had started as teenagers. Older brother Henry then
moved to Chicago, where he became associate editor of the
Populist *Express*. Fred Bailey, who had just purchased the *Guthrie
West and South*, invited Leo Vincent to move to Oklahoma and
become his partner. The opportunity to relocate "amidst thousands of our former *Nonconformist* readers" proved appealing to
the younger Vincent. Although only thirty-two, Leo Vincent
brought vigor and fifteen years of reform-press experience to the
territory's third-party movement. He took over the *West and
South* in March, 1894, and in honor of Ignatius Donnelly's newspaper, the *Saint Paul Representative*, Vincent renamed his new
charge the *Oklahoma Representative*. A few months later Oklahoma Populists named him territorial chairman of the People's
party.[3]

Born in Yorkshire, England, in 1844, Ralph Beaumont was by

far the oldest of Oklahoma Populism's new leaders. Beaumont's parents brought him to the United States when he was four. He attended common school in Webster, Massachusetts, until the age of ten and then was apprenticed to learn the shoe trade. Beaumont volunteered for the Union army in 1862 and served until the end of the war. He then relocated to Elmira, New York, where he practiced his trade and became active in labor union activities.

At the founding convention of the Knights of Labor in 1869 union members elected Beaumont grand worthy foreman. Always a strong advocate of political action, he represented the Knights at the founding convention of the Greenback-Labor party in 1878. In 1884, Beaumont entered journalism as an investigative reporter. Both Democrats and Greenbackers picked up his stridently antiprotectionist broadsides in the mid-1880s. Beaumont was chairman of the Knights of Labor resolution committee, which endorsed opening Oklahoma to settlement in 1886. That year he became the union's Washington lobbyist. Later Beaumont was active in the founding of the People's party, and he campaigned widely for the third-party movement throughout the 1890s. He moved to Oklahoma City in January, 1894, and founded his own paper, the *Oklahoma State*, a month later.[4]

The rise of reform editors to positions of leadership was crucial to the growth of the third-party movement in the Oklahoma Territory. Most Populist editors were relatively young, and the success or failure of their newspapers hinged primarily upon the fortunes of the third-party movement. Because all Populist newspapers in Oklahoma were weeklies, their editors had the time, interest, and, with youth, the energy necessary to assume leadership roles and build up the People's party. The reform editors' importance to the Oklahoma Populist movement grew as the number of third-party papers increased. Oklahoma had one Populist newspaper in 1890, two in 1891, six in 1892, eleven in 1893, twenty in 1894, and twenty-one in 1895. Wherever Populism flourished in the 1890s, reform editors constituted a substantial portion of the third party's leadership.[5]

A new spirit of confidence and vigor emerged in Oklahoma's third-party ranks with the arrival of Beaumont and Vincent early in 1894. Both men were noted Populist spokesmen with strong third-party credentials. Vincent's position, however, was more complicated and delicate. Guthrie was the territorial capital, and Populists looked to Vincent's paper for guidance on Oklahoma matters. In addition, Vincent had replaced fusionist A. G. Copeland as editor of the third party's territorial organ. Midroaders had started their own newspaper, the short-lived *Oklahoma Populist*, in Guthrie the previous July. Part of Vincent's new role was to reconcile the various factions within Oklahoma's Populist party. Although Vincent opposed fusion in principle, he was neither as strident nor as consistent on the subject as John Allan of the *Norman Peoples Voice*. Because his old Kansas nemesis, Frank Greer, whose brother operated the *Winfield Courier*, edited the Guthrie Republican party sheet, Leo Vincent would direct most of his Populistic venom toward the GOP while he was in Oklahoma.

In July, 1894, Vincent and other Populist editors found good reason to turn their undivided attention to the Democratic administrations in both Washington, D.C., and Guthrie. In the wake of the violence associated with the Pullman strike, citizens of Enid and Pond Creek, in the newly opened Cherokee Outlet, began settling their differences with the Rock Island Railroad through acts of sabotage.

Before the September, 1893, land opening, men associated with the Rock Island Railroad, which passed through both towns, manipulated Indian allotments to gain control of land in and around the two proposed townsites. The federal government had selected both as county seats. When General Land Commissioner Silas W. Lamboreau learned of the plot, he moved the location of each county seat three miles to the south. At the time of the opening, rival railroad and government towns appeared. Rock Island officials provided service to their towns but refused to stop at the government sites. The railroad company apparently expected to force citizens of the government towns into relocating to the railroad's townsites.[6]

The citizens of Enid applied pressure of their own upon receiving their city charter in November, 1893. The first act of the Enid City Council was to pass an ordinance limiting trains to a

A NOTE OF WARNING.

Populists consider the growth of their party and confidently look toward the future. From the *Kingfisher Reformer*, July 5, 1894.

speed of four miles per hour while passing through town. Perry, on the Santa Fe line, passed a similar ordinance at the same time. Because the reduced speed would allow patrons to jump on and off the trains at the government townsites, the Rock Island chose to ignore the law. Attempts to arrest the conductor for speeding proved fruitless because the trains carried the U.S. mail.[7]

On September 29, 1893, Representative Joseph Wheeler of
Alabama introduced a bill in the U.S. Congress that required the
Rock Island Railroad to service the government towns. Delegate
Flynn vigorously endorsed the measure. The proposed legislation passed the house quickly, but was sidetracked in the Senate
when opponents successfully fastened to it a county seat election amendment. Vice-President Adlai Stevenson cast the tie-
breaking vote to pass the bill as amended. This blocked passage
of the bill for ten months. Democrats, who controlled the city
council of Enid, claimed that the amendment "will be a death
blow to our party in the territory."[8]

With favorable legislation blocked in Congress, Enid's city attorney attempted a judicial solution to the railroad conflict in the
spring of 1894, but to no avail. In mid-June citizens of Pond
Creek tore up track and wrecked a train. When railroad lawyers
successfully overturned a writ of mandamus favoring Enid on July
11, 1894, the Populist *Enid Coming Events* proclaimed, "It is evident there is no justice to be found in our courts." Another train
was wrecked the next day. At this point Marshal E. D. Nix asked
U.S. Attorney General Richard Olney for authority to raise an
army of deputies. Along with a troop of U.S. cavalry, Nix's deputies arrived in Enid and Pond Creek the next day and placed the
towns under martial law. Two railroad bridges were burned on
July 16. According to Clark Hudson, of the Populist *Alva Review*,
"The Rock Island people are saved the trouble of burning their
bridges behind them by the accommodating people of Oklahoma." The U.S. Senate finally withdrew the county seat amendment on August 1 and settled the whole matter.[9]

Throughout the "Enid Railroad War," Oklahomans of all political faiths supported the government towns' right to secure
railroad service. Only Roy Hoffman's *Guthrie Oklahoma Leader*
sided with the Rock Island. Frank Greer reasoned that the Enid
and Pond Creek situations differed from the events surrounding
the Pullman strike. The railroads had done no wrong at Chicago,
he claimed. In Oklahoma, the Rock Island had defied municipal
law. Greer asserted that if the government was to "make the railroad company obey the municipal laws of Pond Creek and Enid

. . . [there] will be no need to complain of the people." Most mainstream-party editors hoped for legislative relief.[10]

Ralph Bray, editor of the Populist *Enid Coming Events*, put forth the typical third-party critique of the railroad war. A former Greenbacker and an exponent of Bellamy nationalism, Bray contended that government ownership of the railroads was the only solution. He chided the Democratic city council for the ineffectiveness of its speeding ordinance and claimed that legislation pending before Congress was unconstitutional, a position many noted lawyers also took at the time. For Populists, the real issue was whether railroads should be government- or corporate-owned. A court order eventually silenced Bray and more than one hundred other citizens of Enid and Pond Creek. Populist editors elsewhere immediately raised the cry of arbitrary government, but to no avail.[11]

Flynn, Greer, and other Republicans had emphasized a legislative approach to the Enid and Pond Creek situations throughout the conflict. Eventually their contention that relief was possible within the contemporary political system proved valid. Cynics attributed the support of the normally prorailroad Greer to the concerns of Santa Fe officials that the conflict might get out of hand and "Oklahoma, when it gets to be a state, will pass railroad legislation that will be a yoke on the necks of railroads."[12]

Democrats, including Attorney General Olney, Marshal Nix, and acting Governor Thomas J. Lowe (Governor Renfrow was out of the territory during most of the violence) became associated in the popular mind with the Rock Island's cause and were thus discredited. In the wake of the battle, *Oklahoma Leader* editor Roy Hoffman apologized for taking the railroad's side in language so profuse and flatulent that he drew ridicule from almost every quarter. When Leo Vincent noted in December, 1894, that the Choctaw Railroad circumvented Tecumseh on its way from Oklahoma City to Shawnee, mainstream-party spokesmen recognized the propaganda value he expected from the issue and responded with almost uniform silence.[13]

To get the jump on both Democrats and Populists in the turbulent election year of 1894, Oklahoma Republicans scheduled their territorial convention for mid-May in Oklahoma City. Editor Greer proudly reported that the meeting was enthusiastic and harmonious. Former Governor A. J. Seay nominated Dennis Flynn, the incumbent delegate to Congress, for a second term in Washington. He won by acclamation. The GOP territorial platform denounced both the federal and territorial Democratic administrations, praised Flynn for his work in Washington, endorsed the McKinley Tariff, and called for the free and unlimited coinage of American silver. Greer noted that the Oklahoma Republican platform contained "the first straight-out declaration for free coinage of American silver ever made in a Republican platform in this nation" and hoped it would not be the last.[14]

Frank Greer accepted the financial question as the paramount issue of the mid-1890s. The Democratic Wilson-Gorman Tariff, he maintained, was proof that protection was a dead issue. He also expressed fear that his party had drifted away from its original principles and contended that the GOP could no longer rely on the "safe" issues of the previous twenty years for victory. He called for more vigorous prosecution of monopolies and pleaded with Republicans to take the lead on the silver issue.[15]

Greer's seeming turn toward Populism in taking a free-silver and antimonopoly stance was more apparent than real. His commitment to these positions did not constitute a substantial break with the success ethic that Greer, along with most Oklahoma Republicans, espoused. When asked how much money the nation needed, Greer replied, "All we can get, without injuring that we already have, and the way to get it is by using the resources nature has given us," namely, gold and silver. Concerning monopolies, the Republican editor believed that laws that allowed unnatural accumulation of wealth should be abridged, but "the opportunity for a man to accumulate according to his aptitude and his natural powers must not be interfered with." Unlike Populists, Greer believed that differences in people's abilities could naturally result in wide disparities of wealth. He claimed that most Populist leaders were "the disgruntled, disappointed, and defeated elements of the two old parties" and suggested that their idea that legislation "is the panacea for all the ills of mankind, is born of ignorance." According to Greer, laws should give

every man an equal opportunity and "protect him in his consti-
tutional rights and in his accumulations." If some people find
themselves "enslaved," he added, "it is done by their own care-
lessness, perversity, or ignorance."[16]

In contrast to the enthusiasm and harmony within GOP
ranks, Oklahoma Democrats were in almost complete disarray by
the date of their August 1 territorial convention. Feuding between opponents and supporters of President Cleveland had been
rampant for a year. Territorial Democrats removed Leslie P. Ross
as their chairman in January, 1894. Roy Hoffman, however, retained his seat on the executive committee. According to silverite Mort Bixler, of the *Norman State Democrat*, Hoffman continued to insult and drive out of the party every man who failed
to "make a servile and cringing bow to Renfrow." The governor's
friends naturally attributed such attacks to the "kicking" of those
passed over for appointments.[17]

Although silverites easily captured the 1894 Democratic con-
vention's organization, they did not completely control the proceedings. For the Delegate nomination, Democrats named silverite Joseph Wisby over Leslie P. Ross by a two-to-one margin.
Compromises worked out on the platform, however, left the
party with an aura of schizophrenia for the campaign. The 1894
Democratic platform favored the free and unlimited coinage of
American silver, free homes, and immediate single statehood for
Oklahoma. By specifying "American" silver, both Democrats and
Republicans mirrored Cleveland's concern that foreign countries
might flood the American treasury with the white metal and
demand gold in return. Democrats also expressed sympathy for
labor's "just demands, when made in a peaceable and lawful manner," denounced the Rock Island Railroad for its actions in the
Cherokee Outlet, and then endorsed both the national and territorial administrations. Silverites attempted to block the endorsement of Cleveland but failed. The Democrats' opponents made
much of the anomaly of a silverite running on a pro-Cleveland
platform.[18]

Vincent labeled the Democratic and Republican silver planks
"two links of bologna—so alike in smell and complexion . . .
[that they] must be from the same dog." When he published their

silver planks side by side in the *Oklahoma Representative*, Populist
spokesmen cut them out and at debates asked their opponents
which was which. More than once the results proved embarrassing to the third party's opponents.[19]

As Vincent predicted after the Democratic convention, the
race in 1894 was between Republicans and Populists. According
to the Guthrie editor, a greater gap now existed between Populists and Democrats than between Populists and Republicans.
Greer saw great danger for the GOP if large numbers of Democrats converted to Populism. He thus gave Democratic candidate
Wisby much more favorable press coverage than expected. As it
became obvious, however, that Wisby would finish a distant
third, notable Democratic spokesmen dropped from the race.[20]

Leo Vincent put forth his ideas on the Populist campaign of
1894 in an *Oklahoma Representative* article published four days
before the July 10 third-party territorial convention in El Reno.
He suggested that, to lead their 1894 ticket, the People's party
nominate a man who possessed three requisite qualities. The
nominee should have a clean record, should be a known Populist
of stable character, and should not be so partisan as to be offensive. Vincent's first two points were obvious jabs at Samuel
Crocker and N. H. Ward, the third party's previous delegate
nominees. His third point referred to the strategy of securing as
many Democratic votes as possible without actually engaging in
fusion. Vincent eagerly solicited Democratic converts by praising
the old party's rural leaders for supporting silver, a low tariff, and
antitrust legislation. The People's party, he emphasized, had supported each of these issues since its inception, while urban-
oriented Democrats had betrayed their party on these subjects.[21]

Although Vincent claimed his suggestions were not in support
of any particular candidate, he obviously favored Ralph Beaumont for the third party's delegate nomination in 1894. Beaumont's association with the Knights of Labor and his vigorous
lobbying for the opening of Oklahoma to non-Indian settlement
in the 1880s made him widely known in the new territory. As a
longtime–third-party figure, Beaumont was well versed on Populist issues. He was a good speaker, and while his New England

accent may have been a handicap, Oklahoma was still a land of immigrants from the older sections of the nation.[22]

To a certain degree Vincent's statement on party strategy re-kindled the fusion issue among Oklahoma Populists. Fusionists interpreted his article as favoring the nomination of "some conservative man whom the Democrats can endorse." Beaumont vigorously denied the need to nominate a man suitable to Democratic leaders. The Oklahoma County Populist Club, he claimed, had three times the membership of the third party's 1892 vote in the county. According to Beaumont, similar advances elsewhere in the territory ensured the People's party a substantial poll even without Democratic help.[23]

Ninety-nine delegates, two-thirds of whom claimed Civil War service, met at El Reno on July 10, 1894, and nominated Ralph Beaumont as the Populist candidate for delegate to Congress.[24] Although Beaumont had four opponents for the nomination, none were taken seriously. As Leo Vincent noted, most "doubt-less learned many things commendable to themselves that up to that time they were ignorant of." He also proudly noted that less than half of the delegates had taken the train to the convention and that none were officeholders. Vincent was named chairman of the party's central committee, which automatically made him Beaumont's campaign manager.[25]

Oklahoma Populists endorsed the Omaha platform of 1892, called specifically for free coinage of silver, denounced both the Democratic and Republican parties as agents of the money power, called for boards of arbitration for labor disputes, and ex-pressed sympathies for Coxey, Debs, and the people of Enid and Pond Creek. At the territorial level, the third party favored free homes, single statehood, better laws on leasing school lands, and scaling all official salaries "in proportion to the reduction in prices for products and the wages of laborers." Vincent earlier had identified taxation as the "great overshadowing issue in Okla-homa," stating that the territory's tax rate was grossly inflated, "exceeding that of any other state or territory." With drought, debt, and poverty the lot of most Oklahomans, he believed that local and territorial expenditures, especially on salaries, should be reduced. The issue was particularly significant in the older regions of the territory, where land became taxable in 1894. More than a quarter of the taxpayers in the territory were delinquent by this time.[26]

Democrats and Republicans denounced Ralph Beaumont as a "carpetbagger" whom Populist leaders imported for sinister purposes. Nicknames such as "Rollingstone" and "Anarchist" quickly emerged. Frank Greer revived rumors of a Vidette-like secret machine controlling the People's party. He gave Beaumont, Vincent, and Fred Bailey top honors in the order. Vincent and Greer then rehashed the Kansas election of 1888, replete with charges of who was to blame for the infamous Coffeyville bombing.[27]

Beaumont moved to offset his liability as a newcomer with a vigorous campaign. He canvassed the territory with a busy schedule of debates and camp meetings. In Norman the Populist nominee declared the tariff a minor issue. At Perkins he spoke of his Civil War service and how at the end of the war the government had discharged him, but not bondholders. To offset some of the old parties' sectional appeal, Populists ran an "old soldier" campaign. Vincent and Beaumont, for instance, appealed for the kind of money "that came to your rescue during the war." Beaumont also suggested that the easy way to nationalize the railroads was to "simply foreclose the mortgage on the Union Pacific which the Republicans for twenty years have failed to collect." Free silver and taxation, however, proved to be the third party's most important issues.[28]

The "financial question" was one of the most vital political issues of late-nineteenth-century America. The amount of money circulating through the American economy affected prices, availability of credit, interest rates, and income. Because monetary policy established the basic ground rules upon which the economy operated, the stakes were high. Those who controlled the rules of credit and commerce to a great extent determined who got the largest share of America's expanding productive capacity.

Before the Civil War, Americans relied on a metal standad for their currency. The government set the legal ratio between the value of silver and gold at 16 to 1 in 1834. Because the intrinsic value of sixteen ounces of silver was greater than that of one ounce of gold at the time, people generally hoarded the white metal and used gold for currency. The need for money to finance the Civil War caused the federal government to suspend specie payments (the redemption of paper currency with gold and/or silver) in 1862. During the war federal authorities printed approximately $450 million in fiat money, called greenbacks. The result was inflation, commercial liquidity, and general prosperity. Orthodox financial circles, however, looked toward the resumption of specie payments and redemption of greenbacks with metal after the war. The Public Credit Act of 1869 pledged the federal government to such a policy.

Because retirement of greenbacks would cause deflation, unless a major silver or gold strike occurred, bankers and other creditors wrapped their fiscal position in a blanket of moralistic slogans. "Honest money," meaning currency based upon the intrinsic value of some metal, they asserted, was necessary to convince the holders of capital of the long term reliability of the government and the stability of the dollar. Those who had supported the war financially, they claimed, had assumed that the dollar would be returned to par afterward. Investors, otherwise, might be timid and stunt the nation's economic growth. The failure to redeem greenbacks in specie would also destroy foreign confidence in the dollar and, thus, foreign trade as well.

Debtors, particularly in the cash-poor South and West, took the opposite position. Deflation, which decreased commodity prices and wages, was unfair. As each of the scarcer dollars gained in purchasing power, the debt of mortgage-ridden farmers would increase. They would have to sell more and more products to make the same dollar that they had borrowed. With less money circulating through the economy, credit would also be more difficult to obtain, and in a creditor's market, interest rates would soar.

When the federal government revised its coinage list in 1873, silver was eliminated from the schedule of metals to be coined. This made trade with nations on the gold standard easier. Because silver was hoarded at the time, demonetization seemed irrelevant. In the mid-1870s, however, large-scale silver strikes and development of a new technique for processing low-grade ore lowered the value of the white metal. If silver had remained on the coinage list at the ratio of 16 to 1, deflation would not have been as severe as it was in the late nineteenth century. Debtor spokesmen and silver interests immediately labeled it the "Crime of 1873."

Because the free coinage of silver and gold at a ratio of 16 to 1 would have expanded the currency while overcoming the fears many had about fiat money, "free silver" became a popular slogan in the 1870s. In 1878 and 1890, Republicans found it expedient to authorize the limited coinage of silver with the Bland-Allison and Sherman Silver Purchase acts, respectively. Fiscal conservatives believed that uncertainty about the currency resulting from the Sherman Act caused the panic of 1893. When Grover Cleveland accepted their argument and secured repeal of the law in 1893, he catapulted the silver issue into national prominence.

Western and southern spokesmen claimed that Cleveland's repeal of the Sherman Silver Purchase Act in 1893 was a Wall Street plot to advance the interests of bankers and other creditors. Federal expenditures would force the government to float bonds. Banks would use their reserves to purchase these bonds and then place them with the U.S. Treasury as security for bank-issued paper money. The only difference between a government bond and a greenback, Populists claimed, was the interest bankers secured through a bond issue. To Populists, government bonds were a subterfuge that the rich used to concentrate money in their own hands through federal interest payments. This meant that the forces of capital appropriated wealth without human exertion. Populists' producer orientation led them to contend that labor, not investment, speculation, or slick deals, produced wealth. They viewed interest on government bonds as nothing more than legalized thievery. According to Leo Vincent, the old parties wanted interest-bearing bonds in large denominations that only the rich could purchase, while Populists desired non-interest-bearing bonds (greenbacks) in small denominations for the benefit of all.[29]

Populists contended that money was no more than a tool civilized nations used to facilitate exchange. It needed only government fiat, not intrinsic value. As long as the nation remained committed to money with intrinsic value, the rich could keep money scarce and simply watch their purchasing power increase. They could also reap windfall profits from interest on the government bonds that cash stringency had forced. Neither manipulation required the labor that made accumulation valid in Populists' eyes. Third-party spokesmen considered entrepreneurs such as A. J. Seay, who borrowed money at 6 percent in Missouri and loaned it out at 12 percent in Oklahoma, immoral and unfair.[30]

Because the nation's laws favored capital over producers, "the relation between debt-makers and debt-payers is that of master to slave," the Reverend A. G. Copeland wrote when he edited the *Guthrie West and South*. John Allan said that he "would like to see the [other] ministers getting on the Lord's side of the money question" and suggested they start by reading up on usury. Populists believed that those who created wealth through their own labor should receive the full benefits of its value. The difference between what merchants, moneylenders, railroad owners, and other capitalists received and what their workers earned was stolen from the laborer. Leo Vincent proclaimed that "the law that labor recognizes is the law of the great Father above . . . [while] the law that capital works by is Mammon worship." A government-owned banking system that circulated the greenbacks "that freed the chattel slave" during the Civil War would, in time, also "free the wage slave," Vincent believed.[31]

While Oklahoma Populist spokesmen were almost exclusively greenbacker in principle, they found it expedient to promote free silver in 1894. It was only the first step on the "ladder to monetary progression" which led to greenbacks, they claimed.[32] All Oklahoma Populist leaders at one time or another proclaimed greenbacks superior to silver. Fusionists such as Samuel Crocker, A. G. Copeland, and Ralph Bray were every bit as vigorous in promoting greenbacks as middle-of-the-roaders Ralph Beaumont, Leo Vincent, and John Allan.[33] President Cleveland's repeal of the Sherman Silver Purchase Act simply gave the third party an audience it might not otherwise have enjoyed. Because large portions of both old parties opposed coinage of the white

A Populist commentary on the immorality of exploiting others. From the *Guthrie Oklahoma Representative*, May 23, 1895.

metal, Populists logically proclaimed that "the People's party is the only straight silver party in existence" and tried to capitalize on the issue's popularity.[34]

The Populists' 1894 campaign went well until the last month of the race, when another scandal over redistricting emerged. As in 1892, new additions to the Oklahoma Territory had caused the need for a new census and redistricting. Federal legislation authorized Governor Renfrow to appoint a three-man commission to redistrict the territory. The governor appointed Democrat Allen Hall of Perry, Republican W. T. Walker of Norman, and fusion Populist S. B. Oberlander of Enid (formerly of Oklahoma City). The commission selected Hall, the Democrat, as chairman. Renfrow obviously expected a Democratic-Populist fusion on the committee. Oberlander, however, balked at a Democratic plot to secure extra representation for southern-born, presumably Democratic, voters. At one point the governor physically dragged the Populist commissioner into a secret meeting with Hall, but without the desired result. Eventually, Renfrow dismissed Oberlander from the redistricting committee and replaced him with Populist Councillor Fielden S. Pulliam, who proved more pliable. The governor subsequently accepted the Hall-Pulliam plan as the official report of the commission. Oberlander and Walker constructed their own plan, which Renfrow ignored.[35]

In explaining his part in the redistricting controversy, Pulliam claimed that he got a better deal for his party from the Democrats. Charges that he betrayed the People's party to secure a safe council district seemed valid to Populists such as Leo Vincent, who recalled that Pulliam had been one of Beaumont's rivals for the delegate nomination. Pulliam subsequently lost his bid for renomination by a three to one margin at the third party's council convention. He then bitterly charged that Vincent headed a secret organization that ruled the People's party and labeled the new council nominee, B. R. Tankersley, a Vidette. Tankersley won the council seat by only a twenty-four–vote margin in November.[36]

Oberlander also failed to receive his party's nomination for the council. Ralph Bray, editor of the *Enid Coming Events*, defeated him by a four-to-one margin. Oberlander seemed reconciled to his defeat at the time and asked that the nomination be made unanimous. Later, however, he issued a broadside charging fraud in the selection of several delegates to the council convention. Bray lost by thirty votes on election day.[37]

In line with the Populists' middle-of-the-road orientation, the three parties nominated separate candidates in all but one legislative district in 1894. The third-party supported Independent Republican C. H. Tandy, a black, for the Guthrie house district. Regular Republican Cassius Barnes still carried the district easily. Populists also nominated Green I. Currin, the only black member of the first legislature, for a house seat in Kingfisher County. His loss meant that the 1895 legislature would be the first without a black representative.[38]

Even gerrymandering the territory did not help the Democratic party in the election of 1894. Renfrow's party carried only four of the thirty-nine legislative seats, and Wisby came in third in the delegate race with 24.9 percent of the vote. Because Populists constantly made moralistic appeals for support in their campaigns, the redistricting scandal and its aftershocks hurt the People's party most on election day. Beaumont still secured 33 percent of the vote, and Populists won twelve seats in the 1895 legislature. Flynn carried the territory with 42.1 percent of the vote, and the GOP elected twenty-three men to Oklahoma's third legislature.

Better Populist leadership and a more effective third-party campaign combined with the events of the previous summer to increase voter participation in the Oklahoma Territory by 24.5 percent in 1894.[39] The third party increased its share of the vote in every county of the territory and, in fact, became Oklahoma's second party. Democrats, on the other hand, saw their portion of the ballot decline in all but the the western ranching counties of Day and Custer. Republicans increased their share of the vote only in Canadian, Cleveland, and Oklahoma counties, where a number of urban Democrats switched to the GOP.

The most dramatic change in loyalties occurred in the lands opened to settlement in 1891 and 1892.[40] Several years on the land had brought the realization that Oklahoma might not be the "Promised Land." The People's party in the Oklahoma Territory thus drew from two different sources, those who had brought their Populism with them to the new land and those disillusioned by the unfulfilled promises of Gilded Age development after a few years in the territory.

Only minor shifts occurred in the sectional appeal of each party's support in 1894 (see appendix A, table A-1). The mainstream parties still relied heavily on sectional support, while the People's party remained sectionally diverse. The opening of the Cherokee Outlet in 1893 accounts for the changes that did occur. Refugees from Kansas's seventh congressional district brought a new wave of midwestern-born support to the third party. Their exodus from Kansas was a major factor in the defeat of Populist Congressman "Sockless" Jerry Simpson in 1894. Missourians, who entered Oklahoma from the north in 1893, proved to be far less Populistic than earlier white border-state migrants. They lacked the exposure to the Farmers' Alliance that earlier migrants from this region had experienced in their Texas sojourn.

Map 6, which shows the results of the 1894 congressional election by township, graphically demonstrates the rural-urban political cleavage of the early and mid-1890s (also see appendix A, table A-2).[41] The Populist vote was concentrated primarily in the hinterland between Oklahoma's railroads. The third party carried only one township that had a railroad depot; Moore, in heavily southern-populated Cleveland County, where the Democratic party collapsed (see Map 3 for county names).[42] Hinterland townships that the People's party failed to carry consisted mostly of rural commercial centers and areas where blacks were numerous.[43] Map 7 shows that the Republican party carried cosmopolitan Oklahoma, while the Democratic party carried the town of Okarche, which had a significant German population, and a few scattered townships.[44]

With the onset of depression in 1893, Oklahoma's cotton farmers abandoned the Democratic party in large numbers (see appendix A, table A-4). Many enlisted in the Populist cause. Because the value of agricultural products per acre for those engaged in the corn-hog cycle was relatively high, the inclusion of cotton farmers in third-party ranks caused a significant drop in the average agricultural productivity for those supporting the Populist party in 1894 (see appendix A, table A-5). The consequent infusion of formerly Democratic tenant farmers also made the People's party even more the representative of those who had lost out in the struggle for free land.[45]

By 1894 the Democratic party was able to retain the loyalty of ranchers and prosperous farmers of southern heritage. The depression affected beef prices far less than other farm products. Those remaining with the party of Grover Cleveland thus had a much higher value of farm products per acre (productivity) and overall wealth than Democratic voters of previous years. The GOP, on the other hand, remained the party of agribusiness-oriented wheat growers. Farmers engaged in the more diversified corn-hog cycle retained their affinity for the People's party in 1894.

Democrats also lost the support of urban workers in 1894. Most went over to the Republican party. The third party's support for

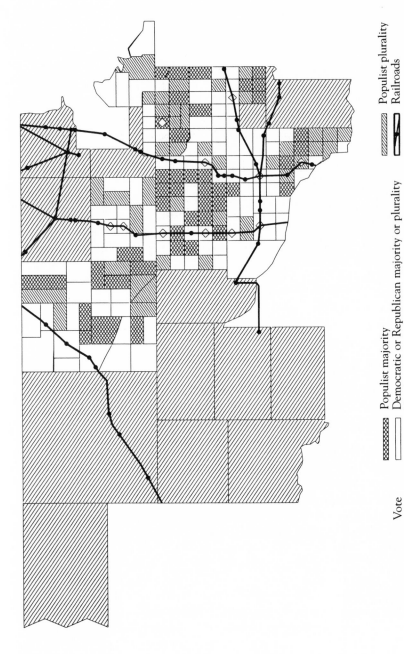

Vote

▨ Populist majority
☐ Democratic or Republican majority or plurality
▨ No data

▧ Populist plurality
▬ Railroads

Map 6. Populist vote for delegate to Congress, 1894.

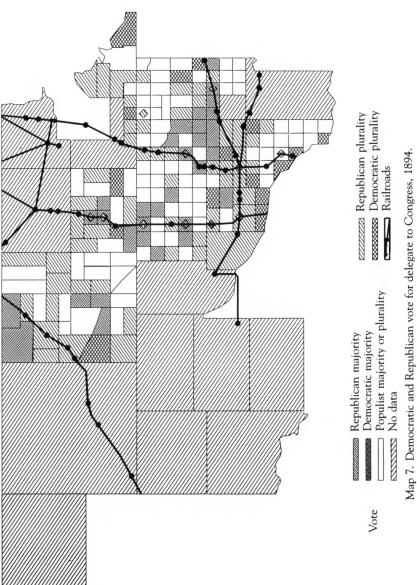

Vote

Republican majority
Democratic majority
Populist majority or plurality
No data

Republican plurality
Democratic plurality
Railroads

Map 7. Democratic and Republican vote for delegate to Congress, 1894.

Coxey and Debs did little to attract industrial workers in Oklahoma. Most of the territory's urban laborers were not unionized. They had come to Oklahoma to secure farms, but were forced into wage-earning jobs until they could acquire land. Because they considered their lot temporary, they failed to unionize or act as a unit in early Oklahoma.[46]

The emergence of a talented and vigorous cadre of new third-party leaders combined with antipathy toward both the federal and territorial Democratic administrations to make the People's party the major opposition to the GOP in the Oklahoma Territory in the mid-1890s. Because new leaders such as Leo Vincent, Ralph Beaumont, and John Allan agitated the old issues in a vigorous fashion, Oklahoma Populists almost quadrupled their poll of 1892.

The Cleveland administration and the depression of the 1890s can be given partial credit for the substantial gains the People's party made in 1894. Populists had already established their basic pattern of support in Oklahoma, however, before Cleveland took office in 1893. Less prosperous hinterland farmers who engaged in a safer, more diversified family-farm setting constituted most of the third party's electoral support in both 1892 and 1894. As in other states the Democratic party began to provide more converts to Populism than did the GOP. The Cleveland administration's perceived closeness to corporate interests led many Democrats to question whether their party really represented them, just as Republicans had done during the Harrison administration.

Although Populists secured the conversion of a number of old-party refugees in 1894, they relied more heavily on mobilizing those who previously had not voted. The third party's message held great appeal for formerly passive citizens who came to the realization that the panaceas of the Gilded Age's cosmopolitan ethos were false. There were limits, however, to the effectiveness of Populist radicalism. Those strongly commited to the late nineteenth century's ruling ideology were unlikely to convert to Populism no matter how far economic conditions deteriorated. A fair number of Oklahoma's urban Democrats, for instance, simply moved into the GOP in the mid-1890s. Those who did convert to Populism were overwhelmingly rural. Their disillusionment with the "Promised Land" came after spending a few years in the territory. Experiencing the realities of Oklahoma in the 1890s was a necessary part of the conversion process. Before this occurred, settlers generally remained loyal to whatever party they had affiliated with before coming to the new land.

CHAPTER SEVEN

Republicans Triumphant: The 1895 Legislature

A number of prominent Populists in both the South and the West went down to defeat in the off-year elections of 1894. Republicans, of course, chose to ignore the 42.4 percent nationwide increase in the third party's popular vote and proclaimed the demise of the People's party. Populists' losses in the West resulted largely from their failure to fuse with Democrats, and the third party's defeat in the South can be attributed, in large measure, to fraud and violence. The People's party, however, displaced one of the mainstream parties to become the major rival of the dominant party in both regions. In 1894, for instance, Democrats received only 9.4 percent of the Kansas vote, while the GOP carried 12.9 percent of the ballot in Texas in 1894.[1] Which of the three parties would survive in the normally two-party American political system was by no means certain in the wake of the 1894 election.

John Allan spoke for most Populists when he claimed that the Democratic party had gone the way of the Whigs. He predicted that the aristocratic elements would go Republican, while the rank and file would join the People's party. In the Oklahoma Territory, Populists captured half of the county offices in the region that had been opened to settlement before 1893 and replaced the Democratic party as the GOP's major rival.[2]

Democratic reverses in the 1894 territorial election delivered the Oklahoma legislature into the hands of the GOP for the first time. The Republican party's margin of victory, however, was small. Populist candidates came within one hundred votes of GOP victors in one council and six house seats. Had the results been reversed, the Democratic party would again have held the

IN WHICH BOX WILL THE VOTER OF '96 PUT HIS BALLOT?

The People's party constituted one of America's major political alternatives by the mid-1890s. From the *Kingfisher Reformer*, November 28, 1894.

balance of power in the assembly. Because the Democratic assemblymen of 1895 were Cleveland supporters, it is not certain that they would have joined a legislative fusion with Populists anyway. As it was, they voted with the Republican party in organizing Oklahoma's third legislature.[3]

Because Republicans feared that Governor Renfrow might veto some of their favorite projects, they moved swiftly to secure a two-thirds Democratic-Republican majority in both houses. They rejected a third-party challenge to the election of Democrat S. A. Waits of Cleveland County. Because this secured the desired margin in the house, they subsequently ignored charges of fraud in the election of Populist R. H. Walling, a Medford physician, and seated him.[4]

In the council, Republican James P. Gandy of Alva contested the election of Populist George Coulson with charges of voter fraud and ineligibility for office. Gandy's fraud affidavit proved to be more questionable than the vote. GOP councillors, however, removed Coulson on a strictly party-line vote (with Democrat Robert Ray siding with the Populists) on the grounds that the third-party candidate was not a legal resident of Oklahoma.[5]

Coulson had been a member of the 1893 Kansas legislature, and according to GOP sources, his family still resided in Kansas. Although he had received a resident's tax exemption on his Kansas farm in 1894, the local tax assessor had conferred it upon Coulson in ignorance of his move to Oklahoma. Coulson was a sixty-nine-year-old farmer who staked his claim in Woods County in September, 1893. Although he still owned and operated his Kansas farm, it was heavily mortgaged, and he expected to lose it.[6] Because Coulson lived in a dugout his first two years in the territory, his wife, who was in poor health, returned to Kansas for the winters of 1893–94 and 1894–95. She was not in the territory when the third legislature met, which made Coulson's true residence seem questionable. Coulson had not bothered to resign from the Kansas legislature, because Kansas law automatically unseated any legislator who moved from the state.[7]

Since Gandy clearly had not received a plurality of the votes cast, Populists saw Coulson's replacement as thwarting the will of the people. Populist Councillor E. H. Spencer of Payne County denounced the "Alabama Methods" used in unseating Coulson, but Republicans refused to allow his statement to be printed in the council journal. GOP Council President John H. Pitzer later admitted that Gandy's seating was purely a partisan move.[8]

Although the Republican mandate of 1894 was hardly overwhelming, GOP legislators found no reason to tread lightly in the 1895 legislature. They quickly denied proportional representation on committees in the council and then excluded third-party councillors from both the judiciary and the railroads and corporations committees. Populists did, however, succeed in getting bills printed after the first reading so that they could be inspected outside committee.[9]

Republicans also moved swiftly to hire what one Democratic editor labeled "an army of committee clerks" for the third legislature. The Democratic-Populist–controlled 1893 legislature had been the least expensive of the territorial years. Only Populists voted against the house's clerk-hire bill in 1895. Republicans also pushed a bill through the council giving Union army veterans preference for government jobs. John Allan, who sat in the third legislature, voted against the measure along with Democrat Robert Ray. Allan claimed that veterans had only performed their duty. Other Populists, however, supported the bill. The measure never came up for a roll-call vote in the house.[10]

Once the third legislature was organized, Populists had some difficulty keeping their colleagues at their posts in Guthrie. In the second week of the session the council adjourned for a junket to Topeka to witness the election of fusion Democrat John Martin to the U.S. Senate. One Republican and three Populists remained in Guthrie. Populist Councillor James E. Doom also declined at first, but later agreed to accompanying the younger councillors as a chaperone. He refused, however, to go on "an irrigation junket to El Reno" the following weekend.[11]

James E. Doom of Pottawatomie County, who was an experienced legislator, quickly emerged as the leader of the third party in the council. Although a man of strong convictions and "proud of the title 'crank,'" he was forever pleasant in demeanor and, on occasion, far more jocular than his name suggested. When asked why legislators were so lackadaisical in debating a probate bill, the elder statesman attributed their passivity to the lack of a sufficient lobby to draw their finest oratorical efforts.[12]

Doom's knowledge of the classics, from which he frequently quoted, quickly made him a close friend of John Allan. The relationship probably served to harness the younger legislator's earnestness in debate. On more than one occasion Allan came to recognize the warmth of his argument before crossing the bounds of propriety and tempered his language. Populists in the house, where no such moderating force emerged, proved far more pugilistic in spirit.[13]

By 1895 the Oklahoma Territory enjoyed a highly partisan political system. Of the thirty-nine members of the third legislature, only one, Republican W. A. Hogan, voted more often with the members of another party than with his own. Hogan's record more closely resembled that of the People's party than the GOP's. He was a northern-born Lincoln County farmer. Certain counties, including Lincoln, near the transition zone between northerners and southerners retained a more sectional orientation than the territory as a whole in the 1890s. This held agrarian Republicans such as Hogan loyal to the GOP, while their counterparts elsewhere joined the People's party. Because the third legislature's Democrats were Cleveland supporters, they sided with the GOP more often than with the People's party.[14]

Populists in the 1895 assembly supported a number of bills designed to benefit the debtor. George Coulson, before his removal from the council, introduced a bill allowing owners of real property sold under decree of foreclosure to reclaim their land within eighteen months by paying the amount of the judgment and the taxes accrued. The bill, however, never got out of committee. Neither did a bill Republican Representative William A. Knipe introduced exempting all land and personal property in the Cherokee Outlet from taxes. Populists called, instead, for an extension on the payment of taxes for all Oklahomans, but in vain. The advice of Frank Greer that "no large changes are needed in our laws" seemed to prevail among GOP legislators. Still, Populists in the house were able to unite with seven Republicans and two Democrats to repeal a law that allowed imprisonment for debt. The bill met with no resistance in the council and became law.[15]

The most important laws to pass the third legislature concerned county expenses and taxes. Republican Representative Robert A. Lowry introduced and pushed to passage a bill that limited county expenses to 80 percent of the year's tax levy. County commissioners were charged with establishing a separate fund for each type of expenditure, estimating all expenses for the coming year, and then adding 25 percent to cover expected delinquencies. This established the sum to be raised through taxes each year. They could then issue county warrants, but only for up to 80 percent of the taxes levied. Lowry designed the measure to create more faith in county warrants, which were heavily discounted in many places. The rigidity implicit in establishing several funds and the overtaxing to cover delinquencies led Populists to believe that Oklahomans would suffer markedly increased taxes to satisfy warrant scalpers. Of the Populists in the house, only R. H. Walling voted for the measure.[16] Democrats and all Republicans except farmer W. M. Smith voted for the bill. John Allan labeled Smith a first-class "capital striker" and invited him to join the People's party. The council passed Lowry's bill unanimously in the rush to finish business on the last day of the session.[17]

Estimating county expenses became much more difficult at the same time, because the legislature simultaneously changed county salaries. Republican Councillor O. R. Fegan introduced a fee-and-salary bill into the 1895 legislature designed to reduce expenses. The bill reduced district clerks' salaries substantially. It also absolved counties from paying court costs in misdemeanor cases and half of the fees in felony cases. The salary of jurors was cut, and the county was required to pay the expenses of witnesses only if they were indigent. The bill, however, did raise the salaries of many minor officials. John Allan, who supported the measure, predicted that the bill would save each county $8,000 to $10,000 a year, which he hoped would free them from the tender mercies of warrant scalpers. Three of the four Populists in the council voted for the bill. Senator Doom later explained that Populists voted for the measure only because it was better than the existing law. Third-party legislators would have prefered to reduce salaries even more, he claimed. In the house, Populists split two-to-two on the fee-and-salary bill, with three absent. With the exception of W. A. Hogan, Republicans supported the measure unanimously. When the Oklahoma Supreme Court declared the district clerks' salary cuts unconstitutional in September, 1895, the effect of the bill was to raise county expenses, and thus taxes, substantially. Although Councillors Allan and Doom claimed that the law was nonpartisan, many Populist spokesmen denounced the "Republican sponsored" measure as typical of the GOP's penchant for extravagance.[18]

As more and more Oklahoma farmers began receiving titles to their land in the mid-1890s, they began to mortgage their farms, and the issue of high interest rates quickly became important. The 1893 legislature defined usury as any interest rate above 12 percent. Cosmopolitan elements considered such laws an intimidation of capital. Populist Councillor B. R. Tankersley, however, introduced a bill reducing the legal interest rate to 7 percent in 1895. Republicans, with Democratic help, amended it so as to repeal all usury legislation and then jocularly complimented Tankersley for sponsoring a piece of "Populist legislation" they could finally support. The Populist councillor angrily disowned the bill, which passed despite third-party protests. Only one Populist (Walling), two Republicans, and one Democrat broke with their parties on this highly partisan measure. Leo Vincent sarcastically predicted that with "the bars to the rapacious money sharks" abolished, "filthy lucre would become plenty, interest rates would jump below zero, and the laboring classes and other poor men would be greatly benefited."[19]

Despite their minority status, Populist legislators were not reticent about introducing their own brand of legislation in the third assembly. Democrats and Republicans, however, quickly tabled Populist-sponsored resolutions memorializing Congress in favor of free silver and denouncing President Cleveland's bonding schemes. Populist Councillor E. H. Spencer managed to push a bill taxing gold-bearing obligations to a vote. Republicans and the council's lone Democrat unanimously opposed the measure. A similar vote killed Spencer's initiative-and-referendum bill. Both old parties, on the other hand, supported B. R. Tankersley's bill prohibiting corporations from hiring private armed detectives (Pinkertons).[20]

Oklahoma City Republican Henry St. John introduced two antirailroad bills to the 1895 house. One required railroads to reimburse farmers for livestock their trains killed. The other required rail lines to pay damages for personal and property losses connected with their operations. Although Populists strongly supported both measures, St. John was unable to secure enough support among his fellow Republicans to pass the bills. Democrats and Republicans likewise unanimously voted down a Populist bill requiring the Choctaw Railroad to establish depot facilities at Tecumseh, which it had circumvented in favor of Shawnee. Republicans also finally pushed a militia bill through the third legislature against the protests of both Democrats and Populists.[21]

Populist legislators, as might be expected, parted company with the mainstream parties on a number of financial issues in the 1895 legislature. They sponsored a bill requiring the registration of promissory notes, which was designed to locate liquid capital for tax purposes, but the measure never got out of committee. Only one Republican joined Populists on the Tankersley Usury Bill, and a Republican bill allowing counties to fund their existing indebtedness into long-term bonds ran the gauntlet of third-party protests and became law. Although Republicans joined the third party on a bill making it illegal for territorial and county officers to speculate in county bonds and warrants, Governor Renfrow vetoed the measure.[22]

Party-line votes, with Democrats joining Republicans, also occurred on several tax exemption measures. The mainstream parties supported tax relief for railroads, while Populists sought a $100 exemption for all taxpayers. Populists also constituted most of the opposition to clerk hire for the legislature and the supreme court and funding for the Oklahoma Historical Society. Historian Karel Bicha contended that "almost without exception the Populist approach to public spending was that of the meat-axe." In Oklahoma, where capital was scarce and most land not taxable, Populist legislators were definitely concerned about controlling government expenses. Their focus, however, was not as indiscriminate as Bicha suggests. Populists consistently opposed only those measures that proliferated the number of appointive offices. B. R. Tankersley, for instance, introduced and pushed to passage a road-construction bill, and Populists in the house provided the margin of victory on a bill establishing a territorial penitentiary. The latter measure never came up for a vote in the council. Only three of the eleven third-party members voted against the 1895 assembly's general appropriations bill. Populists proved quite willing to spend on needed projects but vehemently opposed anything smacking of sinecures. In Populists' eyes, politicians who repaid special favors with patronage appointments shifted the cost of reimbursement to the taxpayer. Their primary function, third-party advocates feared, was to loot the territory's meager treasury.[23]

Morality legislation received a cool reception in the 1895 assembly. Populist Robert J. Nesbitt, who served as a Democrat in the first legislature, introduced a liquor-licensing bill that most Democrats and Republicans supported. Four of the seven Populists in the house voted against the bill, and the council killed it without a roll-call vote. Populists constituted most of the opposition to a bill legalizing prizefighting. The editor of Stillwater's *Payne County Populist* charged that the bill would convert Oklahoma into the "Mexican bull pen" of the United States. Texas Governor Charles A. Culberson had secured legislation that stopped an 1895 world championship fight in El Paso, and Oklahoma boosters hoped to lure the fight to the new territory with favorable legislation.[24]

Republican Representative W. H. Mason introduced a bill into the third legislature prohibiting racial discrimination in public facilities. C. H. Tandy, the black Independent Republican whom Populists supported for the Guthrie house seat in 1894, was the moving spirit behind the measure. Populists split four-to-three in favor of the measure in the house. Only John Allan and Democrat Robert Ray opposed the bill in the council. Governor Renfrow vetoed the measure.[25]

Perhaps the most controversial moral issue to come before the 1895 legislature was the attempt to abolish capital punishment. Oklahoma City black John Milligan, a convicted murderer, was the first man sentenced to hang in the new land. On January 9, 1895, the night before his scheduled execution, John Furlong, the secretary of the Populist territorial central committee, secured a sixty-day stay of execution for the condemned man from acting Governor Thomas J. Lowe. He then appealed to the third legislature to abolish the death penalty and thereby save Oklahoma from what he called "the stain of legal murder." To make his appeal nonpartisan, he secured the support of Angelo Scott, an Oklahoma City Republican councillor. Scott introduced Council Bill no. 134, which gave the governor the option of imprisoning for life anyone sentenced to death. To sway public opinion, Furlong also wrote a number of impassioned pleas for newspaper publication and addressed both houses of the legislature.[26]

Frank Greer, of the *Oklahoma State Capital*, vehemently opposed Furlong's measure and maintained a steady barrage of anti-repeal editorials throughout the controversy. He claimed that there was "too much sympathy for criminals" and that "the law of capital punishment . . . was made by God when the world's human code was handed down in imperishable record." What safety, Greer asked, is there when "mock sympathy helps bloody-handed villains out of the clutch of justice?" Scott's bill narrowly passed the council but was defeated by a single vote in the house. Republicans split badly over the measure, while Democrats opposed it. With the exception of James Doom, all Populist legislators voted to abolish capital punishment. Milligan went to the gallows when his stay of execution expired in March.[27]

The 1895 legislature made several important changes in the Oklahoma election code. Democrats and Republicans increased the number of judges and clerks at each polling place from two to three. Previously only the two largest parties in each county were represented. This frequently excluded Populist representation. With the new law, however, Democrats kept their places on the election boards, thus ensuring a mainstream-party majority.[28]

Oklahoma's legislature also passed the nation's first antifusion law in 1895. Republican Councillor George Orner sponsored the bill, which provided a five-year prison sentence for any candidate, election judge, or official printer who allowed the name of a candidate to appear on more than one ticket. Fusion candidates normally had their names listed under both Democratic and Populist columns. Only a generation after the Civil War, the Democratic party still carried too much secessionist baggage for many former Republicans, no matter what a candidate might otherwise represent. Because the Populists in the third legislature were all middle-of-the-roaders, they joined the GOP in supporting the bill. Democrats constituted the bill's only opposition, and Roy Hoffman immediately proclaimed the measure unconstitutional. Because supporters of the bill clearly had the votes to overturn a veto, Renfrow signed it into law.[29]

The third electoral change to emanate from the 1895 legislature was the most controversial. Because Governor Renfrow had manipulated the 1894 legislative redistricting board, the 1895 legislature took for its own the right to apportion the territory for 1896. Populist Representative N. H. DeFord put forth a reapportioning bill that satisfied Democrats, Populists, and six of the house's sixteen Republicans. Republicans in the council subsequently amended the bill along highly partisan lines. This produced a straight party-line vote in the upper chamber and Populist charges of gerrymandering. Essentially, the amended measure spread out the GOP vote in order to maximize the number of seats Republicans could win in a three-way race. The measure would backfire when Democrats and Populists fused for the 1896 elections.[30]

Assessments of the third legislature largely followed party lines. One Republican editor claimed that "it did splendid work for the territory." A new school land-lease law, which would give leaseholders the right to compensation for improvements, he stated, was the only notable omission. Roy Hoffman's Democratic *Guthrie Oklahoma Leader* charged that most of the legislation passing the assembly in the final three days of the session was "engineered by money and fraud by the Republican members." When the Logan County grand jury returned indictments against thirteen members of the assembly, both Democrats and Populists reveled in the news. Hoffman then published a list of twenty-eight legislators who Guthrie saloon keepers claimed had skipped town before paying their bills.[31]

Although the People's party put the old parties on record as favoring Grover Cleveland's pro-gold monetary policies and established the third party as the GOP's major opposition, they were no more successful in securing Populist legislation than in previous legislatures. The repeal of usury legislation, creation of a territorial militia, and proliferation of patronage positions, in fact, signified a regression from earlier conditions. Middle-of-the-roaders gained both voters and offices for the People's party in 1894, but compared to the third party's influence in previous legislatures, such advances actually translated into less power.

CHAPTER EIGHT

The Road to Fusion

Most Americans, and certainly most Oklahomans, realized that the American party system was highly unstable by 1895. Populists envisioned the election of 1896 as another like that of 1860, when had events catapulted the young and vigorous Republican party to national power. As the important election year neared, intraparty debates over what strategy to use in elevating the People's party intensified. Populist leaders had discovered that the money question, or, more specifically, advocating the unlimited coinage of free silver at a ratio of 16 to 1 with gold, was their most important issue in recruiting converts to the third-party movement.[1]

In February, 1895, the Populist party's Washington, D.C., congressional delegation issued an open letter to the party's rank and file declaring the money question to be the "mightiest and most fundamental controversy of the present century." Although the manifesto was worded vaguely enough to imply greenbacks as well as silver, emphasizing free coinage was clearly the purpose of the address. Because third-party leaders, both nationally and in Oklahoma, were essentially greenbackers, focusing on the silver issue was largely a pragmatic political decision.[2]

How to use the silver issue and what silver coinage came to symbolize differed from man to man as party strategy developed. The popularity of William H. Harvey's free-silver tract, *Coin's Financial School*, reflected the growing importance of the issue in the South and West. According to A. C. Towne, of the *Alva Review*, Harvey's book was "creating a revolution." J. C. Tousley, editor of the *El Reno Industrial Headlight*, advised all voters to read Harvey's book and offered a free copy to new subscribers.

Tousley and John Allan, of the *Norman Peoples Voice* inaccurately proclaimed Harvey a Populist. Both editors were greenbackers, but they believed that Harvey's book would disrupt the old parties. Tousley claimed that many would read Harvey's tract who otherwise would never consider looking at a Populist document. Once the free-silver issue inspired thought in such people, he contended, "there is a chance to convert them to every principle set forth in the Omaha platform.[3] Leo Vincent feared that making silver the main issue might actually backfire. It could so educate and commit people to the principle of intrinsic value that converting them to greenbacks might prove impossible. A. C. Towne, on the other hand, believed that if the public would accept the Populist program only one plank at a time, "we are making progress toward victory." According to Towne, to create confidence in the third party, Populists needed to stand firm on silver while Democrats and Republicans straddled the issue. Otherwise, a new party committed to free silver would emerge and indefinitely postpone Populist success.[4]

Populists also were divided on the meaning of the new Silver party, which appeared in 1895. William McDonald, a member of the Canadian County executive committee, warned *Industrial Headlight* readers that "the leading figures of the movement are invariably either Democrats or Republicans . . . [who] expect the Pops to whoop 'em up by doing the voting, leaving them masters of the field as in the past." Tousley, on the other hand, believed that the party would amount to nothing. Prominent mainstream silverites, such as Richard ("Silver Dick") Bland of Missouri, William Jennings Bryan of Nebraska, and Henry M. Teller of Colorado, refused to join.[5]

Oklahoma Populists were unable to monopolize the silver issue without a strong protest from GOP spokesmen in the mid-1890s. Former Governor Seay proclaimed the Republican party record on silver a good one. The editor of the *Alva Republican* found it peculiar "to hear a Populist ranting about the silver question when they are in favor of paper money." Frank Greer, of the *Guthrie Oklahoma State Capital,* agreed, claiming that the Populist party "had but one object, . . . [propagating] the old greenback idea of irredeemable paper money." Greer, of course, was correct. In a letter to the editor of the *Kingfisher Reformer*, a reader put his finger on what silver came to symbolize to Populists: "If silver . . . can be effectively stricken down, as it is now, then the citadel of the people's power is broken."[6]

The prospect of riding the free-silver issue to power in the mid-1890s colored the thinking of all third-party activists. Populists especially concerned themselves with what their party's exact relationship should be toward the disintegrating Democratic party and those still loyal to it. As the political vehicle of southern-born Oklahomans, the Democracy, as the party was called, represented men excluded from the territory's social and political elite. This, in a sense, made them outsiders. Because the People's party drew overwhelmingly from hinterland farmers, who were likewise underrepresented, it also was a party of outsiders. Most Oklahoma Populists considered the rank and file of the Democratic party to be excellent prospects for conversion to Populism as the old party dissolved. How to wean such men away from the Democratic party, however, became a matter of debate. Should the Cleveland administration be singled out for most of the third party's abuse, or should local Democratic leaders also bear the brunt of the third-party attack?

Most of Oklahoma's Populist editors were middle-of-the-roaders and proud of the gains they had brought to their party in 1894. A National Reform Press Association reprint published in a number of Oklahoma third-party papers in January, 1895, told loyalists that fusion meant death to their movement. Reprints from other midroad sources, such as Tom Watson's *Peoples Party Paper* and the *Chicago Sentinel* (where Henry Vincent worked) graced almost every edition of the *Norman Peoples Voice* after John Allan returned from the third legislature. Ralph Bray, editor of the *Enid Coming Events*, boosted such midroader organs as the *Southern Mercury* and the *Coming Nation* as proper repositories of Populist thought. By 1895 most third-party editors doubted the sincerity of Democratic leaders on the silver issue. John Allan noted that "three-fourths of the Democrats in this [Cleveland] county who signed the call for a silver convention were loud-mouthed gold standard men" less than six months earlier. The editor of the *Alva Republican* summed up the emerging dilemma of Oklahoma Populists when he charged that "so many Democrats and Republicans have crowded on to the Populist platform, recently, that the Pops will have to build an addition, or get off."[7]

Plans for a convention to create a supposedly nonpartisan territorial bimetallic league to promote free silver brought about the first major breach in Populist ranks on how to deal with mainstream-party silverites. Leo Vincent advised Populists to "witness the deliberations of these novice silver politicians" but "to be on the alert." He still opposed fusion or trimming the Omaha platform to emphasize the silver issue. But if a former Republican, Democrat, or single-plank silver man "should go part way with us . . . while he is with us he will be treated courteously and with kind respect." Vincent believed that a crisis of civilization was near and called for Democrats to "return once more to the primitive faith of the fathers" and join the People's party. John Allan saw the meeting as a mainstream-party plot and advised that the convention be "let severely alone."[8]

The Populist debate over how to deal with Democratic silverites reached the level of a formal newspaper debate in January, 1896, when Leo Vincent published an open letter from fusionist S. B. Oberlander entitled "Suggestions for Populists." Vincent had held the controversial letter for more than a week, but finally decided to release it without editorial comment in hopes of completely airing the party strategy debate before the 1896 convention.[9]

Oberlander contended that there was neither logic nor political sagacity in the minority rule of Republicans when Democrats and Populists could unite and evict them from power. Political parties, he asserted, "cannot stand the strain of perpetual defeat." Although the principles upon which parties were based might be eternal, to secure them in law required majorities. The People's party "must have an inning" if it was to perpetuate itself.[10]

Oberlander assumed not only that the Populist and Democratic parties had stabilized in size but also that there was a natural affinity between them. Disaster at the polls, he feared, might destroy the third party's cohesiveness. Northern- and southern-born Populists, for instance, might lose faith in each other and return to their old allegiances. All shades of political opinion that "opposed the centralization of power, class legislation, [and] the monarchial tendencies of plutocracy" should unite against the common enemy. Oberlander even suggested that "Populism is Democracy intensified." He believed that Democrats would make friendly allies if Populists would offer the olive branch and make just concessions. He noted that "in unification there is strength, the result, power." Late-nineteenth-century egalitarians, he contended, had grown battle scarred and gray defending the eternal principles of Populism. He feared that the People's party might miss the opportunity to succeed while so close to victory.[11]

In the weeks following the publication of Oberlander's address, Leo Vincent received numerous letters, both pro and con, on the matter. E. H. Spencer, the third-party councillor from Payne County, wrote what Vincent considered the most able refutation of Oberlander's views. Vincent published Spencer's letter in the *Oklahoma Representative* three weeks after he published the Oberlander address, again without editorial comment.[12]

Spencer contended that "from the very nature of things the Democratic party can never be a natural ally of the Populists." The party was a machine "whose master-wheel is located at Washington . . . a counterfeit presentment of the GOP." While there was an affinity between the "masses of Democracy" and Populism, as there also was between the rank and file of the Republicans and Populists, coalition with either of the old parties was "antagonistic to the principles of Populism." The fusion of two parties, he claimed, "always proves to be the death of the least venal one." If Oklahoma Democrats were sincere in favoring monetary reform, "let them prove their faith by their works and sever their connection with the old party." There was hope in the "unification of the industrial classes of all parties" but not in party fusion.[13]

A week after publishing Spencer's address, Leo Vincent finally provided his own views on the subject of party strategy, which he defined as lying somewhere between the two previously stated extremes. He contended that the common people were fed up with the "corrupt, ring-ridden, decayed relics of a past virtue and usefulness." On all questions concerning Oklahoma voters, he claimed, there were only two sides. The GOP "houses nearly all of the ignorance and vice in Oklahoma." Those disposed to quibble too much "will find the machine Republicans are in again" in 1897. Vincent believed that reformers, however, were too sensitive about the word "compromise." He reminded Oklahoma Populists that "the inception of the People's party was a compromise." It was born in Cowley County, Kansas, when rebelling Republicans, Democratic leaders, and the Union Labor party executive committee compromised on a "People's Convention" in 1889. That combination had carried elections in Cowley County, while three-way races elsewhere in Kansas had left the GOP in control. Vincent claimed that a similar condition existed in Oklahoma in 1896 and added that "no principles were abandoned in Cowley County" in 1889.[14]

Leo Vincent agreed with Spencer that Oberlander's approach implied working with the Democratic machine. Producers, on the other hand, regardless of party, opposed "high taxes, infamously corrupt officials, and the credit wrecking, warrant scalping fraternity." In the name of their common interests, Vincent asked Democrats either to join the People's party at once or to move into the Silver party and help put out a platform in Saint Louis, where both the Populist and Silver parties were scheduled to meet simultaneously in July, "which we can all stand on." With the same urgency found in Oberlander's letter, Vincent told both Democrats and Populists that "our principles are of no avail without the offices through which to enact them into law."[15]

Vincent saw the Silver party as a way station on the road to Populism for Democrats fed up with Cleveland and Renfrow. If the Democratic party had not endorsed free silver and nominated William Jennings Bryan at the Chicago convention of 1896, Vincent's position might have been considered simply a better stated version of Spencer's. Neither brooked fusion. Both wished to recruit the Democratic rank and file for the third party. But the sense of urgency found in Oberlander's address was also present in Vincent's. The belief that victory must come in 1896 was widespread in the Populist movement. As one Oklahoma Populist stated, "Almost every leader in reform favors the mustering of all reform forces before it is too late."[16]

Debate over trimming the Omaha platform to gain support and the degree to which Populists should deal with Democrats continued in Oklahoma Populist ranks until the national conventions of the two parties met in July, 1896. Even Clark Hudson, of the *Oklahoma City Oklahoma Champion*, the most conservative of Oklahoma's third-party editors, believed that "amalgamation of the Populists and the disaffected free silver elements of the old parties . . . [could] be done without the sacrifice of a single principle or forfeiture of name or organization." He did, however, advocate dropping the subtreasury plan, which he considered extraneous, from the Omaha platform but not stripping the platform to a single plank. E. H. Spencer charged that smothering the Omaha platform in favor of free silver would alienate thousands from Populism, and he quickly noted that the infant Republican party had actually expanded the number of planks in its platform from nine in 1856 to seventeen in 1860.[17]

Not only right-wing Populists considered the idea of dropping certain planks from the Omaha platform. Ralph Bray, a labor leader before coming to Oklahoma and a vocal Bellamy nationalist, believed that the subtreasury system was not essential. If the Populists' financial reforms were enacted into law, he claimed, "every farmer's corn crib and wheat bin would be his subtreasury." In April, 1896, Bray ceased publishing the Omaha platform in his paper, although he continued to endorse Bellamy nationalism. N. S. Mounts, editor of the Populist *Tecumseh Leader*, also advocated dropping from the Omaha platform the planks "that the American people will not at this time give serious consideration." Such a trimming of the platform was not designed to promote fusion, which he claimed to oppose, but rather to help recruit converts to Populism. Neither Bray nor Hudson nor Mounts, however, advocated a single-plank platform for 1896.[18] Although there were some exceptions, such as E. H. Spencer, it was considerations of which old party constituted the oppressive local elite rather than a left-right dichotomy that determined the position of most Populists on fusion. Ralph Bray, a full-blown

Bellamy nationalist, for instance, became one of the territory's most rabid fusionists, while John Allan, who after the turn of the century supported agrarian Democrats such as William H. ("Alfalfa Bill") Murray, became the leading middle-of-the-roader in the territory.

Although most Oklahoma Democrats favored free silver, and a silverite had led their ticket in 1894, many of the party's leaders broke with the Cleveland and Renfrow administrations only in 1895. The party's weak showing in the election of 1894 probably accounts for these conversions. Roy Hoffman, the editor of the *Guthrie Oklahoma Leader*, resigned as Governor Renfrow's personal secretary on the eve of the 1894 election. In May, 1895, he turned his paper into a full-fledged free-silver sheet. His animosity toward Wisby for attacks on officeholding Democrats, however, remained. Subscribers to the Democratic *Alva Chronicle* could also obtain a free copy of *Coin's Financial School* beginning in May, 1895. Such conversions led to the belief that the silver crusade had captured the Democratic party by midyear.[19]

The June, 1895, Silver convention in Oklahoma City proved to be a big success for the Democratic party. William Jennings Bryan, who also spoke in Enid, Guthrie, and Purcell on his swing through the region, mesmerized his audience with a three-and-one-half-hour harangue at Smith's Grove, on the outskirts of the city. Estimates of the size of his audience ranged from fifteen hundred to three thousand. Although John Allan and A. J. Seay warned Populists and Republicans, respectively, to stay away, men from all parties attended. Oklahoma City Republican Charles G. ("Grist Mill") Jones, a member of the first legislature, presided over the meeting when fellow Republican David A. Harvey, Oklahoma's first delegate to Congress, suddenly disappeared.[20] To warm up the audience, Democrat Sidney Clarke, the old Boomer leader, preceded Bryan with a speech of his own. Bryan spoke again at the opera house that evening, when the Oklahoma Territory Bimetallic League was founded. Clarke and Mort Bixler were elected president and vice-president, while Populists Asa Jones and Leo Vincent became the order's secretary and assistant secretary. Despite the effort to emphasize the meeting's nonpartisan nature, it was largely a Democratic affair.[21]

Democratic spokesmen, especially where southerners were in the majority, used the Oklahoma City bimetallic convention as an opportunity to wean support away from the People's party. Mort Bixler, editor of the *Norman State Democrat*, charged that Populists only "pretended to be for free silver, but don't want it except by the grace of the People's party." Their failure to join the bimetallic league, he claimed, proved their insincerity. J. C. Tousley, of El Reno, denounced the convention as a fraud to get the Democratic party "right on the silver question." Relations between Democratic and Populist leaders, however, were warmer where northerners dominated. Ralph Bray, of Enid, for instance, strongly supported the formation of local nonpartisan silver clubs in Garfield County.[22]

U.S. Marshal Patrick Nagle put forth the goldbug, or pro-gold, version of the Democratic party's course in the Oklahoma Territory. Although he claimed to speak only for himself, free-silver Democrats and Populists believed he spoke for the territory's Democratic officeholding clique. Nagle proclaimed his loyalty to "sound money" and labeled free silver "a gigantic scheme of repudiation." He warned that those who promoted a fight of the West and South against the East should remember the lessons of Appomattox. Fusionists' real purpose, he charged, was "to sacrifice the national Democracy for the local office."[23]

Nagle saved his most venomous remarks for the People's party. The passions that inspired Populism, he charged, were the same as those that "inflamed the mind of Mirabeau and nerved the hand of Danton." The People's party was "the Siberia of the Republican party." It fostered class conflict and was particularly prejudiced against lawyers, who he believed were the vanguard of peaceful reform. According to Nagle, "the field, workshop, and the streets are the home of the revolution."[24]

Nagle believed that those who could accept free silver could also accept the other tenets of Populism. The party was "rotten with socialism," and Oklahoma Democrats, he feared, were becoming "rotten with Populism." Nagle had no illusions, however, about the relative strengths of silver and gold forces within the territory's Democratic party. His position was in the minority and becoming more so every day. The party's minority status and the events of the mid-1890s pushed Democrats toward "free silver."[25]

Sensing that 1896 would be a difficult year for the GOP in the Oklahoma Territory, Republicans held their territorial convention early to gain an advantage over the opposition. The Republican convention, which unanimously renominated Dennis Flynn for delegate to Congress, was enthusiastic and harmonious. Oklahoma Republicans claimed to be the "party of progress and prosperity" and advocated protection, reciprocity, and bimetallism. As in 1894, Republicans advocated the unlimited coinage of American silver only. Concerning territorial matters, the GOP platform endorsed the Fegan Fee and Salary Act of 1895, criticized the Democratic supreme court for striking down the reduction in district clerks' salaries, and denounced the Democratic board of equalization for "placing a raised and fictitious valuation" on all but railroad property. A week later Republicans met in Oklahoma City to chose delegates to the GOP national convention. Populists charged that the GOP was "true to its masters . . . [choosing] as their representatives six railroad tools." The convention selected an uninstructed delegation with Henry Asp and John I. Dille at its head. They were the Oklahoma general counsels for the Santa Fe and Rock Island railroads, respectively.[26]

The Republican party's position on national issues hurt the GOP in the Oklahoma Territory. Many who associated the GOP with corporate interests found the party weak on the silver issue and far too strong on the protective tariff. Both Democrats and Populists had these negative reference issues in common. When McKinley received the GOP nomination for president, Oklahoma Republican spokesmen could do little more than claim that "a proper adjustment of the tariff will cure most of the existing ills" and insist that free homes and statehood were more important. One Democratic paper claimed that the choice in 1896 would be between "Bland and the masses" and "McKinley and the classes."[27]

The GOP's manipulative style likewise pushed Democrats and Populists together. House Bill no. 1 in the 1895 legislature provided for restoring the records of Payne County, which were destroyed in a January, 1895, courthouse fire. Speculation about those responsible for the conflagration fueled existing charges that the outgoing Republican officeholders feared a Populist investigation of the county's records. In order not to inconvenience anyone, Populists charged, the GOP firebugs had saved the real estate mortgage records, the marriage records, and a few court dockets. All records relating to county warrants, however, were put to the torch.[28]

Republicans also had the charge of gerrymandering the Oklahoma legislative districts hanging over their heads in 1896. Populists concluded that with their 1894 vote they could carry only one council and three house seats with the new apportionment. House District no. 18, in Logan County, for instance, was shaped like a backward h with an L lying on its side appended to it. The two sections connected only at an imaginary point where the corners of two townships touched. Three strongly Populist townships, away from the railroad, on the other hand, were added to Guthrie to make up House District no. 17.[29] District no. 18 surrounded it on three sides. The remaining hinterland sections of Logan County were split into three different districts. In Garfield County, Enid and North Enid, which were only three miles apart, were placed in two separate districts in hopes that urbanites could outpoll hinterland voters in both.[30] Woods County, the only county in the Cherokee Outlet to go Populist in 1894, was divided into six house and three council districts. The only district entirely within the boundaries of the county contained the full extent of the Santa Fe Railroad through the county. Two townships had the misfortune to be completely excluded from the 1896 apportionment, and thus their voters were disfranchised.[31] The more Democrats and Populists considered the apportionment, the more they saw cooperation as the only way to defeat it.[32]

Although the Republican gerrymander was a vital issue in 1896, taxation proved to be even more important in pushing Democrats and Populists into combination. Because county commissioners in several localities had issued warrants in excess of the legal percentage of tax assessments, the territorial board of equalization doubled Oklahoma's tax valuations in 1895. The purpose of this move was to save the territory's credit by legalizing the excess warrants. While a Democratic board of equalization raised the valuations, a Republican law subsequently kept county commissioners from reducing the levy. Both Populists and silver Democrats rapidly came to view Oklahoma's Democratic office-holders as assistant Republicans.[33]

Other factors made the tax situation even more aggravating. The 1895 legislature separated railroad valuations from the board of equalization's jurisdiction. Railroads were underassessed, while landowners faced a doubling of their taxes. The supreme court then lowered the railroad's valuations another 30 percent in 1896. In April, 1896, the Oklahoma Supreme Court ruled that the board of equalization's assessments were unconstitutional but ordered territorial officials to collect them anyway, because most taxpayers had already paid their tax bills. Leo Vincent found the Republican party's territorial platform, which Frank Greer ostensibly wrote, particularly insincere in denouncing the raised taxes. Greer had defended the increased valuations in his paper at a time when he reputedly held a large number of county warrants.[34]

As territorial issues began to loom larger in mid-1896, talk of a coalition of like-minded men replaced conversations about the pragmatic values of fusion. Because Oklahoma had no vote in the presidential race, Leo Vincent advised focusing on local elections. According to the Guthrie editor, high taxes and thieving rings were the main issues in Oklahoma. John Allan agreed that "the greatest portion of the wealth of this country is fast getting beyond the power of taxation and the expenses of government are beginning to press heavily upon the shoulders of industry." Ralph Bray noted in the *Enid Coming Events* that even middle-of-the-roaders had "caught the idea that the issue in this county is not the Omaha platform, but economical county administration and the consequent defeat of the Republican gang." As the Democratic and Populist national conventions drew near, territorial third-party leaders were actively agitating the unifying theme of lower taxes.[35]

Democrats held an exceptionally tumultuous meeting in Oklahoma City on March 26, 1896, to select delegates to their national convention. Administration forces were well represented and supported a minority report endorsing Cleveland's tenure, except on finance, and requiring the Chicago delegates to abide by the convention's results. After the statements of the report's sponsors, Joseph Wisby commenced an antiofficeholder tirade that brought Leslie P. Ross to his feet with documents showing that federal officeholders had financed Wisby's 1894 delegate campaign. A scuffle ensued in which chairs were knocked over and pistols were drawn. Cooler heads called for an adjournment until that evening, when planks endorsing the Cleveland and Renfrow administrations were easily voted down. Generally pro-administration delegates, however, were chosen to attend the Chicago convention. They were charged with voting as a unit for Richard Bland and an unqualified silver platform.[36]

Populist reports on the Democratic convention revealed the widening gap in third-party ranks over relations with the old party. John Allan called it "the most disgraceful convention ever held in Oklahoma" and emphasized its lack of unity. Ralph Bray, on the other hand, focused upon the platform and claimed that Democrats had gone "a fair way to take their organization away from the shysters and to turn the party back toward the doctrines of Jackson and Jefferson." Leo Vincent also focused on the platform, claiming "the only difference observable this year between the Populist and Democratic platforms is in name."[37]

To choose Oklahoma's nine delegates to the Populist party's 1896 national convention, Leo Vincent decided to experiment by holding four regional conventions rather than a single territorywide meeting. His purpose was to cut traveling expenses. Third-party representatives were to meet at Enid, El Reno, Oklahoma City, and Perry on May 22 to choose two delegates and two alternates each. The conventions would also adopt resolutions and vote for an at-large delegate and alternate. Because the meetings represented the various regions of the Oklahoma Territory, they provide a gauge of the sentiments of local Populist leaders on party strategy for 1896.[38]

Leo Vincent and his Logan County colleagues attended the Perry convention, where fusionists and middle-of-the-roaders seemed to compromise. Vincent and fusionist Ralph Bray received the convention's vote for at-large delegate and alternate, respectively, while middle-of-the-roader E. H. Spencer became one of the regional delegates. The Perry resolutions denounced government favoritism toward railroads, governmental extravagance, and the repeal of territorial usury legislation. They also endorsed free silver and were the only set of regional resolutions to specifically mention greenbacks.[39]

The Enid convention overwhelmingly endorsed Ralph Bray for the delegate at-large position. Bray withdrew in favor of Leo Vincent, however, and accepted the convention's vote for the alternate position. For regional delegates, the Enid convention chose George Coulson and William Garrison, a distant relative of the famous abolitionist. Coulson, Garrison, and one of the alternates, R. W. Hurt, had been members of the 1891 Kansas legislature. The Enid resolutions endorsed free silver and called for government control, even government ownership if necessary, of all corporations performing public functions. They also endorsed the "alliance and cooperation of all reform elements of the state and nation." The Enid convention was the most fusion-oriented of the four regional meetings.[40]

Because southern-born Populists were more numerous at El Reno and Oklahoma City, antifusion sentiments were more noticeable at those meetings. The Oklahoma City convention worked out a compromise set of resolutions that endorsed the Omaha platform, the initiative and referendum, and "all honorable means to bring about a patriotic union of all reform forces." A fusionist and a middle-of-the-roader were chosen as delegates, with fusionist Clark Hudson and middle-of-the-roader John Allan as alternates. Cleveland and Pottawatomie counties were able to secure enough votes from the Lincoln and Oklahoma county delegations to select A. D. Hickok, a former president of the territory's Farmers' Alliance, over Leo Vincent for at-large delegate.[41]

At El Reno, where delegates from newly acquired Greer County were prominent, middle-of-the-roaders ruled the proceedings. Convention resolutions endorsed the 1892 Populist platform, free homes, and the initiative and referendum. They were the only resolutions not to mention free silver explicitly. Strict middle-of-the-roaders were chosen as delegates and alternates, and the convention tendered its votes to Leo Vincent for

the at-large delegate slot on the condition that he sign a statement endorsing the Omaha platform. Vincent's recent flirtation
with fusion elements had caused many at the El Reno gathering
to fear that he favored trimming the party platform. Vincent satisfied their concerns and became the at-large delegate to the
Saint Louis convention with Ralph Bray as his alternate.[42]

National events moved rapidly in mid-1896. The Republican
nomination of William McKinley for the presidency in June
helped the GOP in the crucial Northeast but gave silver Democrats and Populists an edge in the West and South. Leo Vincent
was certain that silver elements could not control the Democratic party on the eve of its July national convention. El Reno's
J. C. Tousley, on the other hand, predicted a silver victory and
suggested that Populists make separate nominations and then let
the two parties' executive committees sort out the mess. John Allan apparently agreed and reprinted Tousley's plan in the *Norman
Peoples Voice*.[43]

Fusion elements were elated when the Democratic national
convention endorsed free silver and nominated William Jennings
Bryan for the presidency. W. H. French, editor of the Populist
Chandler Publicist, claimed that "Bryan has been an outspoken
advocate of all the fundamental principles of the People's party
for a number of years" and forgave him for not leaving the Democratic party. Clark Hudson proclaimed that the Democratic party
had "nominated a Populist for president" and attributed the
move to "an outcropping of Jeffersonian principle" among old
party loyalists. Ralph Bray congratulated the Democratic party
for having "broken loose from the grasp of plutocracy." According
to Leo Vincent, the nomination of Bryan was the only instance
in American history when "a political party had succeeded in
correcting and purifying itself."[44]

In the words of Leo Vincent the Republican party had "planted
a Tory fort on American soil" in nominating William McKinley
and adopting the gold standard.[45] The success or failure of Mc-
Kinleyism depended on whether Populists nominated or rejected
Bryan. Although John Allan and the middle-of-the-roaders were
less enthusiastic, they did see McKinley's election as a threat and
charged that his policies had "brought one of the most happy and

prosperous peoples in the world to the very doors of penury and want."[46]

The Oklahoma delegates to the 1896 Populist national convention acted and voted with the majority of their colleagues on most issues. The first test of strength came over the seating of a contesting middle-of-the-road Illinois delegation (mostly Chicago socialists). The Oklahoma delegates voted unanimously in favor of seating the challengers, who secured their seats by a narrow margin. In the contest for permanent chairman, the Oklahomans split down the middle. The election of Senator William V. Allen of Nebraska placed forces favorable to Bryan in control of the convention's machinery.[47]

When it became obvious to middle-of-the-roaders that they could not beat Bryan for the presidential nomination in a straight fight, they fell back upon the tactic of reversing the order of nominations. By choosing the vice-presidential nominee first, middle-of-the-roaders made certain that Bryan's Democratic running mate, Maine banker and shipbuilder Arthur M. Sewall, did not slip through on the Commoner's coattails. They also hoped that Sewall's rejection would cause Bryan to withdraw his name from the nominating process, which he threatened to do. Oklahoma delegates voted six-to-two, with one absent, in favor of reversing the order of nominations and supported the candidacy of Tom Watson of Georgia, who subsequently won the vice-presidential nomination. Bryan, of course, did not fulfill his threat to withdraw from the nomination, and Oklahoma delegates voted unanimously to tender the Nebraskan the Populist nomination for the presidency on the final day of the convention.[48]

The Oklahoma delegation's only major break with the rapidly shifting majorities at the Saint Louis convention came when T. H. Gold of Washita County signed and supported a minority report on the third party's platform. Jerome Kearby, a Texas middle-of-the-roader, wrote the measure. His platform gave equal emphasis to gold, silver, and paper money. The convention, however, adopted the majority report, which made free silver the prime issue. Oklahoma delegates were able to get a strong free-homes plank in the third party's national platform. Guthrie farm journal editor Jules Soule, along with fusionist editors Ralph Bray and W. H. French, were chosen as the Oklahoma members of the national committee. Bray was also named the Oklahoma member of the presidential notification committee, while middle-of-the-roader N. A. Ruggles received appointment to the vice-presidential notification committee.[49]

To Leo Vincent, the Democratic nomination of William Jennings Bryan on a free-silver platform was a dramatic and significant event. Free silver symbolized the third party's battle with plutocracy for control of the nation's future. Populists had worked hard for decades for such a showdown. The fact that a Democrat carried the banner for "the people" was not as important as the fact that the battle finally was being joined. Before Bryan's nomination, fusion with the Democrats in Oklahoma "seemed utterly improbable," according to Vincent. The Nebraskan's victory, however, made an arrangement with local Democrats "wise and expedient for the inauguration of genuine reform." Vincent believed that a complete change had taken place in the Democratic party. The result would be a determination "to revolutionize Oklahoma politics and upset some of the pernicious work of the Republican lawmakers."[50]

A week after the Saint Louis convention adjourned, 235 Oklahoma Populists met in Guthrie to nominate their candidate for delegate to Congress. Party Chairman Leo Vincent told the convention that the Democratic party had regenerated itself through the nomination of William Jennings Bryan, whom he labeled "an idol of the People's party." Because plutocratic forces had captured the Republican party, he claimed, a union of reform forces, "bound together by certain ties of mutual interest," was desirable and necessary.[51]

Vincent believed that fusion was particularly important for the territorial legislative races. He touched upon the gerrymandering controversy, denounced the repeal of usury legislation, and dwelt at length upon the doubling of property valuations. Chairman Vincent proclaimed the 1895 territorial legislature unusually "corrupt and vicious" and called for political purification. He particularly stressed the idea that Oklahoma blacks had provided the GOP with its margin of victory in 1894, an approach that surely warmed the hearts of Democrats. Vincent had become ex-asperated by the blind loyalty blacks showed to the Republican party, although he stopped short of totally rejecting his family's abolitionist heritage.[52]

Before the convention addressed the issue of nominations, the platform committee presented its work, which the convention accepted unanimously. The 1896 Populist territorial platform affirmed loyalty to the party's new national platform and ac-knowledged the financial question as the paramount issue of the national campaign. Specific calls for free silver, pensions for Union soldiers, and free homes were included. Populists also de-nounced the repeal of usury laws, called for revision of the pow-ers of the board of equalization, denounced the 1895 GOP gerry-mander, and again called for official salaries to be "commensurate with the price of labor and its products.[53]

Because a number of counties had favorite sons for the dele-gate nomination, thirteen men received nominations for the party's highest honor. Among them were John Allan, Samuel Crocker, Fielden S. Pulliam, George Gardenhire, E. H. Spencer, N. A. Ruggles, and William Oliver Cromwell, who claimed lineal descent from the famed leader of the English Common-wealth. Party officials gave each man ten minutes to address the convention before the balloting began. Most attacked the GOP, gold, and McKinley. Gardenhire tried to withdraw his name, but Payne County delegates adamantly insisted on his candidacy. Thomas Smith, editor of the *Kay County Populist*, however, suc-ceeded in withdrawing his name. Although not formally nomi-nated for the post, Leo Vincent received votes on all but the last of the twenty-three ballots it took to secure a nominee.[54]

Most delegates remained loyal to their county favorites through the first thirteen ballots. James Y. Callahan of Kingfisher County led on all but the second ballot, but only by a small margin.[55] After the dinner break, which occurred before the fourteenth ballot, the field began to narrow. Southerners began to focus on candidates from their section of the territory and northerners united around candidates from their region. Finally, on the twenty-third ballot, northern-populated Logan County and

southern-dominated Greer County changed their support to
Callahan, which began a stampede resulting in his nomination
by acclamation.[56]

James Y. Callahan was born in Dent County, Missouri, in
1842. He left his native Ozark Mountains at the age of thirty to
settle in southwestern Kansas, where he served two terms as a
Republican registrar of deeds. He returned to Missouri in 1887 to
take up the Methodist ministry. In 1888 he joined the Union Labor party. Callahan moved to Oklahoma at the opening of the
Cheyenne and Arapaho lands in April, 1892. He staked his
claim five miles northeast of Kingfisher, where he engaged in
farming and rode the Methodist circuit. Callahan received the
Populist nomination for the territorial legislature in 1894 but lost
in the general election. The *Kingfisher Reformer* identified him as
"a thorough reformer."[57]

Callahan's first major challenge was to secure the Democratic
nomination for delegate and thus effect fusion. While the Populist convention was in session, Democrats had named four Populists whom they would support for the delegate nomination. Although Callahan's name was not among them, arrangements for
local fusion proceeded as if his endorsement was assured. Both
parties had much to lose if the Democrats failed to nominate the
Kingfisher County Populist.[58]

Opinion within the Democratic party was divided on the
question of fusion. Oklahoma City editor Frank McMaster proclaimed fusion essential if Democrats wanted to "get a single
county office or member of the legislature." He acknowledged,
furthermore, that Democrats would have to concede the delegate
nomination to secure a coalition. Mort Bixler charged that
McMaster enjoyed "the distinction of being the only citizen of
Oklahoma of whom it can truly be said he is neither useful nor
ornamental to the community in which he lives." He boosted
Temple Houston, the flamboyant son of Texas former Governor
Sam Houston, as a straight Democratic candidate and promised
that fusion would never occur in Cleveland County.[59]

The Democratic and Populist territorial committees met in
late August and called for all silverites to unite on the legislative
races. Democrats, however, refused to run under the Populist

banner. Third-party representatives conceded to the name "Free Silver party" for the fusion ticket, and Democrats agreed not to certify any separate legislative nominations before their territorial convention, which was scheduled for September 3 at El Reno.[60]

Democrats Mort Bixler, Temple Houston, and W. S. Denton had broken with fusionists before the party's El Reno convention. Each had supported a nonfusionist for national committeeman at their national convention, despite earlier commitments not to do so. At El Reno, Bixler, Denton, and Roy Hoffman, of the *Oklahoma Leader*, led the antifusion element. When fusion forces narrowly defeated Hoffman for the temporary chairmanship, antifusionists acquiesced, and a fusionist subsequently received the permanent chairmanship by acclamation.[61]

When the platform committee proved unready to present its work at the allotted hour, convention managers invited James Y. Callahan to address the assembly. The Populist delegate nominee consented to answer questions instead. W. S. Denton made the first and most damaging inquiry. He asked whether Callahan had voted in favor of mixed schools while serving on his district school board. Callahan claimed that he had voted for the measure to lower taxes but noted that there were no blacks in his district. His wife was the daughter of a former Confederate, he added, and thus he would never "let her children and mine go to school with colored children." Callahan was then asked whether he was a prohibitionist. He claimed to be commited to temperance but added that liquor was not an issue in the campaign. Denton then asked if he would support Sewall. Callahan replied in the affirmative. J. L. Isenberg, editor of the Democratic *Enid Wave*, then asked about Watson. Callahan said he was for him, too, and believed that the two parties' national committees would work out a deal on the vice-presidential nomination.[62]

To end the debate, a fusionist finally moved that Bixler, Denton, and Hoffman be appointed to ascertain the position of Dennis Flynn on mixed schools, prohibition, and Sewall. Callahan had parried the questions well, and fusionists did not want too deep an inquiry into the candidate's background or beliefs. As Mort Bixler later explained, Callahan was "for and against mixed schools, he was a prohibitionist that did not believe in prohibition, and he was in favor of Bryan and Sewall and Bryan and Watson." Both parties clearly trimmed their positions to effect fusion in 1896.[63] When the platform committee presented a rabidly pro-fusion manifesto, the convention approved it overwhelmingly. Dan Peery, a member of the first two territorial legislatures, then moved that Callahan be endorsed. Democrats nominated Callahan on a voice vote and appointed a committee to meet with Populists and work out the details of a joint campaign.[64]

Roy Hoffman played the part of party loyalist in the wake of the convention and declared that Democrats and Populists "think exactly alike on essential issues." They opposed monopoly, corporate rule, and aggregated wealth, while favoring currency reform. Except for denunciations of mixed schools and the antifusion law, the 1896 Democratic territorial platform was quite similar to its Populist counterpart. Both also rejected the Fegan Fee Bill, repeal of usury legislation, and the GOP gerrymander. According to John Allan, Mort Bixler found that his status in the Democratic party was "about the same as any other Republican."[65]

Callahan immediately embarked on an extensive speaking tour of the territory. He spoke primarily on free silver but also gave time to free homes and single statehood, which both Democrats and Populists endorsed as well. Callahan issued numerous challenges to Dennis Flynn for a joint debate, but the GOP candidate studiously avoided him and campaigned almost exclusively on the free-homes issue.[66]

All Populist leaders and most Democratic leaders supported Callahan's candidacy. Thomas J. Lowe, the second ranking Cleveland appointee in the territory, even spoke in favor of Callahan and bimetallism. Only four Democratic editors, including Mort Bixler, refused to support Callahan. Bixler also blocked the Democratic nomination of John Allan for reelection to the council, which the territorial fusion arrangement required.[67]

Democrats and Populists successfully fused on Free Silver candidates in twelve council and twenty-two house races for 1896. Democrats declined to fuse in Cleveland County, and a three-way race also emerged in House District no. 25, which included Custer, Greer, Roger Mills, and Washita counties. On election day, Democrats won narrow pluralities in Cleveland County, while a Populist carried House District no. 25. In House district no. 23, which included Alva, in Woods County, A. E. Herr ran a straight Populist race against a Free Silver nominee and the incumbent Republican, George W. Vickers, and came within fifteen votes of winning. Middle-of-the-road and renegade Republican candidacies in the Guthrie house and council districts proved inconsequential.[68]

On election day, James Callahan won a narrow victory over Dennis Flynn in the delegate race, carrying fifteen of the territory's twenty-three counties. Because the Republican gerrymander had spread out the GOP vote in anticipation of a three-way race, Republicans elected only three men to the 1897 legislature. GOP candidates received majorities in the Guthrie and Blaine County districts, while George W. Vickers returned to his house seat with a plurality victory in Woods County.[69]

Although fusionists proclaimed a great victory on election day, 1896, a closer look at the returns should have given Populists, at least, cause for concern. Voter participation dropped significantly in 1896. Appendix B, table B-1, shows that Populists deserted the fusion campaigns of 1896 through 1900. In 1894, Beaumont and Wisby carried 57.9 percent of the vote between them. Callahan managed only 51.1 percent in 1896.

Appendix A, table A-1, shows the quite predictable effects of mixing Democratic and Populist votes in the Free Silver victory of 1896. Callahan's correlations with northerners, blacks, and Europeans were substantially lower than Beaumont's, while he gained significantly among white border-state natives in comparison to the 1894 Populist ballot. Likewise, the rural-urban cleavage that had been so important to the third party in the past was moderated substantially in 1896 (see appendix A, table A-2). The only changes in crop, livestock, and economic correlations not explained by fusion were the value of manufactured goods and share tenancy (see appendix A, table A-4). Antifusion Democrats who voted for Flynn in the delegate race are the most likely explanation. The same logic also would explain the reduced south-fusion correlation. Comparison of delegate and house votes in Cleveland and Custer counties, where three-way races developed for the latter, show a significant splitting of Democratic votes between Callahan and Flynn.[70]

Comparison of Callahan's 1896 ballot with Beaumont's in 1894 reveals a disruption of the earlier patterns associated with Populist strength. In 1896 sectionalism increased, the rural-urban cleavage weakened, and correlations with corn and cotton acreage and hogs per farms decreased. This is evidence of the divergent nature of the Democratic and Populist followings. Fusion was not based upon common interests other than opposition to the Republican party's officeholding clique.

The drop in Populist voter turnout reveals disfavor among some third-party elements over coalition with the Democrats. Fusion in 1896 blunted the moral cutting edge that had served as the basis for mobilizing less commercially oriented hinterland farmers to support Populism. The overwhelming victory of silverites in the 1896 legislative races was primarily the product of the Republican gerrymander that backfired. Callahan's victory over Flynn in the delegate race was exceptionally close. According to exponents of fusion, however, the experiment was highly successful. Clark Hudson compared the results of the 1894 and 1896 elections and proclaimed that Populists had learned that "in union there is strength." Other fusionists, such as national committeeman W. H. French, likewise called upon Populists to "continue the combination." All realized that the 1897 legislature would be the litmus test of fusion's worth to the Oklahoma People's party.[71]

CHAPTER NINE

Reformers at Work: The 1897 Legislature

Excitement pervaded the city of Guthrie as the opening of Oklahoma's fourth assembly neared. Reformers would finally have their day. Legislators, party leaders, journalists, lobbyists, and an army of aspirants for appointive offices flooded the capital city. When the house went into session on January 12, 1897, one of its first resolutions called for cutting a large window in the west side of the lower chamber to let in sufficient light for reformers to fulfill their mission. Bold action was expected of the fourth assembly, especially in the house, where Populists had a plurality. Members seemed to be clearing the decks in preparation for a general assault upon the territory's statute books.[1]

The Republican gerrymander of 1895 produced a legislature in 1897 that differed markedly from its predecessor. Twenty-four Republicans sat in the 1895 Assembly. In 1897 the GOP sent only three representatives to Guthrie. Democrats and Populists, on the other hand, increased their delegations from four and eleven, respectively, to eighteen each.[2]

Because Populist voter turnout dropped in 1896, several members of the fourth legislature won narrow victories. Nine candidates (five Democrats, two Republicans, and two Populists) won their seats by fewer than 100 votes. They beat four Republicans and five Populists.[3] Had the results been reversed, the People's party would have gained majorities in both houses of the 1897 legislature. Democrats, however, elected seven councillors, and Populists six. In the house there were three Republicans, eleven Democrats, and twelve Populists. Third-party legislators had the opportunity to secure another seat in the house when S. J.

Fulkerson of Woods County challenged the election of Republican J. P. D. Mouriquand of Blaine County. The house, however, agreed to the findings of a special committee consisting of two Democrats and a Republican, who outvoted two Populists. Fulkerson noted that the third party showed Mouriquand far more consideration than the GOP had exhibited in unseating George Coulson in 1895.[4]

The partisan makeup of the fourth legislature differed substantially from the other assemblies of the period (see appendix C, table C-1). It was the only body of the era not to have at least twice as many northern-born members as southerners. The near absence of GOP legislators, of course, was the reason for this aberration. The 1897 assembly contained twenty northerners (two Republicans, eight Democrats, and two Populists), eighteen southerners (ten Democrats and eight Populists), and one foreign-born legislator (a Republican). Although the proportions of northern- to southern-born Democrats and Republicans were not unusual, the 1897 legislature did contain slightly more southern-born Populists than usual (see appendix C, table C-2). Part of the reason for this was their acceptability to Democrats. All but two of them, however, had come to Oklahoma by way of the Midwest and served constituencies in which northerners were in the majority, although southerners made up significant minorities in several of these districts. The failure of fusion in southern-dominated areas explains the high proportion of southern-born 1897 Populist legislators who entered the territory from the north.

The members of Oklahoma's fourth legislature, on the average, were the oldest of the Populist era (see appendix C, table C-3). Because the literature of the period portrayed Populism as the ideology of old men who could not adapt to the realities of the modern world, this is not surprising. Such literature, however, was misleading. Third-party advocates only seemed older, because their world view owed more to the distant past than their mainstream-party colleagues. Populists actually were the youngest group in the 1897 legislature. Democrats and Republicans in 1897 were, on the average, significantly older than their third-party colleagues.

The greatest divergence between Populists and mainstream-party representatives was in occupation and residence (see appendix C, tables C-4 and C-5). The vast majority of Populist lawmakers, throughout the period, were farmers. Fourteen of the third-party legislators of 1897 lived on farms, while two lived in hinterland small towns, and two resided in county seats (only one of which was a railhead town).[5] Of the Republican representatives, two resided in railhead towns, while the third was a rural merchant and preacher. At least ten of the Democrats lived in railhead towns, while four others resided in townships served by rail.

The most common occupation among mainstream-party legislators in 1897 was that of attorney (two Republicans and eight Democrats). There were no Populist lawyers in the 1897 assembly.[6] Six Democrats claimed to be farmers, but for two of them it was only a sideline. One Populist and three Democratic ranchers sat in the fourth assembly.[7] The occupation and residence data for legislators in Oklahoma's fourth assembly verify the cosmopolitan-hinterland dichotomy found elsewhere in this book, and they diverge very little from the aggregate for all territorial legislators of the Populist era.

The 1897 legislature presented Oklahoma Populists with a moment of truth. Between the Free Silver party victory of November, 1896, and the opening of the fourth legislature on January 12, 1897, assemblymen received much advice on the legislation they should promote. W. D. Hayman, a hinterland Logan County farmer, spoke for most party supporters in a letter to the editor of the *Oklahoma Representative*, in which he declared that the fourth legislature "will either make the Populist party of Oklahoma the majority party or it will completely disorganize it." Another letter stated that the people expected radical legislation. Leo Vincent summed up much of what Populist voters expected when he published shopping lists of reform measures. They included a 12 percent usury law, stricter rules outlining the powers of the board of equalization, heavier taxes on railroad property, the removal of political influence from the school land department, legislation to protect bank deposits, reductions in official salaries, a scaling down of appropriations, and the abolition of useless offices. John Allan, on the other hand, contended that those who believed that the statute books would retain little more than their covers and flyleaves after the fourth legislature ended were too optimistic. He predicted that compromises with Democrats would leave many of the statutes' "running sores" unhealed. Allan had already experienced the questionable charms of dealing with Democrats on their own terms in his unsuccessful 1896 bid for reelection to the council.[8]

Two days before Christmas, 1896, nine Democrats and seven Populists attended a legislative caucus in Oklahoma City to discuss the upcoming assembly. Plans were made to continue the electoral combination in the fourth legislature, prospective legislation was discussed, and the numerous applications for clerkships were canvassed. The proceedings led Roy Hoffman to predict that Democrat J. W. Johnson, an Oklahoma City lawyer, would be named president of the council, while Populist John Hogan, a Pawnee County farmer, would become speaker of the house. Johnson had been a goldbug before 1896 but seemed properly antiadministration thereafter. Hogan had founded the territory's first third-party paper, the *Guthrie Oklahoma State Journal*, in 1890. Hoffman believed that Hogan's elevation to speaker would put Leo Vincent in line to become the chief clerk of the house.[9]

When the fourth territorial legislature convened on January 12, J. W. Johnson duly received the unanimous vote of the council for president. He then divided the council's appointive offices among Democrats, Populists, and free-silver Republicans. He chose a Democrat as chief clerk and appointed three Democrats and two Populists to the rules committee.

In the house of representatives, the Free Silver caucus did not function as smoothly. A rift between James Y. Callahan and Leo Vincent allowed J. C. Tousley of El Reno to put together a westside coalition and secure the speakership. Aside from the north-south cleavage of the 1890s, there was an east-west rivalry centering around people living near or west of the Rock Island line and those residing around or east of the Santa Fe Railroad. Those in the west expressed jealousy over the seeming control of political and economic affairs of those in the east.

In a six-page deposition, Callahan charged Vincent with treachery and unfaithfulness during the 1896 campaign. His charges referred to a proposed debate between Callahan and Flynn at Mulhall, in Logan County. Callahan issued the challenge, but GOP managers wanted to limit the debate to the free-homes issue. When it seemed that no agreement could be reached, Vincent filled out Callahan's schedule with engagements in Blaine and Woods counties, far to the west of Mulhall. Republicans then distributed flyers advertising the Mulhall debate, forcing Callahan to rush back east. When he arrived on the scene, Republicans still would allow only a debate on the free-homes issue. Democrat Virgil Hobbs, the chairman of the Free Silver party's central committee, then declined to share time with the GOP candidate. Callahan eventually came to believe that Vincent had planned the whole debacle to embarrass him. The release of Callahan's charges, which Tousley personally secured from the Populist Congressman, was timed to secure the speakership for the El Reno editor, which it did.[10]

Vincent immediately demanded a hearing before the third party's territorial committee. After surveying the evidence, the committee laid the blame on a misunderstanding and issued a statement that it "unqualifiedly exonerates Chairman Vincent." Callahan refused to accept the central committee's findings. His charges thus sealed a breach that had been growing for months between Vincent and the third party's more rabid fusionists. In the process of moving back to a middle-of-the-road position, however, Vincent received a general roasting from both sides and replied in kind.[11]

Exponents of radical legislation had good reason for joy in the early days of Oklahoma's fourth legislature. Logan County Populist William L. Sullivan gained a quick reputation as an "abolitionist," introducing legislation to eliminate both the territorial militia and the office of oil inspector. Both were the refuge of placemen, according to Populists. The militia, which Leo Vincent labeled the "protege of a shoddy aristocracy," also conjured up visions of a standing army in third-party eyes. The Republican legislation that had established the position of oil inspector, John Allan claimed, was well meant but injurious. The inspection process had the result of establishing a monopoly without keeping dangerous fluids out of the territory. Rejected oils could still be sold in Oklahoma. Unscrupulous dealers knew this and flooded the territory with dangerous-burning fluids, while honest or uninformed oil suppliers avoided Oklahoma. The measure had established an ineffective appointive office, which Populists saw as a sinecure. Although making the office effective would have been a better solution, not enough Democrats would have supported the measure to secure its passage. In line with the abolitionist spirit of the third-party legislators, Populist Councillor William Garrison, the most experienced legislator of the 1897 assembly, brought bills with him to Guthrie for the abolition of capital punishment and contracts requiring payment in gold. The council, where Democrats were in the majority, however, would prove more conservative than the house.[12]

Abolition was not the only theme of the 1897 Oklahoma legislature. As expected, Populists introduced a bill limiting interest rates to 12 percent and strongly supported Democratic Council President J. W. Johnson's bill regulating the operation of railroads. Kingfisher County Populist Thomas Willis, who was studying for the bar at the time, introduced the widely expected bill to revise Fegan's 1895 fee-and-salary act. He also introduced a radical antitrust bill that would fine and imprison violators. Garfield County Democrat William L. Berry, who Vincent came to believe was one of the best "Populists" in the assembly, put forward a bill to limit the authority of the board of equalization, and Guthrie Democrat John DeBois introduced a measure to extend the date for paying 1896 taxes.[13]

Although Populist spokesmen generally lauded the fourth legislature in the early days of the session, as time passed and bills were delayed or compromised, an aura of apprehension spread among third-party observers. The only bills to reach the governor's desk in January related to extra clerk hire. Members of the fusion-controlled 1893 legislature had prided themselves on keeping such expenses to a minimum. The so-called extravagance of the Republican 1895 legislature had been a major campaign issue in 1896. In 1897, however, it seemed that every committee required its own clerk. Third-party legislators were, if anything, worse than their Democratic counterparts on the issue. Although Populists had clearly distrusted the motives of Republican legislators in previous assemblies, they believed that the large amount of work expected of the 1897 legislature warranted more clerks. Leo Vincent, on the other hand, was in no mood to afford them the benefit of the doubt and called upon the legislature to "quickly demonstrate its earnestness in the matter of reform by beginning with itself." [14]

Garrison's anti-gold–contract bill passed the council in early January. The final vote, however, was an ominous note for the so-called free-silver forces. Only two Democrats joined Populists to pass the bill. [15] In the house an even more portentous vote occurred. Only three Democrats joined Populists in passing the third party's usury bill. The council immediately replaced it with a milder substitute. The Populists' antimilitia bill also passed the house with the support of only three Democrats. [16]

By February it seemed clear that Democratic legislators would put a brake upon all reform legislation that they could not claim as their own. Johnson's antirailroad bill easily cleared the council, with five Democrats and all six Populists voting aye. Berry's measure leashing the board of equalization passed the house without a dissenting vote. Only one Democrat and one Republican, however, joined Populists on a woman suffrage bill. Leo Vincent, who had turned over editorial control of a column on women's issues in the *Oklahoma Representative* to his wife, was outraged by the suffrage measure's defeat. House Democrats also pushed through a radical bill outlawing both black-white and Indian-white marriages. The council struck out the latter provision. Old-party legislators also opposed liquor legislation, which most Populists favored. Meanwhile, the legislature wrangled inconclusively with badly needed school-land legislation, official salaries, and a new election law. [17]

As the legislative process began to bog down, some of the more radical Populist editors expressed their impatience. Vincent threatened to disown fusion if the orators who had "dilated to their fullest lingual capacity" in the cause of reform the previous autumn continued to pander to cries of "do nothing rash, preserve the existing order, be careful, ouch!" In early March he proclaimed representative government "inadequate" and began vigorously promoting Populist Representative James K. Graves's referendum bill, which never got out of committee. A week later he published a letter from W. A. Turner that predicted revolution if the masses could not get sufficient relief through the ballot.[18]

As the date for adjournment neared, legislators seemed to awaken to their duties. John Hogan got his bill providing low-cost government insurance through the house, despite cries of anguish from the insurance trust. A Populist-sponsored bill establishing a normal school in Alva, in the Cherokee Outlet, also passed the legislature. A badly needed bill forcing private banks to register with a newly established banking commission and submit to semiannual audits also reached the governor's desk. The Democratic-sponsored measure would end the parade of transient banking institutions that had fleeced Cherokee Outlet residents of their meager savings since the opening. More ominously, however, a fee and salary bill much like the hated Fegan measure of 1895 also emerged from the house.[19] Democrats also substituted their own usury bill for that of the Populists and then struck out the penalty provision before sending it to the governor. A measure giving the "text book trust" an exclusive contract with the territory's schools also emerged from the legislature. Even Roy Hoffman denounced the bill, believing it would surely destroy fusion for the future. In the end Democrats sidetracked or gutted much of the Populist-sponsored reform program. Their foot-dragging, in fact, left more than fifty unresolved pieces of legislation on the calendar when the assembly adjourned on March 12, 1897.[20]

Governor Renfrow pocket-vetoed the textbook bill at the end of the session, along with seven other measures. In all, the Democratic governor vetoed twelve bills. Most were pet projects of Populists or of Democrats who frequently voted with their third-party colleagues. Bills receiving Renfrow's official disapproval were Garrison's anti-gold–contract bill, Speaker Tousley's measure allowing voters to elect nonattorneys to the position of probate judge, Populist Dale Lytton's bill allowing the legislature to remove territorial officials, and a Democratic substitute abolishing the office of oil inspector, a bill most Populists supported.

Measures receiving the pocket veto, in addition to the textbook bill, included Berry's bill limiting the powers of the board of equalization, a Democratic school-land law that Populists supported, Willis's antitrust bill, and a tax on wholesale beer distributors. According to the *Oklahoma Representative*, "About all the reform measures that succeeded in passing a semi-hostile legislature were squelched by the governor." Such power in the hands of an executive, Vincent proclaimed, was "a dangerous prerogative." Republicans immediately pronounced the veto Oklahomans' only safeguard against "ignorant" legislation.[21]

Three measures that Democrats particularly liked and that Governor Renfrow readily signed into law dealt with Oklahoma's black population. The 1897 legislature provided for segregated schools, established a college for blacks at Langston, and passed an election law designed to disfranchise illiterate blacks.[22] Democrats sponsored and unanimously voted for each of these measures. Republicans opposed the election law, which also reversed the antifusion law of 1895.[23]. Only J. P. D. Mouriquand voted against segregated schools. Although several Populists opposed segregation, all third-party members either voted for the discriminatory legislation or were absent from the final vote.[24]

On the eve of adjournment Roy Hoffman proclaimed fusion "a great success." According to the Democratic editor, the fusion parties stood together on the "fundamental principles of economy and progress" and enacted "a large number of wise measures." He predicted that popular demand would keep the coalition intact. As an endorsement of Hoffman's views, Ralph Bray reprinted the Democratic editor's assessment in the *Enid Coming Events*. To drive home his point, Bray also published a comparative study showing the fourth legislature's appropriations to be significantly reduced compared to its predecessor's. Similar comparisons emerged from the *Oklahoma Leader*. John DeBois, the Democratic councillor who represented part of Guthrie in 1897, enumerated the laws he found most important. They included the usury law, banking reform, and reduced appropriations, fees, and salaries. The Democratic *Alva Pioneer* claimed that the only Democratic or Populist editors who denounced the legislature simply had not yet "secured a 'rake off.'"[25]

Critics of the fourth legislature were quick to respond to the flatulent pronouncements of fusionists. The editor of the Democratic *Lexington Leader* found the council "dominated by a set of jackleg lawyers who can't see anything but their own importance." The *Alva Republican* proclaimed the 1897 legislature a blow to Oklahoma's prosperity and predicted that capital would steer clear of the Territory. Leo Vincent took particular exception to Councillor DeBois's claim of being a reformer and pointed to his votes against the anti-gold–contracts bill and Shannon's fee-and-salary measure.[26]

Territorial chairman Leo Vincent, who had been the godfather of fusion in 1896, rapidly became the darling of middle-of-the-roaders in the wake of the 1897 legislature. The Guthrie editor believed that "the logic of events pointed with irresistible force to a cooperation with Democracy" in 1896. But he saw very little of "Jefferson and Jackson reincarnated" in the regenerated Democracy of 1897. Most of his proposed legislation had been defeated, subverted, or vetoed.[27]

Vincent had nothing but adulation for several of the third-party legislators, most notably Garrison and Willis. Other Populist assemblymen, however, received the full brunt of his criticism. Delbert Randolph, for instance, had killed Willis' fee-and-salary bill with a negative vote. A study of roll-call votes in the council shows that both Randolph and D. B. Learned voted with Democrats more often than with members of their own party. Vincent's brother Henry noted that none of the fusion legislatures of 1897 were "composed of the same material as constituted the '89 and '91 [Kansas] legislative bodies." Kansas and Oklahoma legislators, he claimed, had done nothing more significant than "fiddle and snort over the adjustment of fees and salaries."[28]

J. C. Tousley, who had treated Vincent badly at the beginning of the session, received the Guthrie editor's sharpest barbs. According to Vincent, Tousley had killed Johnson's railroad bill the day after he "sat at a princely banquet given by the Santa Fe." Tousley had also proclaimed his desire to see a "reasonable" usury bill at the time Democrats killed a Populist-sponsored measure. Vincent accused Tousley of voting for his own pocketbook, instead of for his constituents, on a measure reducing the price of legal printing. By the end of the session, Vincent claimed that no paper in the Territory, including Tousley's own "little proof-sheet press, . . . [had] the effrontery to arise to the speaker's defence." Vincent labeled the El Reno legislator "the worst of all the Populist failures."[29]

Other evaluations of the 1897 legislature were not as critical. Populist national committeeman W. H. French pointed out that few of the men who served in the fourth assembly were experienced legislators. On the whole, he believed, the 1897 body had made fewer mistakes and passed more wholesome legislation than had its predecessors. Republican Cassius Barnes, who became Oklahoma's fifth governor shortly after he completed his legislative duties in 1897, proudly claimed that "no vicious legislation" had ever emanated from an Oklahoma legislature. He went on to state that Oklahomans could rejoice in the knowledge that "all propositions against the interests of corporate investments have been uniformly defeated."[30] Leo Vincent accorded the third-party legislators' failure to support Populist measures to a lack of grounding in the principles of the People's party. He hoped that "organization and education, the peaceful handmaidens of evolution, will yet remodel our social order on the lines of fraternity and equality." Vincent also promised to have "an egg hatching for every member of the late legislature who betrayed his constituents."[31]

Exponents of fusion had promised a revolution in government but delivered much less. Populist legislators became victims of Democratic negativism, because they did not have a majority in either house. Although certain Democrats, namely Henry Steele Johnston and J. W. Johnson, pushed hard for specific reforms, most of their old-party colleagues subverted or killed the promised reform legislation.

Before 1896 the People's party had represented itself to the voters as a viable alternative to the mainstream parties. Failure to produce promised reforms subsequently discredited third-party leaders. The deepening cleavage over fusion, which became critical with the rift between Callahan and Vincent, accelerated the third party's dissolution. Populists never again spoke with a single voice. This also helped remove their party as a viable alternative.

The problem of assessing exactly what Populists would have done if given power must remain a mystery, because the People's party never controlled the governor's chair and both houses of any state or territory. Mainstream-party officeholders, thus, forever had a brake upon unwanted Populist legislation.

CHAPTER TEN

The Fruits of Expediency

Slightly less than a month after Oklahoma's fourth legislative assembly adjourned, Leo Vincent resigned as chairman of the territorial People's party. His feud with James Y. Callahan and criticism of the do-nothing 1897 fusion legislature had alienated him from much of the third party's leadership. Having changed his mind about fusion, he found himself out of step with his colleagues and stated that intraparty harmony was needed to further the third party's effort.[1]

Vincent recounted his tenure as party chairman in his letter of resignation. When he took office in July, 1894, he found practically no organization, no data on party supporters or contributors, and the "mixed conditions incident to past fusion with the Democrats." Pursuing a middle-of-the-road course in 1894 with an aggressive veteran of past egalitarian crusades at the head of the Populist ticket, Vincent had applied his noteworthy organizational talents to a territorial party stillborn through incompetence and scandal. His efforts resulted in an almost fourfold increase in the third party's vote. Because free-silver forces in the Democratic party triumphed with the nomination of William Jennings Bryan, however, Vincent came to believe that "a united effort seemed a destiny in 1896 under *like* [Vincent's emphasis] platforms."[2]

Vincent threw his "whole force, reputation, and even family interests" into the Free Silver campaign of 1896. Callahan, however, ran behind, rather than ahead of, his ticket and won only a narrow victory over Flynn. Democrats and a few self-seeking Populists, Vincent claimed, then poisoned Callahan's mind against him in the controversy over the Mulhall debate. When the delegate-elect refused to accept the executive committee's findings in the debate controversy, a lasting disharmony entered the reform movement. Although events were different elsewhere, a widening breach appeared between fusionists and middle-of-the-roaders wherever the People's party was active.[3]

According to Vincent, the "superficial and juvenile conduct" of the 1897 legislature "precluded any chance for a successful continuation" of fusion. The nature of fusion, on the other hand, bound Populists and Democrats together for two years. Since he could no longer be helpful in "a repetition of the past nor guarantee sanction of all party conduct in the future," Vincent resigned as party chairman. In reality, Vincent's letter of resignation was more a reaffirmation of his political faith than a concession of victory to fusionists. The real reason he resigned was his plan to take over a proposed third-party paper in Boulder, Colorado, although he did not make his plans public for several months.[4]

Although Vincent planned to leave Oklahoma, he retained an interest in the party he had helped construct. His resignation spurred a plethora of editorial responses from his journalist colleagues. His old nemesis, Frank Greer, feigned an understanding of Vincent's exasperation by labeling Vincent's offspring, the 1897 legislature, a humiliating failure and noting that the expected chief clerkship and printing contracts had gone to others. According to Greer, the ungrateful free-silver legislators "jumped onto their creator and benefactor like a pack of wolves and bore him torn and bleeding to the ground." Vincent had expected a pecuniary interpretation from Greer and attributed it to "the utter absence of a principle in the minds of the average old party advocate."[5]

Roy Hoffman, Guthrie's Democratic editor, also had some acrid comments. He claimed that Vincent had resigned at the request of the third party's territorial committee, an error he was forced to retract the following day. Hoffman, as well as almost all other commentators, freely acknowledged Vincent's organizational talents. The Populist editor, he asserted, was "a good drillmaster, but of no account as a leader." According to Hoffman, Democrats were largely responsible for Callahan's victory in 1896. For this reason, he concluded, Populism and Democracy might have "a direct and common sympathy" with each other, but with Vincent at the helm they had no common aim. With the Populist editor gone from the chairmanship, however, Hoffman predicted future success for fusion.[6]

Vincent reprinted the remarks that most Oklahoma Populist editors made about his resignation, whether complimentary or not. Occasionally he added editorial comment. When A. C. Towne found reason to criticize the chairman's role in fusion, for instance, Vincent noted that Towne's discovery of the middle of the road must have been even more recent than his own. The Alva editor's virulently antifusion tirade was printed directly under an endorsement of William Jennings Bryan for president in 1900.[7]

In returning to a middle-of-the-road position, Leo Vincent found John Allan's comments on his resignation the most noteworthy. The Norman editor lectured the retiring territorial chairman on the pitfalls of working with Democrats. Rather than taking offense at the remarks of the only Oklahoma Populist editor who had remained consistent in his commitment to the middle of the road, Vincent stated that "we like him the better for it." According to Allan, Vincent had lost his Populist principles a year before and "had floundered around ever since on a sea of doubt." As party chairman in 1896, Allan claimed, Vincent had had an enthusiastic and well organized party with a strong, vigorous press "abundantly supplied with justice and truth to shell the works of the enemy." Why, then, asked Allan, had the party chairman shown such signs of distress? Allan answered his own query by noting that "the reformer is prone sometimes to step aside to try and avoid some of the dangers he beholds in the distance." He was pleased, however, that Vincent had found that the smoother path did not lead to reform and had again "set his face to the blast . . . steering neither to the right nor the left for seeming temporary expediency."[8]

Vincent agreed with Allan that enthusiasm, rather than reason, had ruled the third party's deliberations in 1896. The ensuing stampede, Vincent believed, had allowed inferior men to crowd to the front and receive the party's favors. Regaining his balance, Vincent recalled that the success of reform depended on the "intelligent and sympathetic cohesion" that came from education in the principles of Populism. He labeled the Free Silver triumph of 1896 a victory of numbers but not of principles. The 1897 legislature showed that most Democrats, and some Populists, lacked the proper grounding in reform principles to achieve lasting change. The result was disillusionment with the third party's wasted opportunities.[9]

Leo Vincent probably felt some personal responsibility for the destruction of the People's party in Oklahoma. He was one of the first fusionists to recognize the damage that resulted from association with the Democratic party. Vincent did not, however, kill Populism. The most important Populist goals were national in scope. Other men, including national party chairman Herman Taubeneck and 1892 Populist presidential candidate James B. Weaver, were far more instrumental in the third party's move from the justice orientation that had built the party to the expediency orientation that helped to destroy it.

In a sense the People's party always contained the seeds of its own destruction. Because Populists viewed society from the cyclical perspective of Enlightenment thinkers, they were particularly susceptible to the "now or never" appeal of Bryan Democracy. Free silver symbolized the battle against what Populists saw as the forces of monopoly and oppression, and they feared that a devolution from civilization would surely follow a McKinley victory. Vincent's course was symptomatic of the path most other well-meaning Populists took in 1896.

Vincent seemed to prefer either Jesse Dunn, the county attorney of Woods County, or third-party assemblyman Thomas Willis, as his replacement for territorial chairman. When Logan County Populists endorsed their own man, L. F. Laverty, a retiring but widely known preacher, Vincent supported him. Because James Y. Callahan had declined to attend the executive committee meeting which chose Laverty, it was a placid affair. Vincent had announced the sale of the *Oklahoma Representative*, to Clark Hudson, effective July 15, a week before. N. S. Mounts, of the *Tecumseh Leader*, joined Hudson in Guthrie as the paper's new business manager. Fusionists Hudson and Mounts would send the *Oklahoma Representative* into bankruptcy in 1898. In his last edition before moving to Colorado, Leo Vincent prophetically told

Oklahoma Populists to "keep your eye on Eugene V. Debs and his Social Democracy movement. . . . It is the beginning of a far reaching revolution."[10]

Since the vast majority of Populists elected to the 1897 legislature came from the Oklahoma hinterland, it might be expected that they reflected the true sentiments of rank-and-file Populists more closely than a Guthrie editor did. The 1898 election, however, proved this to be a fallacy. In March, 1898, the Populist territorial committee voted to fuse with Democrats in the fall elections. Laverty, Hudson, Bray, and French, who became the movers and shakers of fusion Populism in the late 1890s, met with Democrats in May and agreed to a joint convention.[11]

At the Democratic-Populist territorial convention, held July 13, 1898, in Oklahoma City, the crucial vote on fusion came on a motion to appoint a conference committee to meet with Democrats. Fusionists won the poll by a vote of 148 to 29. The two conventions then merged for the delegate nomination. A two-thirds majority was necessary for nomination. Democrats, who were determined to secure the delegate nomination for themselves, remained adamant throughout the night. Shortly after nine o'clock the next morning, on the seventy-fourth ballot, they finally triumphed and nominated James R. Keaton, an Oklahoma City lawyer and former district court judge, for the delegate slot. Keaton chose Clark Hudson as his campaign manager, and the Populist territorial committee elected W. H. French to replace Laverty as party chairman.[12]

Cleveland County Populists bolted the Oklahoma City fusionist convention and held their own conference in Guthrie on September 1, 1898. A. S. Hankins, a little-known man from Woods County, received the middle-of-the-roader's nomination for delegate. In his memoirs, Dennis Flynn later claimed that his friends had manipulated the middle-of-the-road convention to split the anti-Republican vote. Whether true or not, Hankins did not draw enough votes to affect the outcome of the 1898 election.[13]

On November 8, 1898, Republicans achieved their greatest electoral victory of the territorial years. Dennis Flynn was returned to Congress with a 58.3 to 39.1 percent victory over Keaton. Hankins collected the remaining 2.5 percent of the vote.

The GOP's vote in 1898 was similar to its 1896 poll, and stay-at-home Populists again deserted the fusion ticket, as they had in 1896 (see appendix B, table B-1). Fusion, particularly under the leadership of a Democrat, proved distasteful to those who had constituted the Populist legions in 1894.

Lower voter turnout and the poll of the southern-dominated, middle-of-the-road faction account for the rather minor changes in the birthplace-race correlations of 1896 in comparison to those of 1896. The mixing of Democratic and Populist voters again reduced the significance of the rural-urban cleavage, which had been important to partisan choice in the early 1890s (see appendix A, table A-3). Populist voter dropout even caused the fusion correlation with urban residence to become slightly positive in most cases. Logan County, where blacks made up a substantial portion of urban votes, was the major exception. Fusion under a Democrat proved to be so unpopular among Cleveland County Populists that they also voted for the GOP candidate in the delegate race.[14]

As in 1896, fusion disrupted the agricultural and economic patterns of the early 1890s (see appendix A, tables A-4 and A-5). Democratic-led fusion caused the GOP correlation with wheat farming to increase, along with the Free Silver correlation with ranching. Because stay-at-home Populists were relatively poor, the fusion correlations with tenancy declined. Correlations between the Free Silver vote and the value of agriculture per farm and per improved acre, on the other hand, predictably increased.

Fusionists also met massive defeat in the territorial legislative races. Eighteen Democrats and eighteen Populists had sat in the 1897 legislature; only eight and six, respectively, were elected to the 1899 assembly.[15] In the territorywide elections of the mid-1890s each of Oklahoma's three major parties successively collapsed at the polls. Cleveland's and Renfrow's Democratic party placed a distant third in 1894. The rise of the People's party and the inadequacies of Democratic leaders account for this collapse. In 1896 the GOP carried only three legislative districts. This was largely the result of a Republican gerrymander which backfired. Callahan beat Flynn in the delegate race by the narrowest of margins. In 1898 the Free Silver party, to which Populists tied their future, collapsed at the polls. This time, however, gerrymandering had nothing to do with the outcome of the election. The apportionment of 1895 remained intact until 1902. The People's party was simply in the throes of dissolution and unable to poll its former vote.

Fusion candidates appeared in thirty-one districts, while middle-of-the-roaders fielded thirteen candidates in 1898.[16] Two Cleveland County middle-of-the-road Populists secured enough Republican votes to be elected, while fusion Populists carried one council and three house seats. Democrats, on the other hand, carried three fusion and five nonfusion races. Seven of the fourteen non-Republicans to sit in the 1899 legislature, therefore, were not elected on fusion tickets. By November, 1898, not only voters but also many successful politicians had rejected electoral coalition.[17]

The battle between fusionists and middle-of-the-roaders within the Oklahoma Populist party did not subside when Leo Vincent left the territory. Despite Cleveland County's bolt of the 1898 Populist territorial convention, John Allan retained his position on the third party's territorial committee until 1900. The final break came at the April, 1900, convention of the People's party in Enid. The assembly met to choose delegates to the third party's national convention. When they decided to send delegates to the fusionist, rather than the middle-of-the-road, national convention, the Cleveland and Greer county delegations walked out. Fusionists met in a joint convention with Democrats in August, 1900, in Oklahoma City. They chose Populist Probate Judge Robert A. Neff over Democrat William Cross for the delegate slot on the thirty-first ballot. Middle-of-the-roaders held their own convention in Oklahoma City, on September 1 and chose John S. Allan as their nominee for delegate. Neither of the Populist conventions were heavily attended.[18]

Robert A. Neff was a longtime third-party warhorse. He had edited a Union Labor party paper in Wichita, Kansas, in the 1880s. Still, his candidacy revived only a measure of the old Populist enthusiasm. He carried 45.7 percent of the vote in 1900.[19]

The GOP and Free Silver correlations with agricultural, economic, and birthplace-race factors generally returned to their 1896 levels in 1900 (see appendix A, tables A-1, A-4, and A-5). The major exception was European-born Oklahomans, who showed their strongest correlation of the era with the Republican party in 1900. The remobilization of third-party voters again returned most of the Free Silver–urban correlations to the negative column (see appendix A, table A-3). Cleveland County Populists, for instance, returned to the fold in the delegate race.

Dennis Flynn, who was elected to his fourth and final term in Congress in 1900, received 52.1 percent of the vote, while Allan and Socialist candidate E. T. Tucker split the remainder of the vote evenly. In the legislative races Democrats and Populists fused in thirty-three districts. In Cleveland County, Populists fused with Republicans, and in the far-west ranching country Democrats ran straight tickets. Democrats and Populists again elected both fusion and straight party men to the 1901 assembly.[20] Third-party councillors provided the swing vote and joined Democrats in organizing the upper house of the 1901 legislature. They received little, however, in return for their help. The only third-party issue to pass either house of the 1899 or 1901 legislatures was George Coulson's initiative and referendum bill of 1901. Councillors passed the measure as a courtesy to the aged Populist, but it was quickly killed in the GOP-controlled house.[21]

On March 22, 1902, the Populist territorial committee met in Oklahoma City and accepted a Democratic invitation for rank-and-file Populists to enter the Democratic primaries. Democrats nominated William Cross, who had lost the delegate nomination to Neff in 1900. Cross lost to Flynn's replacement, Bird McGuire, by less than four hundred votes in November, 1902. In the legislative races of 1902, Populists fused with Democrats in five districts, with Republicans in two, and with Socialists in one. In another district they fielded a middle-of-the-road candidate. All lost. The Populist Revolt in Oklahoma was at an end.[22]

With the demise of the People's party in 1902, sectional voting increased substantially (see appendix, A, table A-1). The dramatic rise in all sectional correlations between 1900 and 1902 suggests that the intervening period marks a dividing line between

two substantially different political universes. After 1900 political contention turned largely upon considerations of sectionalism. Before 1902 other factors, most notably the cosmopolitan-
hinterland dichotomy and type of agriculture, had also been
important to partisan choice.

In June, 1895, Populist editors G. C. Halbrooks and Mont
Howard met in the offices of the Populist *Medford Mascot* and
founded the first socialist local in Oklahoma. Since Daniel De-
Leon's Socialist Labor party was the only nationally organized socialist party at the time, they affiliated with the doctrinaire
Marxist's group. After the Socialists' unity convention of 1901,
the Medford local was the first in Oklahoma to organize under
the new Socialist party label.[23]

When Eugene V. Debs founded the Social Democratic party in
June, 1897, press reports identified the movement as a successor
to the American Railway Union. Even mainstream-party sources
noticed that the new party's mode of development paralleled that
of the Populist party. Debs had supported the Populist party in the
mid-1890s and surely knew that the agrarian movement's origins
lay in the transition of the Southern Farmers' Alliance to the
People's party.[24]

The socialism of Edward Bellamy and Lawrence Gronlund,
which had its roots in the same egalitarian tradition as Populism,
permeated Oklahoma Populist papers in the 1890s. The fusion–
middle-of-the-road dichotomy had no bearing upon Oklahoma
Populists' later espousal of socialism. Ralph Bray, one of the third
party's most rabid fusionists, was a strong Bellamy nationalist.
John Allan seemed to agree with Milton Park, of the *Dallas
Southern Mercury*, who defined socialism as "applied Christianity
as taught by Jesus." Park stated that Populists and Socialists differed only on means, not on policy. He saw socialism as the long-
range goal of Populism. Socialists, he claimed, believed in "cutting the dog's tail off close behind the ears, . . . [while Populists]
believe we must grow into the socialist state by piece-meal and
that the shortest cut around is not always the most feasible
route." Allan never formally affiliated with the Socialist party.
He had an antipathy toward shortcuts that surely was the product

of Populism's experience with fusion. Growth would come for the new egalitarian party, as it had for the People's party, only through education and nothing else.[25]

The process of educating the people on socialism began in earnest in Oklahoma, as it did elsewhere, just before the turn of the century. By mid-1899 excerpts from Julius Wayland's Socialist *Appeal to Reason* appeared regularly in the *Alva Review*. Wayland had founded the *Coming Nation* in 1893 and renamed it the *Appeal to Reason* two years later. Both were Populist in affiliation until after 1896. Even fusionist editor Roy Stafford, of the *Oklahoma City Oklahoma Champion*, began publishing Socialist literature in February, 1900. He became a Democrat, however, when he took over the *Daily Oklahoman* later that year. The paper turned decidedly to the right when E. K. Gaylord bought it from Stafford in 1904.[26] In December, 1898, James W. Hadley, a Canadian County Populist elected to the 1899 legislature on a fusion ticket, attended the founding meeting of the El Reno local of Eugene V. Debs's Social Democratic party. When Debs's party perfected its territorial organization in October, 1899, J. N. Clark, who would chair the 1900 middle-of-the-road Populist convention, was in attendance as a delegate. The 1900 Oklahoma Socialist platform endorsed "legal tender treasury notes," or greenbacks. In 1902, Socialists chose Thomas Smith, the editor of the *Kay County Populist* (renamed the *Oklahoma Socialist* in 1901), as their candidate for delegate. The Socialist party became the next logical expression of the late-nineteenth-century egalitarian movement, just as the People's party had replaced the Union Labor party in 1889. In the counties that constituted the Oklahoma Territory in the 1890s, however, Socialists never came close to receiving Beaumont's share of the 1894 vote.[27]

Not all Oklahoma Populists joined the Socialist party after 1900. Reduced voter turnout suggests that many dropped out of active political participation. In their eyes, the plutocrats had won, and nothing significant could be done to alter the nation's course. Other third-party leaders joined the agrarian wing of the Democratic party. Samuel Crocker, the earliest of Oklahoma's Populist leaders, became a Democrat after the turn of the century and received significant Socialist support in a 1912 bid for the state legislature. His endorsement of Theodore Roosevelt for president, however, cost him the election. He died in 1921, never having held public office.[28]

George Gardenhire, the man responsible for importing the Farmers' Alliance to the Oklahoma Territory, returned to southern Kansas in 1898. Nothing is known about the later life of the third party's 1892 delegate nominee, N. H. Ward. Ralph Beaumont, the Oklahoma Populists' standard-bearer in 1894, returned to his duties as a traveling third-party lecturer early in 1895. James Y. Callahan stumped the territory for Keaton in 1898 and for Neff in 1900. Otherwise, he retired from politics and moved to Enid, where he engaged in business.[29]

Populists elected John Allan secretary of their 1908 national convention. He later supported agrarian Democrats, such as Thomas P. Gore, who had been a Populist in the 1890s. Allan continued to edit the *Norman Peoples Voice* until 1910. It may have been the last officially Populist newspaper in the country. In 1917 the *Norman Transcript*, the *Norman State Democrat*, and the *Norman Peoples Voice* (which had been renamed the *Cleveland County Enterprise* in 1911) merged and became the *Norman Daily Transcript*. The consolidation symbolized the decreasing importance of partisan affiliation in the twentieth century. Allan died in 1930.[30]

Leo Vincent became editor of the *Boulder Colorado Representative* in 1898 and chairman of the Colorado Populist party in 1899. He gave up journalism in 1903 to build and sell houses. In 1909 he became assistant insurance commissioner of Colorado, and in 1914 he joined the Internal Revenue Service as a field agent. In 1924 he opened an entertainment hall in the university district of Boulder. A fire ended that venture in 1927, and Vincent moved to California to take up mushroom farming. In 1936, at the age of seventy-four, Vincent took a job as a pilot at a Hayward, California, industrial plant, the only wage-earning job he ever held. He died in 1955.[31]

Henry Vincent, Leo's brother and partner at the *American Nonconformist*, served on the editorial staffs of several midwestern Populist newspapers in the 1890s and wrote the official Populist version of Coxey's march on Washington. He joined Leo at the *Colorado Representative* in 1899 but left a year later. He then worked at the Pueblo Bessemer Steel Plant until 1907, when he moved to Girard, Kansas, the home of Julius Wayland's *Appeal to Reason.* Vincent's home in Girard became a mecca for Socialist dignitaries, most notably Eugene V. Debs. Vincent became district secretary of the Socialist party in 1908. Poverty and frequent moves in search of work characterized his later life. In 1931 he was severely injured in an automobile accident, and he died four years later. In the depths of the depression of the 1930s, Henry Vincent reminisced about his days as a third-party activist. He recalled that Kansas Republican John J. Ingalls, whom Populists retired from the Senate in 1891, had uttered the infamous words, "The purification of politics is an iridescent dream." Looking back on the egalitarian crusades of his lifetime, Vincent wondered if "there isn't more truth than poetry" in the Republican senator's remark.[32]

CHAPTER ELEVEN
Conclusions

The Populist Revolt was the product of the still-vital neorepublican mind of the late nineteenth century as it evaluated the results of the economic, political, and social revolutions of Gilded Age America. Throughout the late nineteenth century, spokesmen representing a series of egalitarian third-party movements put forth an apocalyptic critique of the Gilded Age's cosmopolitan ethos that was rooted in the ideology of the founding fathers. Third-party agitators were especially successful in mobilizing a following where economic and political conditions had discredited major-party spokesmen, as on the Great Plains and in the cotton-belt South during the late 1880s and 1890s.

Whether the course of late-nineteenth-century development constituted an advance of civilization or a degeneration toward barbarism became a major point of contention in America with the coming of the Populist revolt. Cosmopolitan elements looked back to the pronouncements of John Locke, who elevated property rights to an equal place beside human rights, for inspiration in judging contemporary events. These men pointed to such material factors as increased wealth, expanded production, and a proliferation of services as signs of the nation's advance. They were, in essence, system-oriented. They saw the plight of individual victims as a small price to pay for the significant advances of the nation as a whole.

The republican ideal of the founding fathers, which informed the Populists' assessment of late-nineteenth-century events, viewed the protection of individual liberties as the ultimate goal of society. The role of government was to promote social conditions that would aid the individual's God-given right to self-fulfillment. This humanistic orientation was moral in nature and based upon precepts of justice to the individual. It dictated the rejection of any social development that encouraged the debasement of any human. Such a viewpoint naturally had special appeal to those who saw themselves as victims of the contemporary system.

When railroads first appeared in a region, the almost universal response was enthusiasm for the new commercial and industrial world. Farmers and merchants alike wanted to believe that they were on the brink of the sustained prosperity that the philosophies of laissez-faire capitalism and social Darwinism promised. The more aggressive farmers bought machinery, fertilizer, and more land, all on credit, and quickly discovered that they were the most efficient producers of the age. Their agricultural production vastly outpaced the purchasing capacity of other Americans and even the world. Prices for agricultural commodities naturally plummeted. Railroad operators and other middlemen, however, took their profits regardless of the farmers' plight. In spite of this, commercial elements proclaimed the emerging economic system just and laid the blame for agrarian problems on the farmer. He overproduced, they claimed. A crisis in agriculture occurred where mortgages were numerous, credit was tight, and transportation costs were more expensive.

As the economy of the Plains and the South worsened, farmers turned to their elected officials for aid. Government had provided tariffs to protect manufacturers, land grants to aid railroads, and deflation to help creditors. But when farmers put forth their claims upon the political process, they received little more than the worn-out slogans of laissez-faire. The inadequate response of the Gilded Age's political elite to the plight of the farmer produced a political crisis in these outlying regions of the nation.

Many southern and western farmers had never completely committed themselves to the panaceas of Gilded Age enterprise. Although they had entered the world of commercial agriculture, they were primarily family farmers, not agribusinessmen. By the 1890s their operations often were only marginally profitable. Diversification, however, saved them from the worst effects of the late nineteenth century's agricultural crisis. This reaffirmed their commitment to the more traditional agrarian ethos. In the darkest days of the depression of the 1890s, many who had committed themselves to the dominant ideology of the era began to have second thoughts about their new commitment and searched for new answers. Frequently they found the ideology of the People's party more rewarding.

The cyclical interpretation of social development that late-nineteenth-century egalitarians inherited from the founding fathers lent positive connotations to the simplicity, equality, industriousness, and frugality of a developing society and a negative attitude to the hedonism, luxury, venality, and exploitation of a developed nation. Their Whiggish orientation caused them to see the latter as a triumph of power over liberty.

When the founding fathers came to believe that George III conspired to subvert their liberties and impose England's economic and social system on the colonies, they revolted and formed a republic commited to human equality. The Anglicanization process that George III promoted consisted of government favors to banking elites, aid to monopolies, a widening gap between rich and poor, and the driving of farmers off the land and into dependent subservience. Populists also noted that the political leaders of that age used patronage, pensions, and franchises to build majorities and silence critics. They had financed their manipulations through bonding schemes that rewarded insiders and saddled future generations with a seemingly impossible debt. The American Revolution constituted a rejection of this corrupt system and institutionalized the values of equality and liberty in the young republic.

Late-nineteenth-century egalitarians believed that the principles handed down by the founding fathers were universal truths, valid for all times and conditions. Many of the economic and social developments of the Gilded Age, furthermore, appeared to be consistent with the inherited warnings of social degeneration. Lawmakers seemed to abdicate their responsibility for monetary policy to America's, and, worse yet, England's, banker elite. Government policies, such as the protective tariff and land grants to railroads, promoted the ultimate consolidation of wealth and power—monopoly. The gap between the rich and the poor widened distinctly. The process also destroyed the independent family farmer, the bulwark of liberty in a republic. Rather than using the power of government to stem this spreading cancer, Populists believed that America's Gilded Age political elite aided the process through unneeded extravagance, financed by bonding schemes likely to force future generations into economic dependence.

To return America to the path charted at the nation's founding, late-nineteenth-century egalitarians devised a series of remedies that, when combined, formed the Omaha platform of 1892. With the exception of the Alliance's subtreasury plan, each demand cataloged in the document had appeared in previous third-party manifestos. The People's party was only the largest and most successful of a series of late-nineteenth-century egalitarian movements that shared a common spirit rooted in the republican ideology of the American Revolution.

At first glance, Populist remedies appear to reveal an ambivalence between protosocialism and retrogressive small government. Although republicanism provided late-nineteenth-century egalitarians with a common tool for evaluating Gilded Age development, there was some diversity of opinion about the relative importance of specific remedies.

The unity of Populism's arsenal of demands can be understood only in terms of the republican ideology of the American Revolution. One lesson that Populists learned from the American Revolution was that all officeholders must be watched very closely. Power was considered ever-aggressive. Liberty, on the other hand, was easily subverted if not vigilantly defended. When the American revolutionary leaders turned their attention to the problem of retaining their liberties, they visualized a republican government, supported by an independent citizenry, as the best safeguard. Individual economic independence was necessary to withstand the temptations and threats of those with political power. Only an egalitarian society with widespread property ownership could ensure that none would be strong enough to misuse power and none weak enough to fall victim to the encroachments of those wielding it.

With America's vast land reserves, men such as Thomas Jefferson had looked to widespread freehold tenure as the key to maintaining an egalitarian state. Samuel Crocker's origination of the free-homes issue was thoroughly within this tradition. Republican government, according to Populists, should aim solely at promoting personal independence. A degeneration of freeholders into tenancy, on the other hand, foreboded dire consequences for the nation.

Much of the legislation that Populists promoted and supported in the Oklahoma legislatures was designed to stop the ongoing concentration of landownership and protect the small freeholder. Because most homesteaders were poor, Populists advocated economy in government. High taxes to finance government spending could drive small holders into the clutches of mortgage companies or forced sheriff's sales.

Because land was not taxable until homesteaders had proved their claims, local and territorial officials frequently wished to put off the cost of government operations through deficit spending until the tax base expanded. Populists, however, also opposed bonding schemes. They likewise suspected, sometimes correctly, that officials really just did not want to face the voters after significantly raising taxes to finance their own salaries. Populists also sought school land-lease legislation that would secure to renters the value of their improvements, obtain a reasonable rent for the support of government, and parcel out land in small plots suitable for farming instead of in large sections for ranching, as Governor Renfrow had done.

Although Populists were quick to oppose anything they saw as government extravagance, retrenchment was not their panacea, as it was for Democrats. Populists joined Democrats in opposing high salaries and extra clerk hire and in abolishing offices seen as unnecessary. The militia and oil inspector's office, for instance, fit this category. The militia also conjured up visions of a "standing army" in an era that had seen Grover Cleveland use the army to crush the Pullman strike. Third-party legislators were quite willing, however, to spend money on relief to the needy and on education and roads.

When third-party legislators achieved a modicum of power in 1897, many seemed to reverse their stand on clerk hire. This seeming inconsistency points to one of the most important facets of Populism: antielitism. Populists viewed the cosmopolitan ethos as immoral and frequently saw exponents of the new ideology as conspiratorial. Cosmopolitan spokesmen, for instance, forever dwelt upon the virtues of free enterprise, while their disciples sought government aid in the form of tariffs, land grants, and franchises. Considering the circumstances, Populists naturally looked to the founding fathers' warnings about conspiracies to subvert their liberties. Once popular representatives achieved power and expected to rewrite the statute books, however, third-party legislators no longer saw clerk hire in conspiratorial terms.

The Populists' apparent ambivalence about active government was rooted primarily in considerations of who would control the government. As long as elements hostile to their interests remained in power, third-party advocates seemed intent upon leashing them. Populists were particularly opposed to nonelected officers making policy. Independent regulatory agencies implied elite rule without popular control. The board of equalization's doubling of taxes in 1895 and the court's subsequent validation of the levy left taxpayers without direct recourse in a supposedly democratic system. Third-party legislators were not, however, opposed to regulation, and often introduced bills designed to control banks, railroads, and other businesses. They also regularly supported the measures of others on regulating entrepreneurs. Abolishing the oil inspector's office was the only apparent exception. Populists supported that move because Democrats did not agitate the measure in terms of ending regulation but on the grounds that the office was ineffective and, thus, a sinecure.

In the national arena Populists looked to an active government as the salvation of the nation. They called for elected representatives to restore monetary policy to popular control and then to reverse the trend toward concentrated wealth with the graduated income tax. Populists called for greenbacks to reflate the currency and provide needed credit in outlying regions of the nation. They favored postal-savings banks to secure the deposits of average citizens, who often lost everything through the speculations of bankers. Populist spokesmen also called for government ownership of the railroads, telephones, and telegraphs. They reasoned that such monopolies concentrated too much wealth and power in the hands of the few. Although this solution seemed to contradict the Populists' antipathy toward the proliferation of offices, returning the American people to their egalitarian heritage and popular control would make active government acceptable To facilitate the return of popular control, Populists also advocated direct democracy through the initiative and referendum, plus popular election of the president and senators. Where Adam Smith had feared the power of the government, Populists feared the power of the few and saw popular control of an active government as their savior.[1]

The more sophisticated Populists, such as Leo Vincent, recognized that the frontier had closed and that in the future few would be able to maintain their economic independence through freehold tenure. To achieve individual independence in an industrial age, Vincent and others promoted the cooperative industrial schemes of the Knights of Labor. As partners in an enterprise (which implied equality), rather than as wage earners (which meant subservience), industrial workers would be able to maintain their personal independence. This facet of Populism, of course, laid the groundwork for the next egalitarian wave, socialism.

Populist antielitism also manifested itself in other ways. Third-party legislators generally opposed bills to professionalize what today are called the "professions." They believed that such preference amounted to granting a special franchise or establishing an aristocracy. More important, however, Populists wished to deny the Gilded Age elite's claim to special status. Such men were seen as wanting the government to grant them monopoly status because of their superior advantages, namely a better education. Populists believed that the people, rather than the elite, should judge the qualifications of professionals. Because modern medicine was in its infancy, examples of patients knowing better than their doctor were, of course, numerous. Samuel Crocker's refusal to permit the amputation of his arm in 1891 is a prime example. This bias against professionalism did, however, have its bizarre side, such as John Furlong's faith healing. Populists based their antiprofessionalism primarily on a cultural decision to deny their opponents' claim of superior knowledge.

Although the People's party in Oklahoma exhibited some characteristics of both plains and southern Populism, it more closely resembled the Kansas rather than the Texas movement. Although most early Oklahomans were poor, and tenancy was significant in certain areas before 1900, most territorial farmers were able to secure homesteads. The major problem farmers faced in the West was holding on to the land they already owned. Social conditions in the South, on the other hand, frequently resembled class warfare. Furnish merchants and other landlords used their economic power to control a sometimes restive population in postbellum Dixie.

Although important individual exceptions can be found, most Oklahoma Populists in northern-dominated areas supported fusion. Where southerners were numerous, third-party advocates generally became middle-of-the-roaders.[2] This was especially true among the rank and file, which suggests that the cleavage centered more on which major party constituted the local cosmopolitan elite than on major philosophical differences.

How well most Populists understood the workings of the modern industrial economy can be questioned. Some third-party advocates clearly realized that many of the undesirable events in a modern industrial society resulted from the impersonal workings of a complex economic system rather than from conspiracies. Many others did not. Using the conspiracy metaphor, however, Populists could label their opposition immoral, which provided a stronger motivation for action than did appeals not invested with moral overtones. Still, Populists were not unique in their conspiracy-mindedness. The so-called anarchist plots associated with the agrarian and labor troubles of the late nineteenth century played an equally important role in the minds of their cosmopolitan rivals, who might have been expected to know better. Industrialism was in its infancy, and most people struggled to understand the meaning of its impact. In large part, accusations of conspiracy were simply the level upon which politics was played in the 1890s.

Although Populists chose economic policy as their battlefield, morality was their cause. They looked backward to an earlier moral order for their inspiration. Populists did recognize, however, that commercial and industrial society was a permanent part of the American landscape. Instead of engaging in a frenzy of Luddite retrogression, they attempted to address problems within the context of their morally based mind-set. They accepted industrialism but demanded that it be made humane. The adoption of many of their solutions in the twentieth century attests to the practicality of their reforms. Populists wanted both the benefits of industrialization and a moral social order.

Various scholars have noted the almost religious fervor of the Populist appeal. For many, the People's party replaced the church as a vehicle for moral expression. The apocalyptic vision of Populism, however, encouraged a drive for quick victory. Third-party disciples believed that the crisis of the age was upon them in 1896. The result would be either civilization or barbarism. Desperation caused many of Populism's oldest and most noted leaders to temporize their positions and accept the pragmatism of fusion with Democrats. Those not disheartened by this transition from justice to expediency finally lost heart upon the defeat of William Jennings Bryan.

The nomination of Bryan for president in 1896 saved the Democratic party from going the way of the Whigs. Three major parties vied for the allegiance of the American electorate in the 1890s. If men like Grover Cleveland had controlled the Democratic party in 1896, the People's party could well have replaced it as the GOP's major rival. If the People's party had survived as a major force in the political life of the nation, the American electorate would have been presented with a continuing debate over its commitment to capitalism. Instead, the great political debate of twentieth-century America has been over how best to save capitalism.

Appendices

The Bases of Partisan Choice, 1890–1902

The party choice of Oklahoma voters during the Populist era turned upon several identifiable bases of support. The most important factors determining the political affiliation of voters while the People's party was active were sectionalism and race, a railroad world–hinterland dichotomy, and the dominant type of agriculture. Sectionalism has always played a major role in Oklahoma politics. The theme is extensively treated in James R. Scales and Danney Goble, *Oklahoma Politics: A History* (Norman: University of Oklahoma Press, 1982), Stephen Jones, *Oklahoma Politics in State and Nation* (Enid, Okla.: Haymaker Press, 1974), and Oliver Benson et al., *Oklahoma Votes* (Norman: University of Oklahoma, Bureau of Government Research, 1964). In determining exactly how sectionalism and race affected voters during the Populist era, the 1890 U.S. census proved to be almost useless. Oklahoma had seven counties in 1890, fifteen in 1892, twenty-two in 1893, and twenty-three in 1896. In addition, six of the original seven counties were enlarged in the two succeeding years, and all county and township lines were changed slightly after the 1890 federal census. For these reasons, all information on birthplace or race in this study comes from the 1900 U.S. census.

Unfortunately, the published results of the 1900 federal census do not contain information on place of birth. Geographer Michael Owen Roark, of Southeastern Missouri State University, however, conducted a 5 percent sample of the 1900 U.S. census manuscripts for his Ph.D. dissertation, "Oklahoma Territory: Frontier Development, Migration and Culture Areas" (Syracuse University, 1979), and graciously provided me with the data on

Oklahoman's birthplace or race used in this study. For both Roark's dissertation and this study the New England states and New York make up the Northeast; New Jersey, Pennsylvania, Ohio, Indiana, Illinois, Michigan, Wisconsin, Minnesota, North Dakota, South Dakota, Iowa, Nebraska, and Kansas constitute the Midwest; Delaware, Maryland, West Virginia, Kentucky, Tennessee, Missouri, Arkansas, and the Indian Territory constitute the border states; and Virginia, North Carolina, South Carolina, Florida, Georgia, Alabama, Mississippi, Louisiana, and Texas make up the lower South. Oklahomans born in the American West, Canada, and other Western Hemisphere nations were combined in a category labeled "others," which made up only 0.4 percent of the population in 1900. Caddo, Comanche, and Kiowa counties, which were opened to non-Indian settlement shortly after the 1900 census was taken, have been excluded from this study. To compare birthplace-race data with voting patterns, I obtained election returns for the August, 1890, at-large race for the territorial legislature and for the races for delegate to the U.S. Congress between 1890 and 1902 (the only territorywide races). The data came from the following sources: *Guthrie Weekly Oklahoma State Capital*, September 6, November 8, 1890; *Guthrie Oklahoma Representative*, November 8, December 20, 1894, December 3, 1896; *Guthrie Weekly Oklahoma Leader*, November 24, 1898, November 22, 1900; and *Perkins Journal*, November 28, 1902.

All of the census and voting data used in this appendix were transposed into percentages by county (or by township for tables A-2 and A-3) to standardize them for comparison. I then employed Pearsonian product-moment correlation coefficients to measure the relationship between voting and birthplace-race variables. Pearsonian correlations measure the relationship between two variables on a range from +1.00 to −1.00. Correlations close to +1.00 indicate that the two variables rise and fall together as each case is observed. In other words, they are positively correlated. If a correlation is near −1.00, the variables are inversely, or negatively, correlated. In either case the presumption is that the two variables strongly affect each other. Coefficients near zero, on the other hand, indicate little relationship between the two variables and infer that they do not affect each other significantly.

Because I used materials from the 1900 census, the accuracy of my findings relies upon the presumption that the patterns of 1900 are not radically different from those of previous years. Physical mobility was high during the Gilded Age, particularly in Oklahoma. Solon Buck, in "The Settlement of Oklahoma," *Transactions of the Wisconsin Academy of Science, Arts, and Letters* 15, no. 2 (1907): 362, shows that the most heavily populated portions of the territory were substantially settled by 1894. Twelve of the thirteen easternmost (and most heavily populated) counties were 99 percent or more occupied by 1894. The only exception was Pawnee County, which was 95 percent settled. These counties held 69.2 percent of the Oklahoma Territory's population in 1900.

Likewise, a comparison of birthplace-race data from the 1890 and 1900 censuses for those seven counties that existed in both years reveals a remarkable similarity. Midwesterners and border-state natives, Oklahoma's two largest sectional groups, made up 60.2 and 25.1 percent, respectively, of the population in 1890, while they constituted 56.1 and 27.5 percent in 1900. When midwesterners and northeasterners are combined to make up the northern-born category, they constitute 66 percent of the native white population in 1890 and 66.1 percent in 1900. White southerners, conversely, made up 34 and 33.9 percent of native whites in 1890 and 1900 Although there was quite a bit of moving about in Oklahoma during the 1890s, even in the lands opened in 1889, it did not substantially alter the birthplace patterns of the territory's settlers.

Table A-1 presents the correlation coefficients between partisan choice and birthplace-race data for Oklahomans between 1890 and 1902. The "Dem./Fusion" category represents the 1890–94 and 1902 Democratic vote and the 1896–1900 Free Silver party ballot. The 1898 and 1900 listings for the People's party are for the southern-dominated, middle-of-the-road faction, which polled minuscule totals in both years.

Throughout the era, both mainstream parties relied heavily on sectional and race bases of support. The GOP drew substantially from northerners, blacks, and Europeans, while the Democratic

Table A-1. Correlation of Birthplace or Race with Party Choice, 1890–1902 *

Birthplace or Race	Party	1890 Leg.	1890 Del.	1892 Del.	1894 Del.	1896 Del.	1898 Del.	1900 Del.	1902 Del.
North	Republican	+.34	+.57	+.51	+.61	+.59	+.64	+.53	+.84
	Dem./Fusion	−.89	−.79	−.44	−.54	−.59	−.43	−.36	−.86
	People's	+.82	+.37	−.06	+.20	—	−.61	−.73	—
Northeast	Republican	+.76	+.54	+.47	+.28	+.42	+.46	+.36	+.74
	Dem./Fusion	−.85	−.91	−.34	−.21	−.42	−.25	−.18	−.73
	People's	+.51	+.55	−.13	+.03	—	−.55	−.60	—
Midwest	Republican	+.23	+.52	+.44	+.64	+.59	+.64	+.54	+.81
	Dem./Fusion	−.85	−.70	−.40	−.57	−.59	−.44	−.37	−.83
	People's	+.85	+.30	−.03	+.22	—	−.58	−.71	—
White South	Republican	−.68	−.83	−.71	−.80	−.69	−.74	−.66	−.92
	Dem./Fusion	+.79	+.90	+.53	+.68	+.69	+.57	+.51	+.91
	People's	−.49	−.20	+.18	−.17	—	+.59	+.73	—
White border states	Republican	−.77	−.92	−.70	−.59	−.75	−.47	−.64	−.76
	Dem./Fusion	+.69	+.78	+.35	+.39	+.75	+.42	+.56	+.73
	People's	−.32	+.07	+.39	+.03	—	+.26	+.49	—
White lower south	Republican	−.57	−.62	−.57	−.82	−.56	−.80	−.58	−.88
	Dem./Fusion	+.87	+.94	+.58	+.74	+.56	+.58	+.42	+.88
	People's	−.66	−.51	+.06	−.30	—	+.69	+.77	—
Europe	Republican	+.45	+.58	+.41	+.51	+.41	+.44	+.72	+.47
	Dem./Fusion	−.05	−.36	−.06	−.29	−.41	−.35	−.72	−.43
	People's	−.23	−.31	−.40	−.12	—	−.31	−.44	—
Blacks	Republican	+.77	+.43	+.49	+.41	+.25	+.30	+.14	+.38
	Dem./Fusion	−.24	−.46	−.42	−.38	−.25	−.32	−.11	−.35
	People's	−.20	+.09	−.05	+.17	—	−.04	−.16	—
North, blacks, and Europe	Republican	+.70	+.81	+.68	+.77	+.65	+.70	+.62	+.91
	Dem./Fusion	−.80	−.94	−.51	−.65	−.65	−.52	−.47	−.91
	People's	+.49	+.27	−.16	+.20	—	−.58	−.74	—

* The Dem./Fusion column represents the Democratic party vote in 1890, 1892, 1894, and 1902 and the Free Silver vote in 1896, 1898, and 1900. The listings for Populists in 1898 and 1900 are for the southern-dominated, middle-of-the-road faction, which polled minuscule totals in both years.

party primarily received the vote of white southerners. The People's party drew strongly from northerners, particularly midwesterners, in 1890. The steep decline in the northern-Populist correlation for the November, 1890, delegate race reflects the substantial reduction in the third party's poll in Logan and Payne counties because of the fight over where to place the territorial capital. The People's party also made minor gains in Cleveland and Oklahoma counties at the same time.

When third-party support spread among southerners in 1892 and 1894, the Populist correlations with all sectional groups became weak enough to validate the party's claim that it bridged sectionalism to address other issues. Blacks and Europeans, 4.8 and 7.9 percent, respectively, of the population in 1900, consistently show negative correlations with the Democratic and People's parties, except for the black-Populist correlation of 1894, when the third party nominated a black farmer for the territorial legislature. Both blacks and Europeans, however, were unusually urban and Europeans had come to Oklahoma by way of the North.

The 1896 Free Silver party correlations represent the mixing of Democratic and Populist voters in territorywide fusion. Because most Democrats supported fusion, while many Populists did not, the voting pattern for the Free Silver party was closer to that of the Democratic party before 1896. The sharp decline in the Free Silver–border-state correlation for 1898, when a Democrat headed the ticket, suggests that many southern-born Populists did not consider fusion to be simply a return to the Democratic party. When a Populist led the fusion ticket in 1900, all of the sectional and race correlations were moderated, except those of white border-state natives and Europeans.

In 1902, when the People's party dissolved, sectional voting greatly increased. The Dem./Fusion correlations for that year jumped from +.51 to +.91 for white southerners, and the GOP correlations with northerners, blacks, and Europeans climbed from +.62 to +.91. Multiple regression analysis (r-square) indicates that the 1902 vote of white southerners accounts for 82.6 percent of the variation in the Democratic vote, while northerners, blacks, and Europeans combined account for 82.1 percent of the variation in the GOP ballot. This compares with 26 and 38.4 percent, respectively, for 1900. The differences between the 1900 and 1902 votes are so great that they indicate a dividing line between two substantially different political universes.

Map 2 shows that the North Canadian River, which flows through Oklahoma City, formed a dividing line between northern- and southern-dominated areas in Oklahoma.[1] Sectionalism, in other words, was a product of the Territory's settlement. Although it became the overwhelming basis for party support after 1900, another, largely ignored, settlement pattern best explains the reduced sectionalism of the Populist era. Because settlers had the option of making the land runs in Oklahoma either by rail or overland, counties served by rail at the time of the openings developed sharply divergent rural-urban culture areas. The alternative modes of transportation filtered migrants with differing world views into islands of homogeneity. An exceptionally entrepreneurial population settled in and around the Territory's railhead enclaves. Because these settlers were exponents of the cosmopolitan world's panaceas of laissez-faire, social Darwinism, and business boosterism, their regions overwhelmingly supported the mainstream parties. In hinterland Oklahoma, on the other hand, migrants adhered more closely to the neorepublican, egalitarian heritage inherited from the traditions of Jefferson, Jackson, and Lincoln. Here the People's party received most of its support.

Tables A-2 and A-3 present the correlation between urban residence and party choice in the delegate races for those counties where reliable township-level returns are available. Urban areas are defined in this study as those entities that are cited as cities, towns, villages, and boroughs in U.S. Bureau of the Census, *Twelfth Census of the United States . . . 1900*, (Washington, D.C.: U.S. Government Printing Office, 1902), 1:470.

I obtained the township-level election returns from the following Oklahoma newspapers: *Norman Transcript*, November 8, 1890; *Hennessey Clipper*, November 14, 1890; *Guthrie Weekly Oklahoma State Capital*, November 8, 1890; *Kingfisher Free Press*, November 17, 1892; *Guthrie Weekly Oklahoma State Capital*, November 19, 1892; *Oklahoma City Evening Gazette*, November 14, 1892; *El Reno Populist Platform*, November 16, 1894; *Norman Peoples Voice, November 17, 1894; Enid Coming Events*, November 18, 1894; *Kingfisher Reformer*, November 15, 1894; *Chandler Publicist*, November 16, 1894; *Guthrie Weekly Oklahoma State Capital*, November 12, 1894; *Oklahoma City Daily Oklahoman*, November 19, 1894; *Pawnee Times-Democrat*, November 9, 1894; *Stillwater Eagle-Gazette*, November 8, 1894; *Alva Pioneer*, December 14, 1894; *El Reno Democrat*, November 12, 1896; *Nor-*

Table A-2. Correlation of Urban Residence with Party Choice,
            1890–1896

Year and County	Party		
	Republican	Democratic	People's
1890			
Cleveland	−.15	−.34	+.45
Kingfisher	+.39	+.45	−.51
Logan	+.59	+.36	−.71
1892			
Kingfisher	+.28	+.25	−.51
Logan	+.48	+.07	−.62
Oklahoma	+.04	+.17	−.28
1894			
Canadian	+.26	+.22	−.44
Cleveland	+.39	+.40	−.62
Garfield	+.41	+.11	−.49
Kingfisher	+.32	+.43	−.50
Lincoln	+.37	+.02	−.28
Logan	+.45	+.46	−.62
Oklahoma	+.01	+.36	−.45
Pawnee	−.30	+.79	−.85
Payne	−.46	+.52	−.02
Woods	+.03	+.43	−.41

	Republican	Free Silver	
1896			
Canadian	+.49	−.49	
Cleveland	+.00	−.00	
Custer	+.32	−.32	
Grant	+.17	−.17	
Kay	+.33	−.33	
Kingfisher	+.22	−.22	
Lincoln	+.32	−.32	
Logan	+.61	−.61	
Noble	+.41	−.41	
Oklahoma	+.06	−.06	
Payne	−.36	+.36	
Woods	+.01	−.01	

Table A-3. Correlation of Urban Residence with Party Choice,
          1898–1902

Year and County	Party		
	Republican	Free Silver	M-R * Populist
1898			
Canadian	+.11	−.10	−.22
Cleveland	−.60	+.60	—
Custer	+.24	−.21	−.41
Garfield	−.08	+.07	+.06
Grant	−.10	+.12	−.24
Kay	−.18	+.17	+.01
Kingfisher	−.05	+.09	−.12
Lincoln	−.10	+.18	−.21
Logan	+.46	−.41	−.35
Noble	−.09	+.09	−.03
Oklahoma	+.07	−.07	—
Payne	−.22	+.21	−.05
Woods	+.04	−.08	+.38

	Republican	Free Silver	M-R Populist	Socialist
1900				
Canadian	+.07	−.07	—	—
Cleveland	+.66	−.69	−.40	—
Custer	−.45	+.47	−.68	−.43
Garfield	−.09	+.09	—	—
Grant	+.00	−.03	+.41	−.46
Kay	+.11	−.12	−.31	+.24
Kingfisher	+.19	−.18	−.02	−.05
Lincoln	+.32	−.30	−.41	+.35
Noble	+.45	−.46	−.05	+.12
Oklahoma	+.11	−.12	−.20	+.18
Pawnee	+.57	−.41	—	−.48
Payne	−.08	+.09	+.11	−.09
Woods	+.12	−.08	−.09	−.11

	Republican	Democratic		Socialist
1902				
Canadian	+.45	−.45		—
Cleveland	−.44	+.44		—
Custer	−.07	+.15		−.45
Garfield	+.17	−.17		—
Grant	+.06	+.04		−.07

Table A-3. (*continued*)

Year and County	Party		
	Republican	Democratic	Socialist
1902			
Kay	+.07	−.03	−.17
Kingfisher	+.07	−.01	−.17
Lincoln	−.13	+.10	+.21
Logan	+.51	−.51	—
Noble	+.35	−.35	—
Oklahoma	+.16	−.17	+.20
Pawnee	+.87	−.61	−.70
Payne	−.03	+.04	+.01
Woods	−.01	+.22	−.25

* Middle-of-the-road.

man Transcript, November 13, 1896; *Arapahoe Bee*, November 6, 1896; *Medford Weekly Patriot*, November 12, 1896; *Ponca City Democrat*, November 12, 1896; *Kingfisher Free Press*, November 5, 1896; *Chandler News*, November 13, 1896; *Guthrie Weekly Oklahoma State Capital*, November 11, 1896; *Perry Enterprise-Times*, November 4, 1896; *Oklahoma City Daily Oklahoman*, November 15, 1896; *Stillwater Gazette*, November 12, 1896; *Alva Pioneer*, November 20, 1896; *El Reno News*, November 11, 1898; *Norman Transcript*, November 11, 1898; *Arapahoe Bee*, November 11, 1898; *Enid Weekly Wave*, November 17, 1898; *Medford Weekly Patriot*, November 17, 1898; *Blackwell Times-Record*, November 17, 1898; *Hennessey Clipper*, November 17, 1898; *Chandler News*, November 18, 1898; *Guthrie Weekly Oklahoma State Capital*, November 10, 1898; *Perry Enterprise-Times*, November 10, 1898; *Oklahoma City Daily Oklahoman*, November 11, 1898; *Stillwater Gazette*, November 17, 1898; *Alva Pioneer*, November 18, 1898; *El Reno News*, November 8, 1900; *Norman Transcript*, November 15, 1900; *Arapahoe Bee*, November 9, 1900; *Garfield County Republican* (Enid), November 15, 1900; *Medford Weekly Patriot*, November 22, 1900; *Newkirk Republican-News-Journal*, November 15, 1900; *Hennessey Clipper*, November 15, 1900; *Chandler News*, November 15, 1900; *Perry Enterprise-Times*, November 10, 1900; *Oklahoma City Daily Oklahoman*, November

11, 1900; *Pawnee Times-Democrat*, November 16, 1900; *Payne County Populist* (Stillwater), November 23, 1900; *Alva Courier*, November 16, 1900; *Yukon Sun*, November 14, 1902; *Norman Transcript*, November 13, 1902; *Arapahoe Bee*, November 17, 1902; *Enid Weekly Wave*, November 13, 1902; *Medford Weekly Patriot*, November 20, 1902; *Newkirk Republican-News-Journal*, November 14, 1902; *Hennessey Clipper*, November 13, 1902; *Chandler News*, November 13, 1902; *Guthrie Weekly Oklahoma State Capital*, November 15, 1902; *Perry Evening Gazette*, November 7, 1902; *Oklahoma City Daily Oklahoman*, November 12, 1902; *Cleveland Triangle*, November 13, 1902; *Perkins Journal*, November 14, 1902; and *Alva Chronicle*, November 15, 1902.

Table A-2 shows that the People's party received a strongly rural vote in the three-party races of the early 1890s, while the mainstream parties showed positive correlations with urban residence. The major exceptions to this occurred in Cleveland County in 1890 and in Oklahoma County in 1892, where the third party's vote correlated with urban residence, and in Pawnee and Payne counties in 1894, when GOP supporters were unusually rural. The People's party was in its infancy in Cleveland County in 1890 and in Oklahoma County in 1892. It received only 12.3 and 11 percent of the vote, respectively, in these elections. Pawnee and Payne counties did not have rail service in 1894 and thus had not developed the sharp cosmopolitan-hinterland cleavage that other counties exhibited. The 1894 Lincoln County Populist-rural correlation is also rather weak. Although the county did have rail service in 1894, the line was laid after settlement.[2] When all the township votes presented in table A-2 for 1894 were combined, the party correlations with urban residence were: +.33 for the Republican party, +.27 for the Democratic party, and −.51 for the People's party. Using this data, the GOP correlated with northerners, blacks, and Europeans at +.28, while the Democratic vote correlated with white southerners at +.22. The Populist correlations with the two sectional-race groups were an inconsequential −.07 and +.04, respectively.

The Free Silver party in 1896 maintained the Populist-rural correlations at their former strength only in Canadian and Logan counties. Canadian County had the largest ethnic population of the counties listed in tables A-2 and A-3, which helps explain the strongly negative Free Silver–urban correlation in 1896. The cities of Guthrie and Langston (an all-black town) in Logan County had substantial black populations, which voted solidly Republican.[3]

Table A-3 shows that in 1898, when Populist voter dropouts became a serious problem for fusion efforts, the largely Democratic vote for the Free Silver candidate caused his urban correlations to become slightly positive in most counties. The major exception was in Cleveland County, where fusion under Democratic leadership was so unpopular that Populists voted for the Republican candidate in the delegate race.[4] In 1900, silverites placed Robert A. Neff, a longtime third-party editor, at the head of the Free Silver ticket, and he revived fusion Populism one last time. Most of the fusion-urban correlations for 1900, therefore, were negative. Even Cleveland County Populists returned to the fold for the 1900 delegate race, although they fused with the GOP for the territorial legislative races. In 1902, when the People's party collapsed, the rural-urban cleavage became inconsequential in most counties. The exceptions were in Canadian County, where northerners and blacks correlated at +.51 with urban residence, in heavily southern-populated Cleveland County, where Populists filtered into Republican ranks, and in northern-dominated Pawnee County, where they joined the Democratic party. Urban blacks, again, accounted for the Logan County correlations. Voter turnout was unusually high in each of these counties in 1902.[5]

Table A-4, which presents the party correlations with Oklahoma's major agricultural products, shows a definite relationship between party affiliation and type of farming in the early 1890s. I obtained data for crop acreage, hogs, cattle, improved acres, and the number of farms from U.S. Bureau of the Census, *Twelfth Census of the United States . . . 1900* (Washington, D.C.: U.S. Government Printing Office, 1902), 5: 114–15, 293–94, 470–71. Because Oklahoma counties varied widely in size, it was necessary to divide crop acreage by improved acres to create percentages for comparison. Hogs and cattle, likewise, were divided by

Table A-4. Correlation of Agricultural Factors with Party Choice,
            1892–1902 *

Agricultural Factor	Party	1892	1894	1896	1898	1900	1902
Corn acreage	Republican	−.48	−.30	−.35	+.08	−.18	−.27
	Dem./Fusion	+.01	−.08	+.35	−.02	+.20	+.23
	People's	+.55	+.47	—	−.15	−.02	—
Cotton acreage	Republican	−.43	−.09	−.36	−.24	−.35	−.48
	Dem./Fusion	+.22	−.15	+.36	+.11	+.30	+.50
	People's	+.23	+.36	—	+.31	+.31	—
Wheat acreage	Republican	+.25	+.53	+.34	+.41	+.27	+.51
	Dem./Fusion	−.32	−.45	−.34	−.35	−.23	−.49
	People's	+.11	+.15	—	−.23	−.28	—
Corn-hog cycle	Republican	−.42	+.17	+.03	+.29	−.03	+.08
(hogs per farm)	Dem./Fusion	−.19	−.40	−.03	−.22	+.06	−.10
	People's	+.73	+.46	—	−.22	−.17	—
Ranching	Republican	+.22	−.09	+.18	−.21	+.20	+.09
(cattle per farm)	Dem./Fusion	+.24	+.41	−.18	+.26	−.20	−.08
	People's	−.56	−.59	—	−.03	−.05	—

* The Dem./Fusion column represents the Democratic party vote in 1892, 1894, and 1902 and the Free Silver party vote in 1896, 1898, and 1900. The listings for Populists in 1898 and 1900 are for the southern-dominated, middle-of-the-road faction, which polled minuscule totals in both years.

the number of farms. Republican voters were associated most strongly with wheat acreage throughout the Populist era. GOP wheat farmers readily entered the cosmopolitan world of agribusiness, where they expected their larger commercial operations, with substantial investments in machinery, to provide them with a considerable margin of profit (see table A-5).[6] Populists, on the other hand, did best in areas where corn and hogs were the main agricultural products in the early 1890s. In contrast to the agribusiness orientation of Republican wheat farmers, Populist corn farmers engaged in more diversified operations. It is an axiom of agricultural economics that ten bushels of corn will add one hundred pounds to a hog. Corn-hog farmers could either feed their corn to their hogs or place both commodities on the market separately. Between 1865 and 1897 corn and pork prices fluctuated so that one of these options was profitable in all but three years. As wheat and cotton prices plummeted in the early and mid-1890s, the vagaries of the marketplace affected the Populist corn-hog farmers far less than their mainstream-party cousins.[7]

In 1892, Democrats and Populists drew equally from areas where cotton dominated agricultural production. By 1894, however, cotton-producing areas had become Populist. The Dem./Fusion correlations of 1896 and 1900 are closer to the earlier Populist numbers, while the correlations for 1898 are closer to the earlier Democratic levels. The 1898 correlations again suggest that large numbers of third-party voters declined to support a Democrat-led fusion effort.[8] Except for cotton and wheat acreage all of the partisan correlations with type of agriculture became weaker after 1900, as the People's party declined. Ranchers, as might be expected, were strongly anti-Populist. This was a holdover from the Boomer–cattle baron struggle of the 1880s.

Table A-5 shows that, although the depression of the 1890s affected Populist farmers less than their mainstream-party counterparts, they were not prosperous. In fact, Populists came from regions that were considerably poorer than those where Democrats or Republicans lived. They lacked the machinery necessary to bring as much land under cultivation as their Republican competitors could. For this reason, the value of agricultural products per farm for Populists was low. As disenchanted Democratic cotton farmers filtered into the People's party in 1894, the third party's correlation with value of agriculture per improved acre declined, and the correlation with agricultural products per farm increased slightly. Populists received little support among urban laborers in the early 1890s. With the depression of 1893 workers began to show a preference for the GOP.[9] The third party drew strongly from areas where tenancy had developed by 1900. This is attributable to the third party's freehold ideology. Except for the value of agricultural products per farm and the value of farm implements and machinery, which were associated with wheat farming, the correlations between economic factors and party choice become weak after the demise of the People's party. The data used to construct table A-5 were taken from U.S. Bureau of the Census, *Twelfth Census of the United States . . . 1900*, 6: 179–80, 433 and 8: 730–31, and from Secretary of the Interior, *Report of the*

Table A-5. Correlation of Economic Factors with Party Choice, 1892–1902 *

Economic Factor	Party	1892	1894	1896	1898	1900	1902
Taxable wealth	Republican	+.19	+.15	+.26	−.12	+.21	+.29
per capita,	Dem./Fusion	+.30	+.22	−.26	+.20	−.21	−.25
1900	People's	−.60	−.54	—	−.10	−.16	—
Value of manufac-	Republican	+.07	+.39	+.12	+.11	+.03	+.29
tured goods	Dem./Fusion	+.14	−.30	−.12	−.05	+.03	−.24
	People's	−.27	−.06	—	−.14	−.24	—
Value of agriculture	Republican	−.30	−.63	−.43	−.47	−.29	−.27
per improved acre	Dem./Fusion	+.28	+.58	+.43	+.64	+.37	+.29
	People's	+.01	−.25	—	−.16	−.00	—
Value of agriculture	Republican	+.05	+.34	+.32	+.08	+.28	+.41
per farm	Dem./Fusion	+.27	−.07	−.32	+.05	−.23	−.37
	People's	−.40	−.28	—	−.27	−.30	—
Value of farm im-	Republican	+.18	+.56	+.39	+.31	+.33	+.54
plements and	Dem./Fusion	+.04	−.36	−.39	−.23	−.28	−.51
machinery	People's	−.25	−.05	—	−.27	−.35	—
Tenancy, cash and	Republican	−.44	+.18	−.15	+.09	−.21	+.01
share	Dem./Fusion	+.09	−.42	+.15	−.07	+.23	−.00
	People's	+.40	+.49	—	−.07	−.03	—
Cash tenancy	Republican	−.25	+.22	−.01	+.25	+.00	+.13
	Dem./Fusion	−.06	−.40	+.01	−.21	+.06	−.13
	People's	+.38	+.41	—	−.17	−.23	—
Share tenancy	Republican	−.50	+.13	−.22	−.03	−.32	−.08
	Dem./Fusion	+.17	−.38	+.22	+.04	+.31	+.08
	People's	+.38	+.48	—	+.01	+.11	—

* The Dem./Fusion column represents the Democratic party vote in 1892, 1894, and 1902 and the Free Silver party vote in 1896, 1898, and 1900. The listings for Populists in 1898 and 1900 are for the southern-dominated, middle-of-the-road faction, which polled minuscule totals in both years.

Governor of Oklahoma, 56th Cong., 2d sess., vol. 30 (H.D. 5, ser. 4104), 582.

I also ran correlations between partisan choice and member-ship in religious bodies. The latter data were taken from U. S. Census Office, *Bureau of the Census Special Reports: Religious Bodies, 1906*, pt. 1 (Washington, D.C.: U.S. Government Print-ing Office, 1907), 348–49. This produced only a few significant correlations, almost all of which could be explained by sectional-ism. Democrats in the 1890 at-large legislative race, for instance, correlated with northern Methodists at −.95 and with southern Methodists at +.84. The only group to correlate strongly with the People's party was the United Brethren before 1894. These correlations were +.86 for the 1890 legislative race, +.81 for the 1890 delegate race, and +.61 for 1892. With the inclusion of less Populistic settlers from the Cherokee Outlet, the Populist–United Brethren correlation dropped to an insignificant +.29 in 1894.

To check for the liturgist-pietist cleavage that ethnocultural historians find so important to party choice in the Gilded Age, I employed the formula found in Richard Jensen, *The Winning of the Midwest: Social and Political Conflict, 1888–1896* (Chicago: University of Chicago Press, 1971), 87. Those unaccounted for by the religious census were combined into a category labeled "no church." This process produced only two significant correlations for the Populist era: pietists with Republicans in the 1890 legislative race (+.88) and pietists with Democrats in 1894 (-.49). Although religion may have been important to party choice in the Midwest, Civil War–Reconstruction loyalties and race were the overwhelming bases of partisan choice in the late-nineteenth-century South. When northerners and southerners met in the common political arena of the Oklahoma Territory, sectionalism proved far more important than religion. During the Populist era, the rural-urban cleavage and the type of agriculture rivaled sectionalism as the most important indices of partisan choice in the Oklahoma Territory.

NOTES

1. The two exceptions in western Oklahoma, Day and Dewey counties, were sparsely populated in the 1890s.

2. Ayer, *American Newspaper Annual*, (1892), 616.

3. Foreign-born and native-born voters with foreign-born parents made up 20.6 percent of the Canadian County population. Only Blaine County had a higher percentage (22.4) of these groups. Blacks made up 23 percent of the Logan County population.

4. *Norman Transcript*, November 11, 1898.

5. The 1902 voter turnouts for Canadian, Cleveland, Logan, and Pawnee counties were 81.2 percent, 72.3 percent, 67.9 percent, and 75.3 percent, respectively. Turnout for the territory as a whole in 1902 was 61.9 percent.

6. In 1900, wheat, corn, and cotton acreages correlated with the value of implements and machinery per farm at +.88905, −.54633, and −.39434, respectively in the Oklahoma Territory.

7. Shannon, *The Farmer's Last Frontier*, 165–68; U.S. Bureau of the Census, *Histori-*

cal Statistics of the United States: Colonial Times to 1957 (Washington, D.C.: U.S. Government Printing Office, 1960), 290, 296–96, 301–02.

8. In 1900, cotton accounted for more than 10 percent of improved acres in only four Oklahoma counties: Cleveland, Greer, Lincoln, and Pottawatomie. Greer County became a part of the Oklahoma Territory in 1896. In 1900, Oklahoma farmers devoted 1,320,506 acres to corn, 1,279,826 acres to wheat, and 240,678 acres to cotton.

9. Populists seem to gain support among urban workers in 1894, because the party made major gains in Canadian, Logan, and Cleveland counties, which accounted for 48.7 percent of the Territory's manufacturing. In these counties, however, the Populist vote was almost completely rural.

The Effects of
Territorywide Fusion

To discover the effect of fusion on Oklahoma voters in the late Populist era, I ran simple correlations between each party's 1894 vote for delegate to the U.S. Congress (the only territorywide race) and the Democratic and Free Silver ballots for the same office between 1894 and 1902.[1] Predictably, the 1894 Republican vote correlated negatively, while the 1894 Democratic poll correlated positively with the Democratic and Free Silver ballots between 1894 and 1902. The only major aberration was the reduced magnitude of both parties' correlations with the 1900 Free Silver vote.

As might be expected, there is a strongly negative correlation between Democratic and Populist voters in 1894. This indicates that where the People's party fared well, the Democratic party did poorly, and vice versa. If both Democrats and Populists had supported James Y. Callahan's 1896 Free Silver candidacy with equal fervor, the correlation between each party's 1894 ballot and the 1896 fusion effort should have been comparable. On the contrary, however, the 1894 Democratic ballot correlates much more strongly with the 1896 Free Silver vote. Because the Republican party vote was not disrupted between 1894 and 1896, and because voter turnout dropped in the interim, Callahan apparently received most of the Democratic vote, while many Populists declined to participate.[2] The erosion of Populist support became even stronger in 1898, when James R. Keaton, a Democrat, led the fusion ticket. Again, stay-at-home Populists accounted for the decline in non-GOP fortunes. Robert A. Neff's Free Silver campaign of 1900, on the other hand, revived the old Populist fervor to a degree. Voter turnout increased slightly. Neff picked

Table B-1. Correlation of Partisan Choice, 1894, with Democratic-
Fusion Votes, 1894–1902

Year	Party	Republican 1894	Democratic 1894	Populist 1894
1894	Democratic	−.81	+1.00	−.74
1896	Free Silver	−.82	+.60	−.06
1898	Free Silver	−.75	+.67	−.26
1900	Free Silver	−.56	+.35	+.06
1902	Democratic	−.75	+.63	−.19

up some Populist voters who had declined to participate in 1898 and also made slight inroads into GOP ranks.[3] Neff was a long-time third-party war-horse compared to Callahan, who was a latecomer to Populism, and to Keaton, who was a Democrat. Although Neff's 1900 race revived the third party one last time, when the People's party dissolved in 1902, the correlations returned approximately to their 1898 levels.

Fusion significantly disrupted the People's party after 1894. Democrats, who were passionately in favor of fusion, supported the Free Silver efforts of 1896 and 1898 much more uniformly than did Populists, and Neff's poll of 1900 correlated more strongly with the Democratic party's 1894 vote than it did with that year's Populist ballot. In 1894, Democrats and Populists combined to carry 57.9 percent of the territorial vote, while the fusion efforts in 1896 and 1898 secured only 51.1 and 39.1 percent, respectively. The most important factor in this erosion of anti-GOP forces was a decline in voter turnout, particularly among third-party supporters who refused to sanction the Jekyll and Hyde nature of fusion with Democrats.

NOTES

1. Only the twenty-two counties that made up the Oklahoma Territory in 1894 were included in the calculations for appendix B. Four counties were added to Oklahoma between 1896 and 1901: Greer, in 1896, and Caddo, Comanche, and Kiowa, in 1901.

2. Voter turnout for the delegate races was 49.7 percent in 1890, 56.7 percent in 1892, 81.2 percent in 1894, 72.6 percent in 1896, 58.2 percent in 1898, 67.9 percent in 1900, and 61.9 percent in 1902. To determine the number of eligible voters in each elec-

tion, I took the percent of voting-age males for each county from U.S. Bureau of the Census, *Twelfth Census of the United States* 2: 199, and multiplied it by the county's population, which was taken from Secretary of the Interior, *Report of the Governor of Oklahoma* 52nd Cong., 2d sess., vol. 14 (H.D. 1, ser. 3089), 469; 54th Cong., 1st sess., vol. 16 (H.D. 1, ser. 3383), 514; 57th Cong., 2d sess. (H.D. 5, ser. 4461), 392.

3. Keaton, in 1898, and Neff, in 1900, correlated at $-.75$ and $-.56$, respectively, with the 1894 GOP vote.

A Collective Biography of Oklahoma Legislators, 1890–1901

Because politics reflects a variety of economic and social cleavages, a collective biography of the men who sat in the Oklahoma legislatures of the Populist era presents several interesting revelations about the three major party's leaders. Data on partisan affiliation, place of birth, age, residence, and occupation were available on most of the men who sat in Oklahoma's first six legislatures.

Because each assembly had thirty-nine members, there were 234 seats filled between 1890 and 1901. Twenty-six men served in two legislatures, and two men served in three. Robert J. Nesbitt was the only assemblyman to represent more than one party. He was cataloged as a Democrat in 1890 and 1901 and as a Populist in 1895. Table C-1 shows the partisan makeup of each Oklahoma assembly between 1890 and 1901.

To compile the collective biography, I consulted a variety of sources, including WPA indexes of "mug-book" histories and newspapers, which are located at the Oklahoma Historical Society. The former were a valuable source of information. Unfortunately, few newspapers were indexed. Newspaper reports of election returns proved to be a particularly good source for determining the partisan affiliation of legislators. When candidates ran on fusion tickets, returns from earlier elections frequently revealed their party. Because early Oklahoma was a land of strangers, newspapers frequently published short biographies of candidates during campaigns. The Democratic *Guthrie Oklahoma Leader* was so proud of the fusionist 1897 legislature that its editor published short biographies of the members while the assembly

Table C-1. Party Makeup of Oklahoma Legislatures, 1890–1901

Legislature	Republican Party	Democratic Party	People's Party
1890 Council	7	5	1
House	14	8	4
Total	21	13	5
1893 Council	7	5	1
House	12	10	4
Total	19	15	5
1895 Council	8	1	4
House	16	3	7
Total	24	4	11
1897 Council	0	7	6
House	3	11	12
Total	3	18	18
1899 Council	8	4	1
House	17	4	5
Total	25	8	6
1901 Council	5	5	3
House	16	6	4
Total	21	11	7
Total 1890–1901	113	69	52

was in session. For this reason, the most extensive biographical information is on Oklahoma's fourth legislature.

Of the 234 seats filled in the Oklahoma assembly between 1890 and 1901, I located usable data in addition to the legislators' party affiliation for 204. I uncovered the party affiliation of each legislator (234), the place of birth for 75.6 percent (177), the age of 65.4 percent (153), the residence of 82.5 percent (193), and the occupation of 81.2 percent (190). Although several Oklahoma specialists have labeled the territorial period predominantly Republican in politics, GOP dominance was far more apparent than real.[1] Republicans elected only 48.3 percent of the assemblymen in the Populist era and controlled both houses of the legislature only in 1895 and 1899. They also organized the house of representatives in 1901. Only in 1899 did the GOP control both houses of the assembly and the governorship. Fusionists, on the other hand, organized both houses of the 1890, 1893, and 1897 assemblies and the council in 1901. They, of course, required the aid of renegade Republicans to organize the first two legislatures. While the People's party was active in Oklahoma, no single party dominated territorial politics.

Table C-2, which presents the birthplace of Oklahoma legislators during the Populist era, shows that Republicans came overwhelmingly from the North. Only eight GOP assemblymen came from the border states, and one came from the deep South. The diverse birthplaces of Populist legislators reflect the makeup of the party, although southerners were somewhat underrepresented. Voting correlations from appendix A, table A-1, show that rank-and-file Democrats were overwhelmingly southern-born (see appendix A, table A-1). Their northern cousins, however, obviously received more than their share of the party's plums in this era.

Table C-3 shows the average age of assemblymen, by party, for the Populist era. Members of the 1897 fusion legislature were significantly older than their counterparts in the other assemblies. Despite the common perception that Populists were old men who could not adjust to the realities of industrial America, the third-party contingent in 1897 constituted the youngest group of legislators, less than a year older than the average for all assemblymen of the Populist era. On the whole, Populist legislators were only slightly older than their mainstream party counterparts. The small number of cases for Democrats in 1895, Republicans in 1897, and Populists in 1901 helps account for the extreme average ages in these years.

By far the greatest divergence between Populists and mainstream-party representatives was in their occupations. Nine legislators, three from each party, were listed as having two occupations. For those claiming more than one calling, I made a serious effort to find their primary occupation and list it alone for this study. Table C-4, which presents the occupations of Oklahoma

Table C-2. Birthplaces of Oklahoma Legislators by Party, 1890–1901

Region	Republican Party, %	Democratic Party, %	Populist Party, %
North	86.6 (71)*	39.6 (21)	66.7 (28)
South	11.0 (9)	60.4 (32)	33.3 (14)
Foreign	2.4 (2)	0.0 (0)	0.0 (0)

* The numbers of cases are given in parentheses.

Table C-3. Average Age of Oklahoma Legislators by Party, 1890–1901

Legislature	Republican Party	Democratic Party	Populist Party	Average
1890	42.8 (13)*	42.9 (7)	43.3 (4)	42.9 (24)
1893	39.7 (8)	37.9 (9)	42.5 (2)	39.1 (19)
1895	41.5 (14)	33.5 (2)	38.7 (4)	40.1 (20)
1897	50.0 (3)	47.8 (18)	43.8 (18)	45.9 (39)
1899	45.3 (21)	35.2 (6)	41.8 (4)	42.9 (31)
1901	38.9 (11)	36.6 (5)	55.2 (4)	37.9 (20)
Average	42.5 (70)	43.3 (47)	44.2 (36)	43.1 (153)

* The numbers of cases are given in parentheses.

Table C-4. Occupations of Oklahoma Legislators by Party, 1890–1901 *

Occupation	Republican Party, %	Democratic Party, %	Populist Party, %
Farming	16.1 (15)	16.4 (9)	66.7 (28)
Law	35.5 (33)	34.5 (19)	7.1 (3)
Professions†	11.8 (11)	18.2 (10)	19.0 (8)
Trade and commerce‡	28.0 (26)	7.3 (4)	9.5 (4)
Finance and real estate	7.5 (7)	16.4 (9)	2.4 (1)
Ranching§	5.4 (5)	12.7 (7)	2.4 (1)

*Nine men, three from each party, are listed as having two callings (one of the Republicans served in two legislatures). For this reason each column totals more than 100 percent.

†This category includes preachers, teachers, physicians, druggists, journalists, engineers, and postmasters.

‡This category includes merchants, a lumberyard owner, a miller, a brewer, a mechanic, and a railroad contractor.

§Those who listed their occupation as farmer and stockraiser are listed here as farmers. This is the way more diversified farmers identified themselves. Those who listed their calling as stockraising alone were presumed to be ranchers.

Table C-5. Residences of Oklahoma Legislators, by Party, 1890–1901

Residence	Republican Party, %	Democratic Party, %	Populist Party, %
Railroad towns and county seats	62.4 (58)	57.1 (32)	11.4 (5)
Hinterland towns	16.1 (15)	5.4 (3)	15.9 (7)
Rural areas	21.5 (20)	37.5 (21)	72.7 (32)

legislators by party in the Populist era, suggests a distinct cosmo-politan-hinterland cleavage. Lawyers were the most numerous representatives of the Democratic and Republican parties, while farmers constituted the vast majority of third-party legislators. When the largely cosmopolitan occupations of law, trade and commerce, and finance and real estate are combined, they account for 71 percent of the Republican, and 55.3 percent of the Democratic, legislators. Only 18.8 percent of the third party's representatives fall into that category.[2]

To delineate the cosmopolitan-hinterland dichotomy further, the legislators were divided into three residence categories: railroad-town or county-seat residents, hinterland-town residents, and rural residents. Table C-5 shows the results. Hinterland residents constituted 88.6 percent of the third party's assemblymen. Third-party legislators residing in the cosmopolitan world included two editors (Allan and Tousley), two doctors (one apparently was a veterinarian), and a Stillwater farm-implement dealer. Railroads did not serve the county seats of Stillwater or Mangum (where the veterinarian resided) at the time the legislators served in the assembly.

Populist legislators did not appear to be significantly less experienced in holding public office than Democrats or Republicans. At least 50 percent of the third-party legislators claimed prior service in public office. The figures for Republicans and Democrats were 56.6 and 43.5 percent, respectively. Some divergence did exist, however, in the educational level of the men representing the three major parties. At least 29.2 percent of all Republicans and 30.4 percent of all Democrats had attended college. Only 21.2 percent of the Populists definitely went to college.

This is probably a result of the Populists' rural, less commercial background. Unfortunately, information on previous experience and education could be found in only 50 and 45.3 percent of the cases, respectively.

Information on ethnicity, religion, and Civil War service proved to be even less available. Ethnicity and religion data showed no significant patterns that could not be explained by sectionalism. As might be expected from the findings presented in appendix A, the two United Brethren who served in the assembly (Wails and Willis) were Populists. Richard E. P. Messall, the only brewer to sit in the assembly during the Populist era, represented the supposedly pietistic Republican party. In regard to later historians' charges that Populists were ethnocentric and Anglophobic, Robert Anoil, who organized the first Roman Catholic services in the Oklahoma Territory, received the Populist nomination for Cleveland County treasurer in 1892, 1894, and 1896, and both Samuel Crocker and Ralph Beaumont were natives of England, as was Leo Vincent's father.[3] No Republicans had been Confederates, although Virgil A. Wood, the only white Republican from the deep South, was the son of a Confederate soldier. The Democratic and Populist parties claimed veterans from both sides of the Civil War. Most of the legislators, however, had been less than eighteen years old in 1865.

The collective biography validates the Populists' contention that their party, more so than the Democrats' or Republicans', was a party of the people. Both Republican and Populist legislators reflected their rank-and-file supporters in place of birth. In the crucial categories of occupation and residence, however, only the Populists truly represented most Oklahomans. Two-thirds of the voters in the Oklahoma Territory were farmers. The legislators' educational attainments were surely higher than those of their constituents for all parties, but less so for Populists.

The third-party voters' choice of representatives clearly revealed an antipathy toward men who were products of the late nineteenth century's cosmopolitan culture. The only part of the biographical survey that appears to contradict this strain of anti-elitism is the surprisingly high level of political experience Populist legislators claimed. Because mainstream-party spokesmen constantly questioned their fitness to govern, it is likely that third-party candidates emphasized their previous experience, thus leaving better information for historians. There was, however, always something of an egalitarian counterelite present throughout nineteenth-century America. Greenbacker, Union Laborite, and Populist leaders constituted alternatives, presenting men for election who more closely represented the citizen-statesman ideal than did the professional political elite of the old parties.

NOTES

1. Benson, *Oklahoma Votes*, 32; Jones, *Oklahoma Politics*, 16.
2. Three Populist lawyers served in the Oklahoma legislature: A. N. Daniels, Ira N. Terrill, and John S. Allan. Daniels and Terrill lived in hinterland small towns when they served, although Daniels later moved to Guthrie and then to Enid. Allan was primarily a journalist, although he engaged in a real estate business as well.
3. Anoil won in the latter two years. *Norman Transcript*, November 11, 1892, November 13, 1896; *Norman Peoples Voice*, November 17, 1894.

Notes

PREFACE

1. Populists received 17.4 percent of the Oklahoma vote in 1890. In 1914, the Socialist party received 15.8 percent of the vote in the counties that had constituted the Oklahoma Territory in 1890. The People's party received 20.5 percent of the vote in 1892. In those counties that had made up the Oklahoma Territory in 1892, Socialists received 19.6 percent of the vote in 1914. At no other time did the Socialist party's vote come within 10 percent of the Populists' showings.

2. The Oklahoma Territory constituted the western half of the present-day state of Oklahoma. The Indian Territory, which contained the Five Civilized Tribes, did not have a Populist movement, because whites could not vote in that region, and the Indian population's concerns were primarily local.

CHAPTER ONE

1. Arrell M. Gibson, *Oklahoma: A History of Five Centuries* (Norman, Okla.: Harlow Publishing Co., 1965), 299; Danney Goble, *Progressive Oklahoma: The Making of a New Kind of State* (Norman: University of Oklahoma Press, 1980), 4. The Oklahoma Organic Act of 1890 provided for the automatic annexation of Indian lands to the new territory as they were opened to white settlement.

2. Gilbert Fite, *The Farmers' Frontier, 1865–1900* (New York: Holt, Rinehart and Winston, 1966, reprint, Norman: University of Oklahoma Press, 1987), 209.

3. Oklahomans usually refer to the North Canadian River, which flows through Oklahoma City, as the "Canadian River." Settlers moving west from Arkansas generally found homes in the Five Civilized Tribes area of what is today eastern Oklahoma.

4. For such treatments of Oklahoma politics see Oliver Benson, *Oklahoma Votes, 1907–1962* (Norman: University of Oklahoma, Bureau of Government Research, 1964); Stanley Jones, *Oklahoma Politics in State and Nation* (Enid, Okla.: Haymaker Press, 1974); or James R. Scales and Danney Goble, *Oklahoma Politics: A History* (Norman: University of Oklahoma Press, 1982).

5. Norman L. Crockett, "The Opening of Oklahoma: A Businessman's Frontier," *Chronicles of Oklahoma* 56, no. 1 (Spring, 1978): 94; Michael Owen Roark, "Oklahoma Territory: Frontier Development, Migration and Culture Areas" (Ph.D. diss., Syracuse University, 1979), 166.

6. *American Nonconformist* (Winfield, Kansas), April 18, 1889; Henry Vincent, "Henry

Sez" (ca. 1931), manuscript in the possession of Vincent's granddaughter Merrily Cummings Ford, of Glendora, California.

7. *American Nonconformist*, October 7, 1886.

8. Charles Maurice Wiltse, *The Jeffersonian Tradition in American Democracy* (New York: Hill and Wang, 1935), 249.

9. For the progress of this model through American history see Rowland Berthoff, "Peasants and Artisans, Puritans and Republicans: Personal Liberty and Communal Equality in American History," *Journal of American History* 69, no. 3 (December, 1982): 579–614.

10. Drew McCoy, *The Elusive Republic* (New York: W. W. Norton & Co., 1980), 18–21, 40. For the Commonwealth and Radical Whig origins of the American Revolution see Robert Shalhope, "Toward a Republican Synthesis: The Emergence of an Understanding of Republicanism in American Historiography" *William and Mary Quarterly*, 3d ser., 29 (Spring, 1972): 49–80.

11. Gordon Wood, *The Creation of the American Republic* (New York: W. W. Norton & Co., 1969), 52; McCoy, *The Elusive Republic*, 23.

12. McCoy, *The Elusive Republic*, 49–52.

13. Henry Nash Smith, *Virgin Land: The American West as Symbol and Myth* (Cambridge, Mass.: Harvard University Press, 1950), 41.

14. Marvin Meyers, *The Jacksonian Persuasion: Politics and Belief* (Stanford, Calif.: Stanford University Press, 1957), 11, 228, 274–75; Chester McArthur Destler, *American Radicalism, 1865–1901* (Chicago: Quadrangle Paperbacks, 1946), chap. 1; Eric Foner, *Free Soil, Free Labor, Free Men: The Ideology of the Republican Party Before the Civil War* (New York: Oxford University Press, 1970), 109.

15. James Turner, "Understanding the Populists," *Journal of American History* 67, no. 2 (September, 1980): 272–73.

16. Stan Hoig, *David L. Payne: The Oklahoma Boomer* (Oklahoma City, Okla.: Western Heritage Books, 1980), 60–64; William W. Savage, Jr., *The Cherokee Strip Livestock Association: Federal Regulation and the Cattleman's Last Frontier* (Columbia: University of Missouri Press, 1973), 69; Fite, *The Farmers' Frontier*, 203.

17. I. N. Terrill, "The Boomer's Last Raid," *Sturm's Oklahoma Magazine* 8, no. 2 (April, 1902): 37–40; *Oklahoma Chief* (Caldwell, Kansas), February 3, 1885.

18. *Oklahoma Chief*, June 18, August 13, 1885.

19. Samuel Crocker, "The Autobiography of Samuel Crocker" (1913), 1–5, 49, Oklahoma Historical Society, Oklahoma City.

20. Ibid., 49, 59, 110–11. Crocker attributed his lame arm to medical malpractice. When told he would die of blood poisoning without the amputation of his infected right arm in 1890, Crocker ordered the doctor off his property at gunpoint. He died in 1921. Ibid., 319–21.

21. Ibid., 110.

22. Walter T. K. Nugent, *The Money Question During Reconstruction* (New York: W. W. Norton & Co., 1967), 59, 62; Crocker, "Autobiography," 115–16, 119, 128, 144–45.

23. Crocker, "Autobiography," 181; *Oklahoma War Chief* (Arkansas City, Kansas), June 18, 1885.

24. Edward Everett Dale, "The Cow Country in Transition," in Arrell M. Gibson, ed., *Frontier Historian: The Life and Work of Edward Everett Dale* (Norman: University of Oklahoma Press, 1975), 317, 323. The term "cattle baron" possibly originated with the Boomers. It appears in the pages of the *Oklahoma War Chief* more than a decade before the citation listed in *A Dictionary of Americanisms* (Chicago: University of Chicago Press, 1951), 285–86. See the *Oklahoma War Chief*, December 31, 1885, August 17, 1886.

25. Edward Everett Dale, "The Ranchman's Last Frontier," *Mississippi Valley Historical*

Review, 10, no. 1 (June, 1923): 42, as quoted in H. Wayne Morgan and Anne Hodges Morgan, *Oklahoma: A Bicentennial History* (New York: W. W. Norton & Co., 1977), 44.

26. *Oklahoma War Chief, March 2, 1883; Oklahoma Chief*, February 17, 1885.

27. *Oklahoma War Chief*, June 11, 18, 1885. These terms were pseudonyms for woman suffrage and greenbacks. Crocker also called for a democratization of the political system through abolishing America's "House of Lords" (the Senate), the electoral college, patronage, and the president's veto power. *Oklahoma War Chief*, June 18, 25, July 2, August 20, 1885.

28. *Oklahoma Chief*, March 12, 1885; *Oklahoma War Chief*, September 3, 1885.

29. *Oklahoma War Chief*, July 23, August 13, 1885. Although sixty-eight treason warrants were secured, only five or six were actually served. All charges against the Boomer leaders were dropped before the dates of their trials. The government's purpose obviously was intimidation.

30. Ibid., June 25, 1885, April 29, May 13, 1886.

31. Ibid., December 31, 1885, April 29, May 7, 21, 1886.

32. Ibid., July 23, 1885.

33. Ibid., July 23, 1885, March 11, 1886; Gerald N. Grob, "The Knights of Labor, Politics and Populism," *Mid-America* 29, no. 1 (January, 1959): 3–7.

34. Ralph Beaumont, "A Lecture on the Declarations of Principles—Knights of Labor" (Cincinnati, Ohio: George N. Bryan Co., 1886); *Oklahoma War Chief*, February 4, 1886.

35. The "Principles of the Knights of Labor" were reproduced in the *Oklahoma War Chief*, March 11, 1886. The first edition of the *American Nonconformist* published in Winfield appeared October 7, 1886.

36. Harold Richard Piehler, "Henry Vincent: A Case Study in Political Deviancy" (Ph.D. diss., University of Kansas, 1971), 100–105; Merrily Cummings Ford, comp., "The Invincible Vincents" (1939), 2–4. (This is a series of biographies, in the possession of Henry Vincent's granddaughter Merrily Cummings Ford, of Glendora, California, which Leo Vincent wrote for his family using his own reminiscences and letters that his two surviving brothers wrote especially for the purpose.

37. James Vincent, Sr., was formerly a staff correspondent to Greeley's *Tribune, Garrison's Liberator*, and various Iowa reform Journals. The *American Nonconformist* was named after an English Abolitionist paper that had connections to the Chartist movement. Ford, "The Invincible Vincents," 7; Vincent, "Henry Sez," 1; Piehler, "Henry Vincent: A Case Study," 100. Although early editions of the *American Nonconformist* have been lost, a reprint of the first edition can be found in the tenth-anniversary edition. *American Nonconformist*, July 25, 1889.

38. Ford, "The Invincible Vincents," 27, 33–34.

39. *American Nonconformist*, April 14, 1887. Cowley County, Kansas, in which Winfield is located, had five Knights of Labor locals in 1886. Jonathan Garlock, *Guide to the Local Assemblies of the Knights of Labor* (Westport, Conn.: Greenwood Press, 1982), 134.

40. *American Nonconformist*, October 7, 1886; Ford, "The Invincible Vincents," 3, 6.

41. *Colorado Representative* (Boulder), December 7, 1899; Piehler, "Henry Vincent: A Case Study," 105, 121, 122.

42. Vincent, "Henry Sez," 3–4.

43. Ibid., 5; Ford, "The Invincible Vincents," 28; Grob, "The Knights of Labor," 9–12; Harold R. Piehler, "Henry Vincent: Kansas Populist and Radical-Reform Journalist," *Kansas History* 2, no. 1 (Spring, 1979): 16.

44. As testament to the longevity of neorepublican ideology among Populists, it

should be noted that Leo Vincent still used the term "Tory propaganda" more than fifty years after the 1888 campaign. Ford, "The Invincible Vincents," 28.

45. *Winfield Courier* (Kansas), October 4, 1888, as quoted in Piehler, "Henry Vincent: Kansas Populist," 16.

46. W. F. Rightmire, "The Alliance Movement in Kansas—Origin of the People's Party," *Transactions of the Kansas State Historical Society* 9 (1905–1906): 2.

47. Vincent, "Henry Sez," 6.

48. Piehler, "Henry Vincent: A Case Study," 154; Charles Richard Denton, "The *American Nonconformist and Kansas Industrial Liberator*: A Union Labor-Populist Newspaper, 1886–1891" (Master's thesis, Kansas State College of Pittsburg, 1961), 53–74, 93, 95; Joint Committee of the Legislature of the State of Kansas, *Investigation of Coffeyville Explosion* (Topeka: Kansas Publishing House, 1891), 288.

49. Walter T. K. Nugent, *The Tolerant Populists: Kansas Populism and Nativism* (Chicago: University of Chicago Press, 1963), 53; Peter H. Argersinger, *Populism and Politics: William Alfred Peffer and the People's Party* (Lexington: University of Kentucky Press, 1974), 15. In 1888 the Union Labor party polled 45,390 votes in Kansas and 146,137 votes nationwide.

50. Rightmire, "The Alliance Movement in Kansas," 3; *American Nonconformist*, November 28, 1888, July 4, 1889. Because Rightmire is demonstrably wrong on the date of the Vidette meeting, Robert C. McMath doubts the entire story. Robert C. McMath, "Preface to Populism: The Origin and Economic Development of the 'Southern Farmers' Alliance' in Kansas," *Kansas Historical Quarterly* 42, no. 1 (Spring, 1976): 64–65.

51. Stanley Parsons et al., "The Role of Cooperatives in the Development Culture of Populism," *Journal of American History*, 69, no. 4 (March, 1983): 880, 884–85.

52. *American Nonconformist*, July 4, 1889.

53. Rightmire, "The Alliance Movement in Kansas," 4; *American Nonconformist*, July 4, 1889.

54. *American Nonconformist*, July 4, September 26, 1889; *Purcell Territorial Topic* (Chickasaw Nation), June 5, August 21, 1890. The *Territorial Topic* ran an alliance column that originated in Winfield, Kansas.

55. Henry and Leo Vincent, *Populist Handbook for Kansas* (Indianapolis: Vincent Bros. Publishing Co., 1891), 1.

56. *American Nonconformist*, July 4, 1890; *Territorial Topic*, June 5, 1890.

57. Parsons et al., "The Role of Cooperatives," 881.

58. *American Nonconformist*, March 21, 1889.

59. The Union Labor party platform of 1888 was quite similar to the Populist Omaha platform of 1892. The first three planks of the Union Labor platform dealt with land, transportation, and money, with later planks calling for a graduated income tax and the direct election of senators. The money plank called for greenbacks "issued directly to the people, without the intervention of banks or loaned to citizens upon ample security at a low rate of interest." The latter contingency clearly foreshadowed the Populist subtreasury plan. In his collection of family biographies Leo Vincent reveals the connection between the Union Labor and People's party in his own mind by writing that "the *Nonconformist* supported the People's party, whose candidate in 1888 was A. J. Streeter of Illinois." See Ford, "The Invincible Vincents," 10.

60. Ibid., 7; Piehler, "Henry Vincent: A Case Study," 163; *American Nonconformist*, July 30, 1891; Argersinger, *Populism and Politics*, 73–74.

61. *American Nonconformist*, July 30, 1891.

62. Ibid., March 6, 1890; *New York World*, April 13, 1890.

63. *Biographical Record: This Volume Contains Biographical Sketches of Leading Citizens of Cowley Co., Kansas* (Chicago: Biographical Publishing Co., 1901), 181–82.

64. Ibid. Four of the five third-party representatives elected to the Oklahoma legislature in 1890 were from Payne County.

CHAPTER TWO

1. Edward Everett Dale, *Cow Country*, (Norman: University of Oklahoma Press, 1942), 9.

2. *Watonga Republican*, August 9, 1893. All newspapers cited in this work were published in the Oklahoma Territory unless otherwise noted.

3. Dennis Flynn, "Memoir," n.d., 12. Royden Dangerfield Papers, Western History Collections, University of Oklahoma; *Report of the Governor of Oklahoma* (1893), 469.

4. Fite, *The Farmers' Last Frontier*, 206.

5. Ibid.; Solon Buck, "The Settlement of Oklahoma," *Transactions of the Wisconsin Academy of Science, Arts, and Letters* 15, no. 2 (1907): 376; Dora Ann Stewart, *The Government and Development of the Oklahoma Territory* (Norman: University of Oklahoma Press, 1933), 219–20.

6. *American Nonconformist*, September 19, 1889; *Stillwater Oklahoma Standard*, December 28, 1889; Buck, "Settlement of Oklahoma," 376.

7. The most prominent politicians among the Seminoles were William Couch and Sidney Clarke, Democrats; Angelo Scott and D. A. Harvey, Republicans; and James B. Weaver and Samuel Crocker, future Populists.

8. Goble, *Progressive Oklahoma*, 17; Dan W. Peery, "The First Two Years," *Chronicles of Oklahoma* (pt. 1) 7, no. 3 (September, 1929): 296–98; *Norman Transcript*, July 20, 1889; *Stillwater Oklahoma Standard*, December 28, 1889, February 1, 1890.

9. *American Nonconformist*, April 4, 1889.

10. Helen Candee, "Social Conditions in Our Newest Territory," *Forum* 25, no. 4 (June 1898): 431.

11. *American Nonconformist*, April 4, 18, 1889; *Norman Transcript*, July 13, 1889; *Purcell Territorial Topic*, August 29, 1889.

12. Stewart, *Government of the Oklahoma Territory*, 49–59.

13. Kenneth N. Owen, "The Pattern and Structure of Western Territorial Politics," *Western Historical Quarterly* 1, no. 4 (October 1970): 377–81.

14. In late-nineteenth-century Europe only France had universal manhood suffrage. Great Britain adopted it in 1918.

15. Lewis L. Gould, "The Republican Search for a National Majority," in H. Wayne Morgan, ed., *The Gilded Age* (Syracuse, N.Y.: Syracuse University Press, 1970), 171–89; Richard Jensen, *The Winning of the Midwest* (Chicago: University of Chicago Press, 1971), 120–21.

16. The only major out-group not to associate with the Democratic party was blacks. They were the out-group of an even larger out-group, southerners, and therefore fell into the GOP camp through default.

17. While Adam Smith's *Wealth of Nations*, the bible of laissez-faire, was published in 1776, it was widely quoted in America only after 1850. See Rowland Berthoff, "Peasants and Artisans, Puritans and Republicans," 587.

18. *American Nonconformist*, March 21, 1889.

19. *Purcell Territorial Topic*, April 3, 1890.

20. For the political affiliations of newspapers in this era of highly partisan journalism see N. W. Ayer, *American Newspaper Annual* (Philadelphia: N. W. Ayer and Co., 1880–present).

21. The Oklahoma Press Association founded the Oklahoma Historical Society in

1893. After this date newspaper sources for Oklahoma are excellent. Most newspapers published before 1893, however, are missing. Because the Historical Society did not seek out manuscript collections before 1920, little manuscript material pertaining to Populism is available there.

22. *American Nonconformist*, April 11, 1889; *Purcell Territorial Topic*, July 9, 1891.

23. *Purcell Territorial Topic*, August 7, 1890.

24. Ibid., August 7, 1890.

25. Ibid., June 5, 1890.

26. Ibid., August 7, 1890.

27. *Oklahoma City Evening Gazette*, November 19, 1890.

28. Farmers founded the first alliance local in Cleveland County on May 30, 1890. H. C. Randolph organized the meeting. *Purcell Territorial Topic*, June 5, 1890.

29. *Guthrie Weekly Oklahoma State Capital*, November 16, 1890; *Purcell Territorial Topic*, March 20, November 21 1890; Bunky (Irwin Jeffs), *The First Eight Months* (Oklahoma City, Okla.: McMaster Printing Co., 1890), 83; *Stillwater Oklahoma Standard*, March 22, April 5, 1890; *American Nonconformist*, April 10, 1890.

30. *Norman Transcript*, June 28, 1890; *Hennessey Clipper*, August 1, 1890.

31. Thomas Arthur Hazell, "George Washington Steele, 1890–91," *Chronicles of Oklahoma* 53, no. 1 (Spring, 1975): 11; *Guthrie Weekly Oklahoma State Capital*, May 21, 1890.

32. In addition one representative was elected by the entire Oklahoma electorate.

33. Robert E. Cunningham, *Stillwater: Where Oklahoma Began* (Stillwater, Okla.: Stillwater Arts and Humanities Council, 1969), 194; *Hennessey Clipper*, August 1, 1890; *Oklahoma City Evening Gazette*, August 28, 1890; Geo. W. Steele to Hon. John W. Noble, July 1, 1890, Interior Department, Territorial Papers, 1889–1912 (microfilm at the Western History Collections, University of Oklahoma).

34. *American Nonconformist*, August 14, 1890.

35. Ibid.; *Norman Transcript*, May 31, 1890; *Frisco Herald*, July 17, 1890.

36. *Guthrie Weekly Oklahoma State Capital*, July 21, September 13, 1890.

37. *Hennessey Clipper*, August 1, 1890.

38. One of the council seats was elected jointly with Cleveland County. Mort Bixler, of Cleveland County, was the Democratic nominee. A. N. Daniels, the nominee of the Industrial Union (People's) party received the votes of many non–third-party elements with his promise to persuade the legislature to move the Canadian County seat from El Reno to Frisco.

39. *Norman Transcript*, August 9, 1890; *Oklahoma City Evening Gazette*, August 6, 1890; *American Nonconformist*, August 14, 1890; Dan W. Peery, "The First Two Years," *Chronicles of Oklahoma* (pt. 2) 7, no. 4 (December, 1929): 432–33.

40. The primary exception seems to be in Canadian County, where Republicans who voted for Arthur N. Daniels returned to their original allegiance. On August 23, Republicans received 39 percent of the vote, Democrats 34.8 percent, and the People's party 26.2 percent.

41. Roark, "Oklahoma Territory," 174–79, 253.

CHAPTER THREE

1. W. H. Merten, "Oklahoma Territory's First Legislature," *Sturm's Oklahoma Magazine* 5, no. 5 (January, 1908): 37.

2. Kingfisher *New World* as quoted in the *Purcell Territorial Topic*, January 30, 1890.

3. *Guthrie Weekly Oklahoma State Capital*, November 1, 1890.

4. The population of Guthrie was 39.1 percent northern, 30.4 percent black, 10.9 percent European, and 19.6 percent white southern. Logan County was 50.4 percent northern, 20.1 percent black, 7.3 percent European and 22.2 percent white southern. All references to race or place of birth in this work are derived from Roark's 5 percent sample of the 1900 U.S. Census (see appendix A).

5. Logan County returned Republican majorities even in the three-way races of the early 1890s.

6. The population of Oklahoma City was 45.3 percent northern, 16.8 percent black, 8.4 percent European, and 29.8 percent white southern. The Republican party carried Oklahoma County in 1894, when the Democratic party collapsed, and in 1898 and 1900, when Populist voters became dissatisfied with fusion.

7. The People's party polled 22.2 percent of the vote in the legislative race but held only 12.8 percent of the legislative seats.

8. Gardenhire later charged that Guthrie interests offered him a $2,000 bribe for his services. See *Norman Transcript*, September 20, 1890.

9. Marion Tuttle Rock, *Illustrated History of Oklahoma* (Topeka, Kans.: O. B. Hamilton & Son, 1890), 220; Peery, "The First Two Years," (pt. 2): 451. As Republicans had hoped, protests did emanate from Payne County, but to no avail. See *Norman Transcript*, September 6, 1890.

10. The Oklahoma Normal College of Edmond, founded by the 1890 legislature, is today known as Central State University. Peery, "The First Two Years," (pt. 2): 452–56. Representative Jones was from Oklahoma City, and Representative Trosper resided on a claim a few miles southeast of the city.

11. *Oklahoma City Daily Oklahoman*, February 6, 1921; *Hennessey Clipper*, July 25, 1890; Rock, *Illustrated Oklahoma*, 210–12.

12. *Guthrie Weekly Oklahoma State Capital*, October 4, 1890. As Terrill expected, the governor vetoed the Payne County agricultural bill. A later bill placed the college in Stillwater. Most accounts of Adair's motives center upon the liberal use of money to change his mind. He left the territory shortly after the session ended.

13. Terrill, "The Boomer's Last Raid," 39–40.

14. In fairness to his party it should be noted that the speaker he drew the revolver on, and the sergeant at arms who subsequently confiscated the firearm and ejected Terrill from the chamber also represented the People's party. Terrill's association with firearms led to his downfall shortly after the legislature ended. He holds the dubious honor of being the first Oklahoman convicted of murder under the criminal code that he himself prominently supported in the legislature. Legal battles and a series of jail breaks kept him out of prison until 1894. He was judged insane in 1904 and paroled in 1906. Terrill spent the rest of his life campaigning for prison reform. As long as he remained at large, his actions did little to further the cause of the party he represented. See Merten, "Oklahoma Territory's First Legislature," 37.

15. To prevent later reconsideration, sponsors of a bill frequently called it up for reconsideration immediately after its passage and then voted not to reconsider it. In this case Clark and Terrill attempted to get an adjournment but failed. *Journal of the First Legislative Assembly of the Oklahoma Territory* (Guthrie: State Capital Printing Co., 1890): 218–19.

16. Peery, "The First Two Years," (pt. 3), 108–12.

17. *Guthrie Weekly Oklahoma State Capital*, October 18, 1890. Grimmer and Beaver County, however, never got their promised railroad.

18. *Oklahoma City Evening Gazette*, October 2, 1890.

19. Peery, "The First Two Years," (pt. 3): 103–107.

20. Ibid., 122. Brown of Oklahoma County was actually the second bill's most vocal opponent.

21. Four of the six votes against the bill in the council came from members of the Oklahoma City combine. *Journal of the First Legislative Assembly*, 995, 1014–15. The original copy of the open letter to Mathews can be found in the Robert A. Lowery Collection, Oklahoma State University, Stillwater.

22. Thomas J. Nemshon to the Secretary of the Interior, August 16, 1890, Territorial Papers; *Journal of the First Legislative Assembly* (1890), 62; *Guthrie Weekly Oklahoma State Capital*, September 6, 1890; *Purcell Territorial Topic*, September 18, 1890.

23. *Journal of the First Legislative Assembly* (1890), 105. Representative Clark opposed "social equality for blacks." *Purcell Territorial Topic*, November 30, 1890.

24. *Journal of the First Legislative Assembly* (1890), 404–405; *Guthrie Weekly Oklahoma State Capital*, November 1, 1890; *Purcell Territorial Topic*, November 13, 1890. Although he was a Republican legislator in the 1890 assembly, Currin deserted the GOP in 1894 and ran for the legislature on the Populist ticket.

25. George Eldon Norvell, "A History of the First Legislative Assembly of the Territory of Oklahoma" (Master's thesis, University of Oklahoma, 1946), 40–41.

26. *Guthrie Weekly Oklahoma State Capital*, October 11, November 29, 1890; *Journal of the First Legislative Assembly* (1890), 820. Populists uniformly supported the woman suffrage measure in the house. Republicans split five to five, with four absent, and Democrats uniformly opposed the measure.

27. *Guthrie Weekly Oklahoma State Capital*, September 6, 1890; *Journal of the First Legislative Assembly*, 926–27.

28. *Guthrie Weekly Oklahoma State Capital*, November 15, December 6, 1890; *Journal of the First Legislative Assembly* (1890), 674–75, 716, 825, 901.

29. *Oklahoma City Evening Gazette*, December 23, 1890.

30. *Guthrie Weekly Oklahoma State Capital*, September 6, 1890; *Oklahoma City Evening Gazette*, December 13, 22, 23, 1890; Norvell, "A History the First Legislative Assembly," 51.

31. They also chastised him for attending the Democratic nominating convention.

32. Crocker was involved with the Seminole Townsite Company, which attempted to control Oklahoma City at the time of the opening. He apparently believed that his services to the Boomer movement warranted repayment in the form of a secure homestead in the new land.

33. Dennis Flynn, "Memoir," n.d., 14, Royden Dangerfield Papers, Western History Collections, University of Oklahoma; *Purcell Territorial Topic*, October 23, 1890; *Oklahoma City Evening Gazette*, September 27, November 8, 10 1890, August 6, 1892; *Guthrie Weekly Oklahoma State Capital*, September 6, October 13, November 8, 1890; Crocker, "Autobiography," 322–27. It should be noted that David A. Harvey was also a Sooner. Such matters seemed less important to Republican voters.

CHAPTER FOUR

1. U.S. rail mileage in 1860 consisted of 33,000 miles of various-gauged tracks. In 1890 the United States had 166,000 miles of standard-gauge track. Samuel P. Hays, *The Response to Industrialism, 1885–1914* (Chicago: University of Chicago Press, 1957), 126–29.

2. Ibid.

3. Ibid.

4. Only the depression of the 1930s can be considered worse than those of 1873–79 and 1893–97.

5. Sheldon Hackney, *Populism: The Critical Issues* (Boston: Little, Brown and Co., 1971), xi.

6. This is particularly true of Vernon Louis Parrington, who was active in the People's party in Kansas before joining the faculty of the University of Oklahoma in 1897. Richard Hofstadter, *The Progressive Historians: Turner, Beard, Parrington* (New York: Alfred A. Knopf, 1968), 369–70. See Parrington's *Main Currents in American Thought: The Beginnings of Critical Realism, 1860–1920* (New York: Harcourt, Brace and World, 1930; reprint, Norman: University of Oklahoma Press, 1987) for an early and lively exposition of the Populist revolt in the progressive vein.

7. John D. Hicks, *The Populist Revolt* (Minneapolis: University of Minnesota Press, 1931), 207–29.

8. Ibid., 229–37.

9. H. Roger Grant, "Populists and Utopia: A Neglected Connection," *Red River Valley Historical Review* 2, no. 4 (Winter, 1975): 482.

10. *American Nonconformist*, June 27, 1889; Samuel Crocker [Theodore Oceanic Islet, pseud.], *That Island* (Oklahoma City, Okla.: C. E. Streeter and Co., 1892), 2–4, 6. Crocker's novel contained several testimonials, including one from his old Boomer friend, Democrat Sidney Clarke.

11. Although the Omaha platform met with almost universal derision from the establishment in the 1890s, including a number of future progressives, many of the reforms contained in the document became law in the early twentieth century.

12. *Seventeenth Annual Report on the Statistics of Railways in the United States* (Washington, D.C.: U.S. Government Printing Office, 1905), 99.

13. Harry E. Henslick, "Abraham Jefferson Seay: Governor of Oklahoma Territory, 1892–93," *Chronicles of Oklahoma* 53, no. 1 (Spring, 1975): 29–32, 42, 44; A. J. Seay, "Autobiographical Sketch of Abraham Jefferson Seay's Public Life," 6–7, Abraham Jefferson Seay Papers, Western History Collections, University of Oklahoma.

14. Henslick, "Abraham Jefferson Seay," 33–34.

15. Angie Debo, *A History of the Indians of the United States* (Norman: University of Okahoma Press, 1970), 70.

16. *Norman Transcript*, October 10, 1891.

17. *Oklahoma War Chief*, September 10, 1885.

18. Ibid., September 3, 1885.

19. *Norman Peoples Voice*, September 30, 1892; *Guthrie Weekly Oklahoma State Capital*, February 1, 1894, February 23, 1895.

20. *Stillwater Payne County Populist*, March 30, 1894; *Norman Peoples Voice*, November 11, 1893, October 27, 1899.

21. *Stillwater Payne County Populist*, March 30, 1894; *El Reno Industrial Headlight*, May 2, 1895; *El Reno Populist Platform*, December 21, 1894; *Norman Peoples Voice*, February 17, 1894; Goble, *Progressive Oklahoma*, 69–86.

22. *Oklahoma War Chief*, September 3, 1885; *Norman Peoples Voice*, November 17, 1899.

23. *Alva Pioneer*, June 7, 1895; *Oklahoma City Evening Gazette*, October 23, November 6, 1890; *Guthrie Weekly Oklahoma Leader*, December 10, 1896.

24. *Guthrie Weekly Oklahoma State Capital*, August 17, November 30, 1895.

25. *Norman Peoples Voice*, December 30, 1893; *Guthrie Weekly Oklahoma State Capital*, December 2, 1890, February 3, 1894; *Perkins Journal*, February 7, 1895.

26. *Guthrie West and South*, January 11, 1894; *Kingfisher Reformer*, March 1, 1894; *Home, Field and Forum* (December, 1895), 184. Populist Jules Soule edited *Home, Field and Forum*.

27. A. M. Colson, the councillor-at-large, returned to Kansas after the 1890 legislative session.

28. Henry E. Asp to Hon. John W. Noble (Secretary of the Interior), July 8, 1892, Territorial Papers, 1889–1912.

29. Henslick, "Abraham Jefferson Seay," 37–38; Seay, "Autobiographical Sketch," 4; Henry E. Asp to Hon. A. J. Seay, June 27, 1892, Territorial Papers.

30. Samuel Crocker, "Autobiography," 331–39; Seay, "Autobiographical Sketch," 11–12; Henslick, "Abraham Jefferson Seay," 38.

31. Crocker, "Autobiography," 336–39; Dan W. Peery, "Colonel Crocker and the Boomer Movement," *Chronicles of Oklahoma* 13, no. 3 (September, 1935): 294–95; *Tecumseh Herald* as quoted in the *Oklahoma City Evening Gazette*, September 20, 1892.

32. Victor Murdock, "Dennis T. Flynn," *Chronicles of Oklahoma* 18, no. 2 (June, 1940): 106–13.

33. *Purcell Territorial Topic*, January 22, February 12, 1901; *Norman Transcript*, January 12, February 7, 28, 1891; *Oklahoma City Evening Gazette*, January 28, 1891.

34. *Oklahoma City Evening Gazette*, December 23, 1890.

35. Ibid., December 23, 1890, January 28, 1891.

36. Hicks, *The Populist Revolt*, 178; *Oklahoma City Evening Gazette*, August 12, 1892.

37. *Oklahoma City Evening Gazette*, August 17, 1892.

38. Ibid.

39. Frank McMasters to Leslie P. Ross, June 29, 1892, Leslie P. Ross Papers, Western History Collections, University of Oklahoma; *Norman Transcript*, August 18, 1892; *Norman Peoples Voice*, December 23, 1892; *Oklahoma City Evening Gazette*, January 19, July 19, 1892.

40. *Oklahoma City Evening Gazette*, August 17, 1892.

41. Ibid.

42. Leander Pitman to Hon. Sidney Clarke, September 19, 1892, Sidney Clarke Papers, Western History Collections, University of Oklahoma; *Oklahoma City Evening Gazette*, September 19, October 7, 1892; *Norman Peoples Voice*, October 21, 1892; *Oklahoma City Evening Gazette*, July 29, August 17, 1892. Although the Democrats' statehood issue had sentimental appeal, it was clearly impractical in 1892. Land was tax-exempt until homesteaders proved their claims. Since they had five years to do this, the territorial tax base was minuscule until 1894, when settlers in the Unassigned Lands region proved their claims, and inadequate before 1898, when Cherokee Outlet land became taxable. In a more practical vein the Populist platform called for home rule and denounced federal interference "in matters justly pertaining to local territorial government."

43. Fusionist tickets appeared in one council and three house districts. Democrats also declined to field tickets in one council and two house districts, while Populists returned the favor in another council and two other house districts.

44. *Oklahoma City Evening Gazette*, September 10, 24, October 25, 26, November 14, 1892. In the sparsely populated west the GOP carried the council seat but split the two house seats with the Democrats.

45. *Guthrie Oklahoma Representative*, November 8, 1894. Flynn (a Republican) carried 44.7 percent of the vote to Democrat Travers's 34.8 percent and Populist Ward's 20.5 percent.

46. Midwesterners were Oklahoma's largest sectional group, constituting 41.2 percent of the territorial population. White border-state natives constituted 26.8 percent in 1900. See appendix A for definitions of each sectional group.

47. Of the fifteen "core" Populist counties of Texas identified in James Turner, "Understanding the Populists," 360, nine of those located outside the eastern woodlands of Texas were populated primarily by border state natives. See Terry Jordan, "Population Origin Groups in Rural Texas," *Annals of the Association of American Geographers* 60, no. 2 (June, 1970), map supplement 13. Roscoe C. Martin, in *The People's Party in Texas* (Austin: University of Texas Press, 1931), 62, identifies the eastern woodlands of Texas as a particularly fertile field for agrarian insurgency. Turner adopted Martin's definition of "core" counties.

48. The most significant drop in Populist-midwestern correlation occurred between the August legislative elections and the November delegate election in 1890. The actions of the third party's 1890 legislative contingent are the most likely explanation for this. The major difference between the votes in the two elections was a significantly reduced turnout of Populists in Logan and Payne counties, where the third party's deal with Democrats to move the capital to Oklahoma City was quite unpopular.

49. In 1900, cotton acreage accounted for more than 10 percent of improved acres only in Cleveland, Greer, Lincoln, and Pottawatomie counties. Greer County became a part of the Oklahoma Territory in 1896. In 1900, Oklahoma farmers devoted 1,320,506 acres to corn, 1,279,826 acres to wheat, and 240,678 acres to cotton.

50. Because of poor soil, little farming occurred beyond the twenty-six–inch rainfall line in the Oklahoma Territory. The rail line passing through the northwestern section of the Oklahoma Territory traversed the Gypsum Hills, a region largely unsuitable for farming.

51. David S. Trask, "Nebraska Populism as a Response to Environmental and Political Problems," in Brian C. Blouet and Frederick C. Luebke, eds., *The Great Plains: Environment and Culture* (Lincoln: University of Nebraska Press, 1979), 65, 75. In the 1890s, Oklahoma Populists showed real strength in only three of the nine corn-belt counties west of the thirty-inch rainfall line: Woods County, in the Cherokee Outlet, which the government opened to white settlement only in 1893; Dewey County, in the Cheyenne and Arapaho lands; and Greer County, which was separated from Texas and attached to Oklahoma in 1896.

52. Argersinger, *Populism and Politics*, 62; Walter T. K. Nugent, "Some Parameters of Populism," *Agricultural History* 40, no. 4 (Spring, 1966): 264. In 1900, wheat, corn, and cotton acreage in the Oklahoma Territory correlated with the value of implements and machinery per farm at .88905, $-.54633$ and $-.39434$, respectively.

53. Fred A. Shannon, *The Farmer's Last Frontier: Agriculture 1860–1897* (New York: Rinehart and Co., 1945), 165–68. U.S. Bureau of the Census, *Historical Statistics of the United States: Colonial Times to 1957* (Washington, D.C: U.S. Government Printing Office, 1960), 290, 296–96, 301–302. Cotton is also a safer crop than wheat because it has a greater drought resistance. The stronger Populist correlation with hogs per farm than with corn acreage verifies the fact that third-party voters were diversified operators. Subsistence farmers grew corn for human consumption, and some commercial farmers grew small amounts for livestock feed without entering the corn-hog cycle. These people were not likely to vote Populist, however, and thus reduced the third party's correlation with corn acreage below that of hogs per farm.

54. The 1892 Populist correlation with the value of manufactured goods was $-.53$; with the value of farm implements and machinery it was $-.25$; and with hogs per farm it was $+.73$.

55. Both cash and share tenancy correlate positively with urban residence, which confirms that they were products of the cosmopolitan culture surrounding the railhead towns.

56. The correlation of black voters with share tenancy was $+.46$.

57. Crocker, "Autobiography," 345; Leslie P. Ross, "The Second Territorial Legislature," *Sturm's Oklahoma Magazine* 6, no. 3 (May, 1908): 80–82.

58. Ross, "The Second Territorial Legislature," 80–82; *El Reno Daily Herald*, December 7, 1892; *Oklahoma City Evening Gazette*, November 16, 1893.

59. Democrats and Populists, therefore, also received most of the house patronage in the second legislature.

60. Crocker, "Autobiography," 345–46; Ross, "The Second Territorial Legislature," 80–82.

61. *Journal of the House Proceedings of the Second Legislative Assembly of the Territory of Oklahoma: Beginning January 10, 1893* (Guthrie: State Capital Printing Company, 1893), 132.

62. Three of the Populists in the house voted in favor of the measure. Populist Councillor Fielden S. Pulliam opposed the measure because clerks would have been paid more than janitors. *Journal of the House Proceedings* (1893), 72, 128; *Journal of the Council Proceedings of the Second Legislative Assembly of the Territory of Oklahoma: Beginning January 10, 1893* (Guthrie: State Capital Printing Company, 1893), 44–45.

63. *Journal of the Council Proceedings (1893)*, 317–18; *Journal of the House Proceedings* (1893), 396.

64. *Journal of the House Proceedings* (1893), 325, 452–71; *Journal of the Council Proceedings* (1893), 330–66.

65. *Journal of the Council Proceedings* (1893), 182, 289.

66. Populist-sponsored laws passed by the 1893 legislature included House Bill no. 59, on contracts on conditional sale of real estate and street railroad equipment; House Bill no. 75, on liquor; and Council Bill no. 108, on townships. *Journal of the Council Proceedings* (1893), 365–66.

CHAPTER FIVE

1. H. Wayne Morgan, *From Hays to McKinley, National Party Politics, 1877–1896* (Syracuse, N.Y.: Syracuse University Press, 1969), 445–46.

2. Hicks, *The Populist Revolt*, 255–57, 265–69.

3. "List of Letters, Petitions and Papers, etc., Recommending Hon. Sidney Clarke for Governor of Oklahoma Territory"; E. P. McCabe to the President, March 23, 1893; D. A. Harvey to the President, March 27, 1893; Dennis T. Flynn to the President, March 3, 1893, Sidney Clarke Papers, Western History Collections, University of Oklahoma.

4. A. N. Daniels to Grover Cleveland, n.d. (received March 23, 1893); Samuel Crocker to the President, March 6, 1893, "List of Letters, Petitions and Papers, etc., Recommending Hon. Sidney Clarke for Governor of the Oklahoma Territory," Sidney Clarke Papers.

5. James F. Morgan, "William Cary Renfrow, Governor of Oklahoma, 1893–1897," *Chronicles of Oklahoma* 53, no. 1 (Spring, 1975): 48.

6. Morgan, "William Cary Renfrow," 47.

7. Perhaps Smithville, North Carolina, was the only true home Renfrow ever knew. He was buried there in 1922 after living the last fifty-six years of his life in Arkansas, Missouri, and Oklahoma. Morgan, "William Cary Renfrow," 64.

8. Roark, "Oklahoma Territory," 350; Morgan, "William Cary Renfrow," 47.

9. Morgan, "William Cary Renfrow," 47–48.

10. *Guthrie Daily Oklahoma State Capital*, June 5, 1893; Morgan, "William Cary Renfrow," 48–49.

11. Morgan, "William Cary Renfrow," 49–50; *Guthrie Daily Oklahoma State Capital*, April 11, 1893.

12. Morgan, "William Cary Renfrow," 50–52.

13. Ibid., 52–53.

14. John Spalding, *Great Depressions: 1837–1844, 1893–1897, 1929–1939* (Glenview, Ill.: Scott, Foresman & Co., 1966), 58–59.

15. Harold U. Faulkner, *Politics, Reform and Expansion, 1890–1900* (New York: Harper & Row, 1959), 141–45.

16. Spalding, *Great Depressions*, 61–62; Faulkner, *Politics, Reform and Expansion*, 145–46.

17. Morgan, *From Hayes to McKinley*, 446–47; Faulkner, *Politics, Reform and Expansion*, 146–47.

18. Helen Candee, "Social Conditions," 431.

19. Oklahoma Agricultural Experiment Station, *Oklahoma Agricultural Statistics, 1894–1947*, Miscellaneous Publication MP-14 (Stillwater: 1947), 13, 15.

20. Clifford Geertz, "Ideology as a Cultural System," in David Apter, ed., *Ideology and Discontent* (New York: Free Press, 1964), 47–76.

21. For further readings on the Old Radicalism theme in Populism, see Christopher Lasch, *The Agony of the American Left* (New York: Random House, 1969); Gene Clanton, "Populism, Progressivism, and Equality: The Kansas Paradigm," *Agricultural History* 51, no. 3 (July, 1977): 559–81; and John L. Thomas, *Alternative America: Henry George, Edward Bellamy, Henry Demarest Lloyd and the American Adversary Tradition* (Cambridge, Mass.: Harvard University Press, 1983).

22. Lawrence C. Goodwyn, *The Populist Moment* (New York: Oxford University Press, 1978), 208; *Guthrie Oklahoma Representative*, April 2, 1894; Morgan, *From Hayes to McKinley*, 465–67.

23. Morgan, *From Hays to McKinley*, 466–68.

24. Cassidy had given up his editorship of the *Guthrie West and South* by this time.

25. *Guthrie Weekly Oklahoma State Capital*, April 14, 1894; *Norman Peoples Voice*, March 10, April 16, 1894; *Kingfisher Reformer*, June 15, 1894; *El Reno Industrial Headlight*, March 24, May 30, 1894. The Canadian County Populist executive committee forced Howard out of the editorship at El Reno in 1895. He moved on to the Populist *Medford Mascot* and later that year founded Oklahoma's first Socialist Labor party local. J. C. Tousley took over the *El Reno Industrial Headlight* shortly thereafter.

26. *Guthrie Oklahoma Representative*, July 14, 1896; *Guthrie Weekly Oklahoma Leader*, October 10, 1896; *Guthrie Weekly Oklahoma State Capital*, May 20, 1894. Something of a political gadfly, John Furlong followed Leo Vincent to Boulder, Colorado, in the late 1890s. *Oklahoma City Oklahoma Champion*, March 25, 1898.

27. *Guthrie Weekly Oklahoma State Capital*, April 21, 1894; *Norman Peoples Voice*, May 25, 1894; *Kingfisher Reformer*, May 17, 1894.

28. *Guthrie Weekly Oklahoma State Capital*, April 28, May 5, 1894; *Mulhall Chief*, August 3, 1894; *Alva Pioneer*, March 30, May 18, 1894; *Guthrie Weekly Oklahoma Leader*, April 16, 1894.

29. *Guthrie Daily Oklahoma State Capital*, August 18, 1895; *Guthrie Weekly Oklahoma State Capital*, August 24, 1895; *Perkins Journal*, August 24, 1895.

30. Ray Ginger, *Age of Excess: The United States from 1877 to 1914* (New York: Macmillan & Co., 1965), 167; Morgan, *From Hayes to McKinley*, 468–69.

31. Ginger, *Age of Excess*, 167–69; Morgan, *From Hayes to McKinley*, 469–72.

32. Morgan, *From Hayes to McKinley*, 469–72; Ginger, *Age of Excess*, 167–69. Illinois Governor John Peter Altgeld, himself a German immigrant, vehemently protested

the use of federal troops without his consent (which was unconstitutional), but in vain.

33. *Guthrie Weekly Oklahoma State Capital*, July 21, 1894; *Guthrie Oklahoma Representative*, June 21, 1894; *Perkins Excelsior*, September 7, 1894; *Norman Peoples Voice*, February 10, 1895.

34. *Alva Pioneer*, July 27, 1894; *Guthrie Weekly Oklahoma State Capital*, July 14, 1894; *Alva Pioneer*, September 7, 1894; *Norman State Democrat*, July 14, 25 1894.

35. *Stillwater Payne County Populist*, June 22, 1894; *Guthrie Oklahoma Representative*, July 5, 1894; *Norman Peoples Voice*, September 16, 1892.

36. *Alva Review*, August 18, 30, 1894; *Norman Peoples Voice*, September 20, November 8, 1895, April 3, 1896; *Kingfisher Reformer*, November 8, 1894.

CHAPTER SIX

1. Nadine Runyun, ed., *Pioneers of Cleveland County, 1889–1907* (Norman, Okla.: Cleveland County Historical Association), 11–12; *Norman Transcript*, August 27, 1939.

2. *Norman Peoples Voice*, November 13, 1892.

3. Ford, "The Invincible Vincents," 35–36.

4. Grob, "The Knights of Labor," 5, 9, 16, 17; *Guthrie Oklahoma Representative*, July 19, 1894.

5. *American Nonconformist*, March 26, 1891; Ayer, *American Newspaper Annual* (1892), 616–17; (1895), 637–41, (1898), 668–72; *Pawnee Appeal*, April 26, 1895. Populists still claimed twenty-one reform papers in 1897. *Guthrie Oklahoma Representative*, January 7, 1897. Some short-lived newspapers never appeared in Ayer's directory. The *El Reno Populist Platform*, founded in 1894 and retitled the *Industrial Headlight* in 1895, is a good example.

6. Berlin B. Chapman, "The Enid 'Railroad War': An Archival Study," *Chronicles of Oklahoma* 43, no. 2 (Summer, 1965): 126–38.

7. *Norman Peoples Voice*, November 18, 25, 1893; Chapman, "The Enid 'Railroad War,'" 151.

8. Chapman, "The Enid 'Railroad War,'" 141, 151–62.

9. Ibid., 169–89; *Enid Coming Events*, July 12, 1894; *Alva Review*, July 21, 1894.

10. *Guthrie Weekly Oklahoma State Capital*, July 28, August 18, 1894.

11. *Norman Peoples Voice*, June 4, 1897; *Enid Coming Events*, March 2, 1894; *Guthrie Weekly Oklahoma State Capital*, August 4, 1894; *Alva Review*, July 14, 1894.

12. *Enid Daily Wave*, July 18, 1894.

13. *Guthrie Weekly Oklahoma State Capital*, August 18, 1894; *Guthrie Oklahoma Representative*, December 13, 1894. The Choctaw Railroad later built a spur from Shawnee to Tecumseh, but only after Populists brought up the subject in the 1895 legislature.

14. *Guthrie Weekly Oklahoma State Capital*, May 19, 1894.

15. Ibid., June 23, July 28, 1894.

16. Ibid., October 27, November 3, 1894.

17. Ibid., January 20, 1894; *Norman State Democrat*, February 3, 1894; *Oklahoma City Press-Gazette* as quoted in the *Norman State Democrat*, August 11, 1894.

18. *Guthrie Oklahoma Representative*, August 9, 1894; *Guthrie Weekly Oklahoma State Capital*, August 11, 1894; *Norman State Democrat*, August 4, 1894; *Payne County Populist* (Stillwater), August 10, 1894.

19. *Guthrie Oklahoma Representative*, September 6, 20, 1894.

20. Ibid., August 9, September 13, October 25, 1894.

21. Ibid., June 6, 1894, August 25, 1894.

22. Ibid., September 27, 1894.

23. *Oklahoma City Oklahoma State* as quoted in the *Guthrie Oklahoma Representative*, June 28, 1894.

24. Fifty-six former Union soldiers and ten former Confederate soldiers attended the convention. This exceeded the number of Civil War veterans attending both of the old-party conventions in 1894.

25. *Guthrie Weekly Oklahoma State Capital*, June 2, 1894; *Guthrie Oklahoma Representative*, July 12, 1894. John Allan was permanent secretary of the convention.

26. *Guthrie Oklahoma Representative*, May 21, July 12, 1894.

27. *Alva Chronicle*, July 20, 1894; *El Reno Democrat* as quoted in the *Norman State Democrat*, June 13, 1894; *Norman State Democrat*, August 11, 18, 1894; *Guthrie Weekly Oklahoma State Capital*, September 22, 1894; *Guthrie Oklahoma Representative*, September 20, 1894.

28. *Norman Peoples Voice*, May 25, 1894; *Payne County Populist*, September 7, 1894; *Guthrie Oklahoma Representative*, September 27, 1894; *Guthrie Weekly Oklahoma State Capital*, September 22, 1894.

29. *Guthrie Oklahoma Representative*, October 3, 1895; *Norman Peoples Voice*, November 12, 1892.

30. Clark Brown, "Biography of Abraham Jefferson Seay," n.d., 13, Abraham Jefferson Seay Collection, Western History Collections, University of Oklahoma.

31. *Guthrie West and South*, October 19, 1893; *Norman Peoples Voice*, December 2, 1893; *Guthrie Oklahoma Representative*, November 8, 1894, December 12, 1895.

32. *Kingfisher Reformer*, September 27, 1894; *Guthrie Oklahoma Representative*, October 4, 1894; *Kingfisher Reformer*, August 31, 1893; *Enid Coming Events*, December 24, 1896.

33. Goodwyn, *The Populist Moment*, 228–45, 251–58. Goodwyn portrays middle-of-the-roaders as greenbackers and fusionists as silverites.

34. *Guthrie West and South*, July 6, 1893; *Alva Review*, May 16, 1895; *Guthrie Weekly Oklahoma State Capital*, September 1, 1894; *Norman State Democrat*, February 5, 1896.

35. Populists and Republicans claimed that the legislation establishing the committee did not provide for the removal of members, once appointed. *Guthrie Weekly Oklahoma State Capital*, September 22, 1894.

36. Ibid., September 29, October 13 1894; *Guthrie Oklahoma Representative*, December 6, 1894.

37. *Enid Coming Events*, October 4, November 18, 1894; *Alva Pioneer*, December 14, 1894.

38. *Guthrie Oklahoma Representative*, December 20, 1894.

39. Voter turnout for the general elections held during the Populist era in the Oklahoma Territory was: 49.7 percent in the August 27, 1890, legislative race; 56.1 percent in the 1890 delegate race; 56.7 percent in 1892; 81.2 percent in 1894; 72.6 percent in 1896; 58.2 percent in 1898; 67.9 percent in 1900; and 61.9 percent in 1902.

40. The correlations between the 1892 and 1894 votes for delegate to Congress in the seven original counties of Oklahoma were: +.97 for Republicans, +.84 for Democrats, and +.92 for Populists. In the lands opened to non-Indian settlement in 1891 and 1892, the correlations were: +.63 for the GOP, +.25 for Democrats, and −.29 for the People's party.

41. The correlation coefficients between urban residence and the partisan vote for the cities and townships represented in maps 6 and 7 are: +.33 for the Republican party, +.27 for the Democratic party, and −.51 for the People's party.

42. None of the three townships that the Rock Island rail line crossed in Kingfisher and Canadian counties had a depot in the 1890s.

43. Hinterland commercial centers that the People's party failed to carry included

Stillwater, in Payne County; Pawnee and Cleveland, in Pawnee County; Crescent, in
Logan County; and Cleo, in Woods County. Blacks were numerous in eastern Logan,
northeastern Oklahoma, and northwestern Lincoln counties. They were also numerous
in east-central Kingfisher County, but the People's party ran a black farmer, Green I. Currin, for the territorial legislature in this district.

44. W. A. Willibrand, "In Bilingual Old Okarche," *Chronicles of Oklahoma* 29, no. 2
(Summer, 1951): 352–53.

45. The late-nineteenth-century egalitarians' tradition of promoting freehold tenure
made the Populist party an obvious repository for farmers unable to secure a homestead.
The third party's consistent correlations with tenancy suggest that the assertions of historians of Oklahoma socialism that the People's party failed to face the land issue is not
valid. The land issue was a major issue for the People's party, although not its only concern. See James R. Green, *Grass-Roots Socialism: Radical Movements in the Southwest,
1895–1943* (Baton Rouge: Louisana State University Press, 1978), 7.

46. The Republican and Populist correlations with the value of manufactured goods
increased significantly in 1894. The Populist advance, however, represented third-party
gains in only three counties: Canadian, Logan, and Oklahoma. These counties accounted for 48.7 percent of the value of manufactured goods in the Oklahoma Territory.
Appendix A, table A-2, shows that the third-party vote in these counties was exceptionally rural.

CHAPTER SEVEN

1. Argersinger, *Politics and Populism*, 184 *Texas Almanac and Industrial Guide, 1974–
75* (Dallas : A. H. Belo Publishing Co., 1974), 536. If the vote of the Lily-White Republican candidate is combined with that of the GOP's regular candidate in Texas, the Republican share of the ballot was 14.1 percent in 1894.

2. *Norman Peoples Voice*, November 17, 1894; *Alva Review* as quoted in the *Guthrie
Oklahoma Representative*, November 22, 1894.

3. *Guthrie Oklahoma Representative*, December 6, 1894. Populists lost four of the
house seats by less than twenty votes. Populist and Republican candidates, for instance,
tied in one race. The GOP candidate won the seat by lot.

4. *Guthrie Weekly Oklahoma State Capital*, January 19, 1895; *Guthrie Oklahoma Representative*, February 7, 21, 1895.

5. *Guthrie Weekly Oklahoma State Capital*, January 19, February 9, 1895; *Norman
Peoples Voice*, February 16, 1895. As a consolation, Republican Councillor O. R. Fegan of
Guthrie appointed Coulson clerk of the committee on school lands.

6. Coulson lost his Kansas farm to a mortgage company in 1894.

7. *Guthrie Oklahoma Representative*, February 7, 14, 1895.

8. *Guthrie Weekly Oklahoma State Capital*, January 19, February 9, 1895; *Guthrie
Oklahoma Representative*, February 7, 21, 1895; *Norman Peoples Voice*, February 16, 1895.

9. *Norman Peoples Voice*, January 12, 1895; *Guthrie Oklahoma Representative*, January
17, 1895.

10. *Guthrie Oklahoma Representative*, January 31, 1895; *Norman State Democrat*, February 13, 1895. The 1893 legislature had two committee clerks in each house; in 1895
almost every committee had a clerk.

11. *Guthrie Oklahoma Representative*, January 24, 31, 1895.

12. *Guthrie Weekly Oklahoma State Capital*, March 16, February 23, 1895.

13. *Norman Peoples Voice*, March 16, 1895; *Norman State Democrat*, January 26, 1895;
Guthrie Weekly Oklahoma State Capital, February 2, 1895.

14. Populists in Lincoln County in 1894, for instance, correlated with white south-erners at +.64. In this instance, the People's party simply replaced the Democratic party as the party of southerners.

15. *Guthrie Oklahoma Representative*, January 31, 1895; *Guthrie Weekly Oklahoma State Capital*, January 12, 26, February 2, 1895; *Journal of the Council Proceedings of the Third Legislative Assembly of the Territory of Oklahoma, Beginning January 8, 1895 and Ending March 8, 1895* (Guthrie: State Capital Printing Co., 1895), 954–55; *Journal of the House Proceedings of the Third Legislative Assembly of the Territory of Oklahoma, Beginning January 8, 1895 and Ending March 8, 1895* (Guthrie: State Capital Printing Co., 1895), 1057.

16. Walling, a Medford physician, was the only nonfarmer Populist in the 1895 house.

17. *Alva Pioneer,*, March 29, 1895; *Alva Review*, November 28, 1895; *Journal of the House Proceedings* (1895), 954–55; *Journal of the Council Proceedings* (1895), 1057.

18. *Guthrie Weekly Oklahoma State Capital*, February 9, 1895; *Norman Peoples Voice*, March 9, 16, September 13, 1895; *Journal of the Council Proceedings* (1895), 1055; *Norman Peoples Voice*, October 2, 1896; *Journal of the House Proceedings* (1895), 958–59; *Alva Review*, January 2, 1896; *Chandler Publicist*, May 1, 1896.

19. *Guthrie Weekly Oklahoma State Capital*, February 23, 1895; *Norman Peoples Voice*, February 9, 1895; *Payne County Populist*, March 8, 1895; *Journal of the Council Proceedings* (1895), 1055; *Journal of the House Proceedings* (1895), 1058–59; *Guthrie Oklahoma Representative*, February 21, 1895. Three of the assembly's four Democrats voted to repeal the usury legislation.

20. *Journal of the Council Proceedings* (1895), 1055–57; *Journal of the House Proceedings* (1895), 956–59.

21. *Norman Peoples Voice*, January 26, 1895; *Guthrie Weekly Oklahoma State Capital*, February 2, 9, 23, March 2, 1895; *Journal of the Council Proceedings* (1895), 1012, 1014, 1055–56; *Norman State Democrat*, February 13, 1895.

22. *Journal of the House Proceedings* (1895), 954–55, 958–59; *Journal of the Council Proceedings* (1895), 1055, 1057; *Guthrie Weekly Oklahoma State Capital*, March 16, February 2, 1895.

23. *Journal of the House Proceedings* (1895), 954–57; *Journal of the Council Proceedings* (1895), 1012, 1055–56; Karel Bicha, *Western Populism: Studies in an Ambivalent Conservatism* (Lawrence, Kans.: Coronado Press, 1976), 123. The funds for the Oklahoma Historical Society were designated for binding the newspaper collection, a task Populists believed could wait for better economic times. William Campbell, the president of the society at the time, had been a Republican member of the first legislature and thus was viewed as a typical placeman.

24. *Guthrie Weekly Oklahoma State Capital*, February 23, 1895; Alwyn Barr, *Reconstruction to Reform: Texas Politics, 1876–1906* (Austin: University of Texas Press, 1971), 161; *Payne County Populist*, March 8, 1895; *Journal of the House Proceedings* (1895), 954–57; *Journal of the Council Proceedings* (1895), 1057.

25. *Payne County Populist*, February 15, 1895; *Norman State Democrat*, March 20, 1895; *Journal of the House Proceedings* (1895), 956–57; *Journal of the Council Proceedings* (1895), 1056–57.

26. *Guthrie Weekly Oklahoma Leader*, October 10, February 2, 1895; *Guthrie Oklahoma Representative*, February 14, 1895.

27. *Guthrie Weekly Oklahoma State Capital*, February 2, March 2, 16, 1895; *Journal of the Council Proceedings* (1895), 1055.

28. *Alva Pioneer*, April 5, 1895; *Guthrie Weekly Oklahoma State Capital*, March 30, 1895.

29. *Guthrie Weekly Oklahoma State Capital,* March 16, 30, 1895; *Journal of the House Proceedings* (1895), 958–59; *Journal of the Council Proceedings* (1895), 1056.

30. *Guthrie Oklahoma Representative,* November 14, 1895; *Journal of the House Proceedings* (1895), 956–57; *Journal of the Council Proceedings* (1895), 1057.

31. *Alva Chronicle,* March 15, 1895; *Norman Peoples Voice,* March 16, 1895; *Guthrie Daily Oklahoma Leader,* March 22, 1895. The federal government gave each territory land for the support of schools.

CHAPTER EIGHT

1. *McMaster's Weekly Magazine* as quoted in the *Norman Peoples Voice,* May 22, 1896.

2. *El Reno Populist Platform,* February 28, 1895.

3. *Alva Review,* May 2, 1895; *El Reno Industrial Headlight,* May 9, June 27, 1895; *Norman People's Voice,* June 29, 1895.

4. *Guthrie Oklahoma Representative,* September 12, 1895; *Alva Review,* June 13, 1895.

5. *El Reno Industrial Headlight,* May 9, 1895.

6. *Guthrie Weekly Oklahoma State Capital,* June 1, 1895; *Kingfisher Reformer,* January 3, 1895.

7. *Payne County Populist,* January 4, 1895; *Chandler Publicist,* January 4, 1895; *Coming Nation* as quoted in the *El Reno Industrial Headlight,* March 29, 1895; *Enid Coming Events,* July 4, 1895; *Norman Peoples Voice,* June 1, 1895; *Alva Republican,* June 7, 1895. Julius Wayland edited the *Coming Nation* before renaming it the *Appeal to Reason* in 1895. In the twentieth century the paper was the nation's leading Socialist party paper.

8. *Guthrie Weekly Oklahoma Leader,* June 27, 1895; *Guthrie Oklahoma Representative,* February 6, January 30, 1895; *Norman Peoples Voice,* June 1, 1895.

9. *Guthrie Oklahoma Representative,* January 16, 1896.

10. Ibid.

11. Ibid.

12. Ibid., February 6, 1895.

13. Ibid.

14. Ibid., February 13, 1895.

15. Ibid. Ignatius Donnelly put forth the idea that Populists should meet at the same time as the Silver party, adopt a platform, and then have a conference committee meet with silverites and choose a presidential candidate. The National Reform Press Association met in January, 1896, and issued a resolution calling for the People's party to hold its national convention after the other parties to pick up silverite renegades and adopted Donnelly's plan for consolidating reform elements. Ibid., December 5, 1895, January 16, 1896.

16. Ibid., January 16, February 6, 13, May 7, 1896. The last quote is from Miles Allen, a veteran of the Greenback and Union Labor parties, who feared the People's party might go the way of its predecessors. He was elected to the 1897 legislature on the fusion ticket.

17. *Oklahoma City Oklahoma Champion* as quoted in the *Guthrie Oklahoma Representative,* February 17, March 26, 1896.

18. *Enid Coming Events,* June 11, April 2, 1896; *Tecumseh Leader* as quoted in the *Guthrie Oklahoma Representative,* March 5, 1896.

19. Norbert R. Mahnken, "Bryan Country," in Paul W. Glad, ed., *William Jennings Bryan: A Profile* (New York: Hill & Wang, 1968), 136–37; James F. Morgan, "William

Cary Renfrow," 50; *Alva Chronicle*, May 3, 10, 1895; *Guthrie Weekly Oklahoma Leader*, May 16, 1895.

20. Harvey explained later that his wife had suddenly become ill.

21. *Oklahoma City Daily Times-Journal*, June 26, 1896; *Guthrie Weekly Oklahoma Leader*, June 27, 1896; *Norman State Democrat*, June 29, 1896. Democratic papers such as the *Oklahoma City Daily Oklahoman* and the *Norman State Democrat* notably failed to mention Vincent's appointment, which seemed rather insignificant considering that he was the chairman of the territory's largest free-silver party. *Oklahoma City Daily Oklahoman*, June 26, 1896; *Norman State Democrat*, June 29, 1896; *Norman Transcript*, June 28, 1896.

22. *Norman State Democrat*, June 19, July 3, 1896; *El Reno Industrial Headlight*, June 20, 1896; *Enid Coming Events*, August 8, 1896.

23. *Guthrie Weekly Oklahoma Leader*, May 28, 1896.

24. Ibid. Nagle was a lawyer.

25. Ibid. Ironically, Nagle reversed his opinions in the twentieth century. In 1914 he became the Socialist party's candidate for U.S. Senator from Oklahoma.

26. Ibid.; *Enid Coming Events*, April 2, 1896.

27. Oklahoma Democrats favored Senator Richard ("Silver Dick") Bland of Missouri for the 1896 presidential nomination. *Silver Knight* as quoted in the *Norman Peoples Voice*, May 22, 1896; *Alva Republican*, June 26, 1896; *Alva Pioneer* July 3, 1896.

28. *Payne County Populist*, January 4, 1895.

29. Two of the townships had returned Populist majorities in the three-way race.

30. Enid was the Oklahoma Territory's third-largest city in 1896.

31. The two townships were Hickory, in Grant County, and Cedar Valley, in Blaine County.

32. *Guthrie Oklahoma Representative*, December 5, 1895; *Norman Peoples Voice*, August 14, 21, 1896; *Guthrie Weekly Oklahoma State Capital*, November 12, 1894; *Enid Coming Events*, August 6, 1896; *Chandler Publicist*, July 24, 1896; *Payne County Populist*, as quoted in the *Guthrie Oklahoma Representative*, August 27, 1896.

33. *Enid Coming Events*, November 28, 1895. Greer reputedly was a large holder of county warrants. The value of taxable property in the Oklahoma Territory rose from $19,947,922.86 in 1894 to $39,275,189.21 in 1895. Secretary of the Interior, *Report of the Governor of Oklahoma*, 54th Cong., 1st sess., vol. 16 (ser. 3383, August 28, 1895), 515.

34. *Norman Peoples Voice*, November 22, December 20, 1895, June 26, 1896; *Alva Republican*, April 17, 1896; *Guthrie Oklahoma Representative*, April 9, 1896; *Guthrie Oklahoma State Capital* as quoted in the *Guthrie Oklahoma Representative*, April 23, 1896; *Guthrie Oklahoma Representative*, August 13, 1896.

35. *Guthrie Oklahoma Representative*, June 11, 1896; *Enid Coming Events*, June 11, 1896; *Norman Peoples Voice*, December 20, 1895; *Guthrie Oklahoma Representative*, May 14, 1896.

36. *Norman Peoples Voice*, May 29, 1896; *Guthrie Weekly Oklahoma Leader*, May 28, 1896. The vote on endorsing Bland was 125 to 123. Many Democrats believed an uninstructed delegation could secure more for Oklahoma.

37. *Norman Peoples Voice*, May 29, June 5, 1896; *Enid Coming Events*, June 4, 1896; *Guthrie Oklahoma Representative*, June 4, 1896.

38. The People's party in the Indian Territory was finally organized at this time for the purpose of sending representatives to the Saint Louis convention. Since whites were ineligible for office in the Indian Territory, the Farmers' Alliance had not developed into the People's party there. *Guthrie Oklahoma Representative*, June 11, 1896.

39. Ibid., May 29, 1896.

40. *Enid Coming Events*, May 21, 1896; *Alva Review*, May 21, 1896. The Enid convention was moved ahead to May 16 because of scheduling problems with the convention's meeting place.

41. *Norman Peoples Voice* as quoted in the *Guthrie Oklahoma Representative*, June 4, 1896. The vote in the delegate-at-large election was forty-five for Hickok and forty-four for Vincent.

42. *Watonga Condor* as quoted in the *Guthrie Oklahoma Representative*, June 4, 1896. The U.S. Supreme Court ruled that Greer County was part of Oklahoma in 1896. It was formerly considered part of Texas, where middle-of-the-roaders were strong. Bray won the alternate slot by only five votes.

43. *Guthrie Oklahoma Representative*, July 9, 1896; *El Reno Industrial Headlight* as quoted in the *Norman Peoples Voice*, July 9, 1896.

44. *Chandler Publicist*, July 17, 1896; *Oklahoma City Oklahoma Champion* as quoted in the *Guthrie Oklahoma Representative*, July 23, 1896; *Enid Coming Events*, July 16, 1896; *Guthrie Oklahoma Representative*, July 16, 1896.

45. The Republican national platform actually called for bimetallism through international agreement, which Populists considered a dodge.

46. Republicans, of course, attributed what prosperity the nation had seen since 1861 to the protective tariff. *Guthrie Oklahoma Representative*, July 16, 1896; *Norman Peoples Voice* as quoted in the *Guthrie Oklahoma Representative*, July 30, 1896.

47. *Saint Louis Republic*, July 24, 1896.

48. Ibid., July 25, 26, 1896.

49. *Houston Post*, July 25, 1896; Kirk Harold Porter and Donald Bruce Johnson, comps., *National Party Platforms, 1840–1960* (Urbana: University of Illinois Press, 1961), 105; *Nebraska State Journal* (Omaha), July 26, 1896.

50. *Guthrie Oklahoma Representative*, September 10, 1896.

51. *Norman Peoples Voice*, August 14, 1896.

52. Ibid.

53. *Guthrie Weekly Oklahoma Leader*, August 6, 1896.

54. Ibid.

55. Cromwell received forty-two votes to Callahan's forty-one on the second ballot.

56. *Guthrie Weekly Oklahoma Leader*, August 6, 1896; *Norman Peoples Voice*, August 7, 1896.

57. Elmer L. Fraker, "The Election of J. Y. Callahan," *Chronicles of Oklahoma* 33, no. 3 (Autumn, 1955): 353; *Guthrie Oklahoma Leader*, August 6, 1896; *Kingfisher Reformer*, November 18, 1894. Fraker interviewed Callahan's daughter for this article and claims Callahan left the Republican party in 1888. But the article contains so many other factual errors that this may not be true.

58. *Chandler Publicist*, August 7, 1896; *Alva Republican*, August 14, 1896; *Guthrie Weekly Oklahoma Leader*, August 6, 1896; *Guthrie Oklahoma Representative*, July 30, 1896. A fusion arrangement was secured in Garfield County even before the Populists' territorial convention. In Logan County fusion was arranged immediately after the convention.

59. *McMaster's Weekly* as quoted in the *Norman Peoples Voice*, July 24, 1896; *Norman Peoples Voice*, August 21, 1896; *Norman State Democrat*, August 13, 1896.

60. *Chandler Publicist*, August 28, 1896; *Norman Peoples Voice*, August 28, 1896.

61. *Alva Pioneer*, July 31, 1896; *Norman State Democrat*, September 10, 1896; *Norman Peoples Voice*, September 11, 1896.

62. *Norman Peoples Voice*, September 11, 1896; *Norman State Democrat*, September 10, 1896.

63. *Norman State Democrat*, September 10, 1896.

64. *Norman Peoples Voice*, September 11, 1896; *Norman State Democrat*, September 10, 1896.

65. *Guthrie Weekly Oklahoma Leader*, September 10, 17, 1896; *Norman Peoples Voice*, September 11, 1896.

66. *Guthrie Weekly Oklahoma Leader*, September 24, 1896; *Norman Peoples Voice*, October 2, 1896; *Guthrie Oklahoma Representative*, October 29, 1896; Elmer Fraker, "The Spread of Populism into the Oklahoma Territory" (Master's thesis, University of Oklahoma, 1938), 57–58; *Guthrie Oklahoma Representative*, August 27, 1896; *Norman Peoples Voice*, October 16, 1896; *Alva Republican*, August 14, 1896.

67. *Guthrie Weekly Oklahoma Leader*, November 12, 1896; *Norman State Democrat*, October 29, September 10, 1896. Other Democratic newspapers that refused to endorse Callahan were the *Noble County Sentinel* (Perry), the *Shawnee Chief*, and the *Yukon Weekly*.

68. *Guthrie Weekly Oklahoma Leader*, November 26, 1896; *Alva Republican*, November 22, 1896. In House district no. 26, which included Beaver and Woodward counties in far-western Oklahoma, an independent candidacy appeared, but a straight Democrat won a plurality victory. No Free Silver or Populist candidates appeared in this ranching district.

69. The official vote in the delegate race was 27,435 for Callahan to 26,267 for Flynn.

70. *Norman Transcript*, November 13, 1896; *Arapahoe Bee*, November 6, 1896.

71. *Oklahoma City Oklahoma Champion* as quoted in the *Guthrie Oklahoma Representative*, December 3, 1896; *Chandler Publicist*, December 4, 1896.

CHAPTER NINE

1. *Guthrie Oklahoma Representative*, January 14, 1897; *Guthrie Weekly Oklahoma Leader*, January 14, 1897.

2. Seventeen Populists and fourteen Democrats were elected on fusion tickets.

3. Three of the winners (a Democrat and two Republicans) defeated Populist candidates by less than twenty votes.

4. *Guthrie Oklahoma Representative*, January 28, 1897.

5. J. C. Tousley, editor of the *El Reno Industrial Headlight*, was the only Populist legislator in the fourth assembly to reside in a railhead town.

6. Populist Thomas Willis was studying for the bar at the time of the 1897 session but took his exams after adjournment.

7. Levi M. St. Clair listed his occupation as a stock raiser, which usually meant rancher. As a child he had known Abraham Lincoln personally, which may account for his commitment to neorepublicanism. *Guthrie Weekly Oklahoma Leader*, March 4, 1897.

8. *Guthrie Oklahoma Representative*, January 7, 1897, December 3, 31, 1896; *Guthrie Weekly Oklahoma Leader*, December 24, 1896; *Norman Peoples Voice*, January 8, 1897. Cleveland County Democrats ignored the territorial fusion agreement that accorded Allan a second term in the council and narrowly defeated him in a three-way race.

9. *Guthrie Weekly Oklahoma Leader*, December 24, 1896; *Norman Peoples Voice* as quoted in the *Norman State Democrat*, July 30, 1896.

10. *Guthrie Oklahoma Representative*, October 15, 1896, January 14, 28, 1897.

11. Ibid., January 28, 1896. Ralph Bray and N. S. Mounts proved to be Vincent's most vocal critics. Bray even denied that Vincent was chairman of the People's party, stat-

ing that he had been superseded by Virgil Hobbs when the Democrat was named chairman of the Free-Silver party. *Enid Coming Events*, February 4, 1897.

12. *Guthrie Weekly Oklahoma Leader*, January 21, 1897; *Guthrie Oklahoma Representative*, January 28, February 11, March 19, 1897; *Norman Peoples Voice*, March 19, 1896; *Guthrie Weekly Oklahoma Leader*, February 25, 1897; *Journal of the Council Proceedings of the Fourth Legislative Assembly of the Territory of Oklahoma: Beginning January 12, 1897* (Guthrie: Leader Publishing Co., 1897): 1320, 1328. On final passage of the bill abolishing the office of oil inspector, three of the five Populists present in the council abstained. *Journal of the Council Proceedings* (1897), 1371.

13. *Journal of the House Proceedings of the Fourth Legislative Assembly of the Territory of Oklahoma: Beginning January 12, 1897* (Guthrie: Leader Publishing Co., 1897), 1143, 1148; *Journal of the Council Proceedings* (1897), 1322; *Guthrie Weekly Oklahoma Leader*, January 21, 1897; *Guthrie Oklahoma Representative*, January 28, February 4, 18, March 18, 1897; *Enid Coming Events*, February 25, 1897.

14. *Journal of the Council Proceedings* (1897), 1129–32, 1371; *Guthrie Weekly Oklahoma Leader*, January 21, 1897; *Journal of the House Proceedings* (1897), 1090–91; *Guthrie Oklahoma Representative*, January 14, 18, 1897; *Norman Peoples Voice*, January 22, 1897.

15. One of the two Democrats was Henry Steele Johnson, who voted with the third party more often than with the Democrats in the 1897 assembly. *Journal of the Council Proceedings* (1897), 1371–71.

16. Ibid., 1371–72; *Guthrie Oklahoma Representative*, February 4, 11, 1897; *Journal of the House Proceedings* (1897), 1192–93; *Guthrie Weekly Oklahoma Leader*, February 4, 11, 1897; *Norman Peoples Voice*, February 5, 1897.

17. *Journal of the Council Proceedings* (1897), 1371; *Journal of the House Proceedings* (1897), 1192–93; *Guthrie Weekly Oklahoma Leader*, February 25, 1897; *Guthrie Oklahoma Representative*, February 18, 25, 1897.

18. W. A. Turner was the Free Silver candidate for the Guthrie house seat in 1896. *Guthrie Oklahoma Representative*, February 25, March 4, 11, 1897.

19. The fee-and-salary bill that passed the house and eventually became law removed the pauper provisions for the witness fees and put a ceiling on the total fees an official could earn. The salaries and fees, however, remained much as they had been before. *Norman Peoples Voice*, March 5, 1897.

20. *Guthrie Weekly Oklahoma Leader*, March 25, 1897; *Alva Republican*, January 29, 1897; *Guthrie Weekly Oklahoma Leader*, March 4, 18, 1897. Although a Populist introduced the Alva college bill, voting on the measure was largely along regional rather than party lines.

21. *Guthrie Weekly Oklahoma Leader*, March 18, 1897; *Guthrie Oklahoma Representative*, March 18, 1897; *Alva Republican*, February 26, 1897.

22. The election law abolished the use of devices on ballots, arranged names in a single column under each office and alternated the order of candidates by party for each office.

23. The antifusion law of 1895 may have been a factor in the reduced voter turnout of 1896. Some scholars attribute much of the reduced voter participation of the twentieth century to legal manipulation. In Oklahoma, however, removal of the antifusion legislation did not reverse the trend toward lower voter participation. Voter turnout in Oklahoma in 1898 was significantly lower than it was in either 1896 or 1894, despite the repeal of the 1895 antifusion law. A bibliography of the debate over legal manipulation of the voting process, along with a discussion of antifusion legislation, can be found in Peter H. Argersinger, "'A Place on the Ballot': Fusion Politics and Antifusion Laws," *American Historical Review* 85, no. 2 (April, 1980): 287–306.

24. *Guthrie Weekly Oklahoma Leader*, March 18, 1897; *Alva Republican*, April 2, 1897;

Journal of the House Proceedings (1897), 1192–93; *Journal of the Council Proceedings* (1897), 1371, 1373.

25. *Guthrie Weekly Oklahoma Leader*, March 11, 1897; *Enid Coming Events*, April 8, 1897; *Guthrie Daily Oklahoma Leader*, March 25, 1897; *Alva Pioneer*, March 26, 1897. Appropriations from the third legislature (1895) totaled $170,896, while the fourth legislature (1897) appropriated $150,322.

26. *Lexington Leader* as quoted in the *Norman Peoples Voice*, March 19, 1897; *Alva Republican*, March 19, 1897; *Guthrie Oklahoma Representative*, March 18, 1897.

27. *Guthrie Oklahoma Representative*, March 18, 1897.

28. Ibid., March 25, 1897; *Journal of the Council Proceedings* (1897), 1371–73.

29. *Guthrie Oklahoma Representative*, March 18, April 22, 1897.

30. *Chandler Publicist*, April 30, 1897; *Report of the Governor of Oklahoma*, 55th Cong., 2d sess (ser. 3642, July 1, 1897), 557.

31. *Guthrie Oklahoma Representative*, March 25, April 1, 1897.

CHAPTER TEN

1. *Guthrie Oklahoma Representative*, April 8, 1897.

2. Ibid.

3. Ibid.

4. Ford, "The Invincible Vincents," 36. Evidence that Colorado was already on Vincent's mind came in the form of small filler on the editorial page of the edition that contained his resignation letter. Vincent identified Colorado as "one of the most progressive states" and noted that it had woman suffrage and had abolished capital punishment. *Guthrie Oklahoma Representative*, April 8, 1897.

5. *Guthrie Daily Oklahoma State Capital* as quoted in the *Guthrie Oklahoma Representative*, April 15, 1897.

6. *Guthrie Daily Oklahoma Leader* as quoted in the *Guthrie Oklahoma Representative*, April 15, 1897.

7. *Alva Review* as quoted in the *Guthrie Oklahoma Representative*, April 22, 1897. It was not uncommon for Democratic and fusion Populist editors to run endorsements of Bryan for president in 1900 in the wake of his 1896 defeat. This was a way of reaffirming their loyalty to the "Great Commoner" even in defeat.

8. *Norman Peoples Voice* as quoted in the *Guthrie Oklahoma Representative*, April 22, 1897.

9. *Guthrie Oklahoma Representative*, April 8, 15, 1897.

10. *Guthrie Weekly Oklahoma Leader*, April 22, 1897; *Guthrie Oklahoma Representative*, April 29, July 8, 15, 1897.

11. *Oklahoma City Oklahoma Champion*, March 11, May 13, 1898.

12. *Norman Peoples Voice*, July 15, 1898; *Oklahoma City Oklahoma Champion*, July 15, 1898; *Norman Transcript*, July 15, 1898; *Blackwell Times-Record*, July 21, 1898.

13. *Alva Pioneer* as quoted in the *Chandler Publicist*, September 16, 1898; Dennis Flynn, "Memoir," 40–41, Royden Dangerfield Papers, Western History Collections, University of Oklahoma.

14. The Populist correlations with urban residence in the three-way Cleveland County council and house races, however, were typically negative. *Norman Transcript*, November 11, 1900.

15. Only one of the men who served in the 1897 legislature was reelected in 1898. Democrat Thomas Doyle of Perry, in Noble County, won in a three-way race.

16. Both fusion and middle-of-the-road tickets appeared in three house and two council districts (in Lincoln, Logan, and Payne counties). A fusion Democrat won one seat, and Republicans carried four. Six of the eight three-way races without fusion candidates occured in predominantly southern-populated areas. Democrats won five, Populists two, and the GOP one.

17. *Norman Transcript*, November 11, 1898.

18. *Alva Review*, April 12, 1900; *Guthrie Weekly Oklahoma State Capital*, April 12, 1900; *Norman Peoples Voice*, April 13, August 3, 1900; *Oklahoma City Daily Oklahoman*, September 2, 1900.

19. *Transactions of the Kansas State Historical Society, Embracing the Fifth and Sixth Biennial Reports: 1886–1888* (1890): 222. Neff is listed as the editor of the *Wichita Weekly Express*, a Union Labor paper, in a January, 1889, survey.

20. Populists elected four fusionists to the house and two fusionists and one middle-of-the-roader to the council. Democrats, on the other hand, elected three fusionists and three straight Democrats to the house and four fusionists and one straight candidate to the council.

21. *Alva Review*, January 17, 1901; *Norman Peoples Voice*, March 8, 1901.

22. *Alva Review*, March 27, 1902. The vote in the 1902 delegate race was 45,803 for Republican McGuire and 45,499 for Democrat Cross. Middle-of-the-roaders did field a delegate candidate, H. E. Straughen, in 1904. He received only 1.7 percent of the vote, and his vote shows none of the correlations common to the votes for earlier third-party candidates.

23. Green, *Grass-Roots Socialism*, 13–14; *Appeal to Reason* (Girard, Kansas), September 5, 1903.

24. *Guthrie Weekly Oklahoma Leader*, June 24, 1897.

25. *Dallas Southern Mercury* as quoted in the *Norman Peoples Voice*, July 27, 1900; *Norman Peoples Voice*, December 28, 1900.

26. Stafford brought his old partner, Clark Hudson, back to Oklahoma City to edit the *Daily Oklahoman* in 1902. *Oklahoma City Weekly Oklahoman and Champion*, March 29, 1900; Walter M. Harrison, *Me and My Big Mouth* (Oklahoma City: Britton Publishing Co., 1954), 52–53.

27. *El Reno News*, December 16, 1898; *Norman Peoples Voice*, October 27, 1899, February 16, 1900; *Oklahoma City Daily Oklahoman*, September 2, 1900. Smith received 2 percent of the vote in 1900.

28. Crocker, "Autobiography," 375; Peery, "Colonel Crocker," 276.

29. *Biographical Record*, 282.

30. *Norman Transcript*, August 27, 1939; Runyun, ed., *Pioneers of Cleveland County*, 11–13; Ayer, *American Newspaper Annual* (1911), 765. The *Peoples Voice* was renamed the *Cleveland County Enterprise* by its new editor, but it was still listed as a Populist paper in the 1911 edition of the *American Newspaper Annual*. A few broadsides and information about speaking engagements during Thomas P. Gore's 1922 campaign can be found in the Allan papers, which are in the possession of his daughter Mrs. Marjorie Lenore Allan Garrett, of El Reno, Oklahoma.

31. Ford, "The Invincible Vincents," 36–37.

32. Piehler, "Henry Vincent: A Case Study," 215; Mary Vincent Cummings, "Memories of Girard, Debs and Me," 1–10 (manuscript in the posession of Vincent's granddaughter Merrily Cummings Ford, of Glendora, California). Harold Piehler, "Henry Vincent: Kansas Populist," 25; Vincent, "Henry Sez," 4.

CHAPTER ELEVEN

1. The Organic Act, which opened Oklahoma to non-Indian settlement, provided for the secret ballot, which Populists elsewhere had also endorsed.

2. This assessment is based on the nomination and support for middle-of-the-road and fusionist candidates for the territorial legislature rather than on voting in the race for delegate to Congress. Neither the 1898 nor the 1900 middle-of-the-road delegate nominee mounted an active campaign. The two most notable exceptions were northern-born middle-of-the-roaders E. H. Spencer and John Allan. Allan, however, served an overwhelmingly southern-born constituency.

Bibliographical Essay

Manuscript Collections

The major reason Oklahoma Populism has been largely neglected as a field of research is the dearth of pertinent manuscript materials. Henry Vincent's granddaughter, Merrily Cummings Ford of Glendora, California, possesses several typescripts useful on the Kansas origins of Oklahoma Populism, namely, Henry Vincent's "Henry Sez" (ca. 1931) and Leo Vincent's family biographies, which Ford compiled under the title "The Invincible Vincents" (1939). Samuel Crocker's autobiography, which was written in pencil but later typed under the direction of Royden Dangerfield, of the University of Oklahoma, contains much useful information on the author's activities as an egalitarian spokesman both in the Oklahoma Boomer movement and later as a Populist leader. Although the manuscript was never published, it is located in the book collection of the Oklahoma Historical Society, in Oklahoma City.

The Royden Dangerfield Papers, in the Western History Collections of the University of Oklahoma, also contain a number of interesting and useful typescripts, particularly Dennis Flynn's short "Memoir." The Western History Collections also hold the Sidney Clarke Papers, which contain significant information on his activities in the Boomer movement and his effort to be appointed governor of the Oklahoma Territory in 1893. The Interior Department's Territorial Papers (1889–1912), which are on microfilm at the Western History Collections, University of Oklahoma, also contain a limited amount of useful information about politics in the territorial period. The papers of Frederick S. Barde and Fred L. Wenner, in the Oklahoma Historical Society, and Leslie P. Ross and Milton L. Turner, in the Western History Collections of the University of Oklaoma, also contain information on major-party affairs in the territorial era, but little on Populism.

Newspapers

Because individual Populists left so few resources for historians and because it took less than $150 to establish a small newspaper in the 1890s, most studies on the People's party rely heavily upon the period's highly partisan press. Students of Oklahoma history are blessed with one of the finest state newspaper collections in the nation. The Oklahoma Press Association founded the Oklahoma Historical Society in 1893. Since that date the society has been on the exchange lists of most Oklahoma papers. Although many papers published between 1889 and mid-1893 have been lost, the society holds almost every edition of most papers published in Oklahoma after mid-1893. Those from the pre–World War I period are now all on microfilm.

Most nineteenth-century newspapers rejected the charade of nonpartisanship prevalent in America today and openly represented the viewpoint of a political party, much as present-day European papers do. In the 1890s most of Oklahoma's major towns had at least three newspapers, one for each active party. Frank Greer's *Guthrie Oklahoma State Capital* was the territorial mouthpiece of the Republican party. Because Guthrie was the territorial capital and the GOP the largest party in the territorial days, and because most editions of Greer's paper, even between 1889 and 1893, have survived, it is the most useful source on Oklahoma politics in the 1890s. Its Democratic counterpart was Roy Hoffman's *Guthrie Oklahoma Leader*. Both the *State Capital* and the *Leader* appeared in daily and weekly editions. Because the weekly versions were normally compilations of the previous week's daily editions for farmers, most information about Populism can be found in the weekly editions. Populists sponsored a series of weekly newspapers in Guthrie beginning with the *Oklahoma State Journal* in 1890. No copies of this paper are known to exist. The *Guthrie West and South* succeeded the *Journal* in 1891 and was, in turn, succeeded by Leo Vincent's *Oklahoma Representative* in 1894 and the fusionist *Oklahoma State Register* in 1898. John S. Allan's *Norman Peoples Voice*, which first appeared in 1892, was the most notable third-party paper in southern Oklahoma. Its Democratic and Republican rivals were the *Norman State Democrat* and the *Norman Transcript*, respectively. Other Populist newspapers of note were the *Payne County Populist* (Stillwater), *Alva Review*, *El Reno Populist Platform* (which was renamed the *Industrial Headlight* in 1895), *Kingfisher Reformer*, *Enid Coming Events*, *Chandler Publicist*, and *Tecumseh Leader*. Many of the smaller Populist organs, such as Thomas Smith's *Kay County Populist* (Newkirk), primarily contained "ready-print" articles from larger third-party papers and the Populists' news service, the National Reform Press Association. Most "ready-prints" originated in the Midwest and also appeared in the larger Populist papers, even in southern-dominated areas.

Almost every town that had a Populist paper in the 1890s also had a Democratic and a Republican rival. Information on the partisan affiliation, day of publication, editor, and number of subscribers for each newspaper can be obtained from N. W. Ayer, *American Newspaper Annual* (Philadelphia: N. W. Ayer and Co.). Ayer's also provides useful information on commercial facilities, terrain, and crops.

For information on the southern Kansas origins of the Oklahoma and Kansas People's parties, two newspapers are particularly important. Samuel Crocker's *Oklahoma War Chief* (Arkansas City and Caldwell, Kansas) was the official organ of the Oklahoma Boomer movement. It also contained substantial doses of greenback and antimonopoly propaganda. Henry and Leo Vincent's *American Nonconformist and Kansas Industrial Liberator* (Winfield, Kansas) was relocated to southern Kansas from their southwest Iowa home in 1886 and successively promoted the fortunes of the Greenback, Union Labor, and People's parties. The Vincents moved the paper to Indianapolis in 1891. The *Nonconformist's* Republican rival was Ed Greer's *Winfield Courier.* Ed Greer was the older brother of Frank Greer, the editor of the *Guthrie Oklahoma State Capital.*

Government Documents

The published results of the 1900 U.S. census (U.S. Bureau of the Census, *Twelfth Census of the United States . . . 1900* (Washington, D.C.: U.S. Government Printing Office, 1902)) are far more useful than those of the 1890 U.S. census for determining the agricultural, commercial, and population patterns of the Oklahoma Territory during the Populist era. Because Oklahoma was opened to non-Indian settlement only in 1889 and farmers suffered drought conditions the first two years, patterns derived from the 1900 census are probably more accurate for Oklahoma in 1892 or 1893 than those gleaned from the 1890 census. Oklahoma also contained only seven counties in 1890 (six of which were enlarged in the two succeeding years), while all twenty-three counties listed in the 1900 census were opened to non-Indian settlement by the fall of 1893 (part of Lincoln County was opened in 1895). The most important problem with the 1900 census is its lack of birthplace information on residents of the territory. Geographer Michael Roark, of Southeast Missouri State University, however, was kind enough to furnish me with the results of a 5 percent sample of the 1900 census manuscripts, which he conducted for his Ph.D. dissertation, "Oklahoma Territory: Frontier Development, Migration and Culture Areas" (Syracuse University, 1979).

Each annual *Report of the Governor of Oklahoma* to the secretary of the interior contains the biennial territorial census used for redistricting the Oklahoma legislature during the territorial period and a tabulation of the value of taxable property. Although the population information is highly useful, property values taken from this source must be used carefully. The land of homesteaders was not taxable for the first five years of residence. The governor's report also contains information on transportation, commerce, and government expenses. The house and council Journals for all but the first legislature contain highly useful tabulations of roll-call votes and action taken on specific bills. The *Journal of the First Session of the Legislative Assembly of the Territory of Oklahoma* (Guthrie: State Capital Printing Co., 1890) combines both the house and council journals without tabulation, and is quite rare. A copy can be found in the legislative library in the capitol building in Oklahoma City.

Farm-commodity prices were secured from several sources. *Oklahoma Agricultural Statistics, 1894–1947,* Miscellaneous Publication MP-14 (Stillwater: Oklahoma Agricultural Experiment Station, 1947), contains some useful data, as does U.S. Bureau of the Census, *Historical Statistics of the United States, Colo-*

nial Times to 1957 (Washington, D.C.: U.S. Government Printing Office, 1960). Data on agriculture can also be found in the Guthrie farm journal, *Home, Field and Forum* (August, 1895), which Populist George Soule edited.

Works Progress Administration (WPA) indexes of turn-of-the-century "mugbook" histories and newspapers are located at the Oklahoma Historical Society in Oklahoma City. These were essential in compiling the collective biography of territorial legislators, as well as for providing useful information on other men prominent in Oklahoma politics in the 1890s. Although the "mug-book" index is quite extensive, the newspaper index contains citations from only a few papers.

Published Primary Sources

There is a substantial amount of published primary material pertinent to the settlement of Oklahoma and territorial days. Dan Peery, "The First Two years," *Chronicles of Oklahoma* (pt. 1) 7, no. 3 (September, 1928): 278–322; (pt. 2) 7, no. 4 (December, 1928): 419–57; (pt. 3) 8, no. 1 (February, 1929): 94–128, provides a vivid portrayal of early Oklahoma and the first legislature. As a Democratic member of the 1890 assembly representing Oklahoma County, Peery was understandably critical of those Populists who deserted Oklahoma City in the capital fight. A more favorable treatment can be found in Marion Tuttle Rock, *Illustrated History of Oklahoma* (Topeka, Kans.: O. B. Hamilton and Son, 1890). Rock was a Populist.

Other useful sources on early Oklahoma local history include E. Bee Guthry, "Early Days in Payne County," *Chronicles of Oklahoma* 3, no. 1 (April, 1925): 74–80, and Irwin Jeffs (Bunky), *The First Eight Months* (Oklahoma City: McMaster Publishing Co., 1890). Guthry was a Cleveland Democrat. Little is known of Jeffs, who left the Territory shortly after the publication of his book. Information on the 1890 legislature also can be obtained from W. H. Merten, "Oklahoma Territory's First Legislature," *Sturm's Oklahoma Magazine* 5, no. 5 (January, 1908): 36–41, and on the 1893 assembly from Leslie P. Ross, "The Second Territorial Legislature," *Sturm's Oklahoma Magazine* 6, no. 2 (May, 1908): 80–82. Both authors were prominent members of the legislatures about which they wrote. Merten was a Republican and Ross a Cleveland Democrat. Perhaps the best primary account of living conditions in the Oklahoma 1890s is Helen Candee, "Social Conditions in Our Newest Territory," *Forum* 25, no. 4 (June, 1898): 426–37. Internal evidence suggests that Candee was a Democrat. W. F. Rightmire, "The Alliance Movement in Kansas—Origins of the People's Party," *Transactions of the Kansas State Historical Society* 9 (1905–1906): 1–8, provides information, some of it inaccurate, on the southern Kansas origins of the People's party.

Between 1888 and 1900, nearly 200 novels of the apocalyptic and utopian variety were published in America. Kenneth M. Roemer, *The Obsolete Necessity: America in Utopian Writings, 1888–1900* (Kent, Ohio: Kent State University, 1976), contains a selective bibliography of 160 such novels. Samuel

Crocker's (Theodore Oceanic Islet), *That Island* (Oklahoma City: C. E. Streeter and Co., 1892), was surely one of the more detailed, and thus boring, of this genre. Crocker wrote his novel specifically for an Oklahoma audience. It maps out the transition of a bountiful island nation (a thinly disguised version of the Populist view of America in the 1890s) from oppressive capitalism to Populism. The transformation occurs in a single day when the masses read a book on political economy written by a genius of old wealth (Crocker was born on an English estate, although he was not wealthy) and distributed by a secret reform group (reminiscent of the Union Labor party's Videttes). The book is useful for discerning the details of how a Populist state might operate and provides insight into the third-party expectation that education would cause a sudden, massive political revolt against those in power. This is useful in understanding the Populist move to fusion in 1896. Crocker was a fusionist.

Secondary Sources on Oklahoma

The most useful general studies of Oklahoma history are H. Wayne Morgan and Anne Hodges Morgan, *Oklahoma: A Bicentennial History* (New York: W. W. Norton & Co., 1977), and Arrell M. Gibson, *Oklahoma: A History of Five Centuries* 2d. ed. (Norman: University of Oklahoma Press, 1981). A number of fine studies exist on the Boomer-rancher conflict that preceded the opening of the Oklahoma Territory to non-Indian settlement. Arrell M. Gibson, editor of Edward Everett Dale, *Frontier Historian: The Life and Work of Edward Everett Dale* (Norman: University of Oklahoma Press, 1975), combines essays on historian Dale, who was a cowboy in the 1890s, and reprints several of Dale's best sketches of cowboy life. Carl Rister, *Land Hunger: David L. Payne and the Boomers* (Norman: University of Oklahoma Press, 1942), still provides valuable insights into the Boomer movement, and Stan Hoig, *David L. Payne: The Oklahoma Boomer* (Oklahoma City: Western Heritage Books, 1980), is useful for the activities of this early boomer leader. William W. Savage, Jr., *The Cherokee Strip Livestock Association: Federal Regulation and the Cattlemen's Last Frontier* (Columbia: University of Missouri Press, 1973), details ranchers' attempts to resist the encroachments of farm interests. Dan W. Peery, "Colonel Crocker and the Boomer Movement," *Chronicles of Oklahoma* 13, no. 3 (September, 1935): 273–95, gleans information from Royden Dangerfield's typescript of Crocker's autobiography. The article downplays Crocker's egalitarian political activities.

There are numerous sources relevant to the settlement and development of Oklahoma. Older studies, such as Solon Buck, "Settlement of Oklahoma," *Transactions of the Wisconsin Academy of Science, Arts and Letters* 15, no. 2 (1907): 325–80, and Gilbert Fite, "Pioneering in West Texas, the Indian Territory, and Oklahoma, 1865–1900," in *The Farmers' Frontier, 1865–1900* (New York: Holt, Rinehart and Winston, 1966; Norman: University of Oklahoma Press, 1987), are still quite useful. Norman Crocket, "The Opening of Oklahoma: A Businessman's Frontier," *Chronicles of Oklahoma* 55, no. 1 (Spring, 1978): 85–95, provides insight into the activities of those scrambling for advantage in the cosmopolitan areas in early Oklahoma. Jerome O. Steffen, "Stages of Development in Oklahoma History," in H. Wayne Morgan and Anne Hodges Morgan, eds., *Oklahoma: New Views of the Forty-sixth State* (Norman: University of Oklahoma Press, 1982), sets the economic development of the Oklahoma Territory in the context of broad national trends. Because Michael Frank Doran's, "The Origin of Culture Areas in Oklahoma, 1830–1900" (Ph.D. diss., University of Oregon, 1974) was completed before the 1900 census manuscripts were opened to scholars, Michael Owen Roark's "Oklahoma Territory: Frontier Development, Migration and Culture Areas" (Ph. D. diss., Syracuse University, 1979) supersedes the older study. Both provide valuable insights into the mingling of cultures in Oklahoma. N. James Wilson, "Oklahoma and Midwestern Farmers in Transition, 1880– 1910," and Donald E. Green, "Beginnings of Wheat Culture in Oklahoma," in Donald E. Green, ed., *Rural Oklahoma* (Oklahoma City: Oklahoma Historical Society, 1977), provide useful studies of the development of agriculture in Oklahoma.

A number of sources deal with political development in the Oklahoma Territory. Most focus at least as much attention on intraparty maneuvering as on interparty conflict. Danney Goble, *Progressive Oklahoma: The Making of a New Kind of State* (Norman: University of Oklahoma Press, 1980), which also provides insightful chapters on settlement and development, is the best. Goble's ideas are also summarized in the opening chapter of James R. Scales and Danney Goble, *Oklahoma Politics: A History* (Norman: University of Oklahoma Press, 1982). Older studies, such as Dora Ann Stewart, *The Government and Development of the Oklahoma Territory* (Norman: University of Oklahoma Press, 1933), and Roy Gittinger, *The Formation of the State of Oklahoma, 1803–1906* (Norman: University of Oklahoma Press, 1942), are also useful. *Chronicles of Oklahoma* 53, no. 1 (Spring, 1975), contains biographies of each of the territorial governors. Most are quite good. Other works valuable to the study of territorial politics are George Eldon Norvell, "A History of the First legislative Assembly of the territory of Oklahoma" (Master's thesis, University of Oklahoma, 1946); Eldon L. Clemance, "A History of the Democratic Party in Oklahoma Territory" (Master's thesis, Oklahoma State University, 1966); and Victor Murdock, "Dennis T. Flynn," *Chronicles of Oklahoma* 16, no. 2 (June, 1940): 106–13. Glen Shirley, *Temple Houston, Lawyer with a Gun* (Norman: University of Oklahoma Press, 1980), provides insight into the life and character of a prominent Cleveland Democrat. Berlin Chapman, "The Enid 'Railroad War:' An Archival Study," *Chronicles of Oklahoma* 43, no. 2 (Summer, 1965): 126– 79, is a definitive study of this important subject.

The best secondary source on the Kansas Origins of Oklahoma Populism is Harold Richard Piehler, "Henry Vincent: A Case Study in Political Deviancy," (Ph. D. diss., University of Kansas, 1971). Piehler summarizes his findings on Vincent's Kansas sojourn in Harold Piehler, "Henry Vincent: Kansas Populist and Radical-Reform Journalist," *Kansas History* 2, no. 1 (Spring, 1979): 14–25. Charles Richard Denton, "The American Nonconformist and Kansas Industrial Liberator: A Union Labor-Populist Newspaper, 1886–1891" (Master's thesis, Kansas State College of Pittsburg, 1961), also provides some interesting information. James R. Shaber, "An Interpretation of the Agrarian Reform Movement in Oklahoma from 1890–1923" (Master's thesis, University of Tulsa, 1959) is based largely upon secondary materials. John Edward Thompson, *Closing the Frontier: Radical Response in Oklahoma, 1889–1923* (Norman and London: University of Oklahoma Press, 1986), provides an interesting contrast between radical and reform oriented agrarian political expression.

Secondary works on Oklahoma Populism are thin and sometimes inaccurate. Elmer Fraker, "The Spread of Populism into the Oklahoma Territory" (Master's thesis, University of Oklahoma, 1938), is based mostly upon secondary materials. Elmer L. Fraker, "The Election of J. Y. Callahan," *Chronicles of Oklahoma* 33, no. 3 (Autumn, 1955): 350–59, benefits from an interview with the subject's daughter, but is so riddled with factual errors that it must be considered unreliable. Donald K. Pickens, "Oklahoma Populism and Historical Perspective," *Chronicles of Oklahoma* 43, no. 4 (August, 1965): 275–83, assesses the validity of Richard Hofstadter's *The Age of Reform: Bryan to F. D. R.* (New York: Alfred A. Knopf, 1955) in the Oklahoma context and rightfully contends that the findings of C. Vann Woodward, Norman Pollack, and Walter T. K. Nugent are more applicable. Pickens also contends that middle-of-the-roaders moved into the Socialist party after the turn of the century. At least two of the five examples he presents (Bray and Smith), however, were fusionists.

H. L. Meredith, "The Agrarian Reform Press in Oklahoma," *Chronicles of Oklahoma* 50, no. 2 (Spring, 1972): 82–94, provides useful information on the operation of several Populist newspapers, and his "The 'Middle Way,' The Farmers' Alliance in the Indian Territory, 1889–1896," *Chronicles of Oklahoma* 47, no. 4 (Winter, 1969–1970): 377–87, is a useful study. His contention that a leadership decision, rather than the lack of elections, prevented the formation of a Populist party in the Indian Territory, however, is debatable. Terry Paul Wilson, "The Demise of Populism in Oklahoma Territory," *Chronicles of Oklahoma* 43, no. 3 (Autumn, 1965): 365–74, fails to recognize the significance of the 1896 Free Silver ticket as a means of circumventing the antifusion law. He rightfully attributed fusion to economic desperation, the free-silver panacea, and a penchant for pseudoreligious causes but neglects causes more specific to Oklahoma, such as the doubling of taxes and the Republican gerrymander of 1895. He also inaccurately assumes that southern-born Populists returned to the Democratic party immediately after 1896.

Secondary Sources on American Populism

The secondary materials available on American Populism are both extensive and quite diverse. As with all other historical subjects, interpretations have varied with the environments in which they were produced. In the 1890s, eastern-oriented scholars largely dominated American historical writing and gave agrarian unrest little attention. When they did focus on the protest movements of the Great Plains and the South, they were usually either condescending or openly hostile. The earliest scholarly work on Populism is Frank Le Rond McVey, "The Populist Movement," *American Economic Association: Economic Studies* 1, no. 3 (August, 1896): 131–209. McVey believed that Populism was a response to the problems of industrialism and pointed to nine planks in the third party's platform that he labeled socialistic. He disapproved of this paternalistic policy and contended that Populism was rooted in the past. He did, however, acknowledge that it was the American past from which Populists drew their inspiration.

At the time Populism focused attention on the South and the West, a number of young scholars from the affected regions were beginning their careers. Frederick Jackson Turner became the most notable historian of the Progressive generation. Very much in the mode of the Populists, Progressive historians tended to recast American history in a series of dualisms roughly paralleling the "people" versus "interests" struggle they associated with their own era. Sometimes they saw struggles between sections, such as North versus South during the Civil War and Reconstruction. The conflict of the Populist era, however, was between East and West, with the South joining the latter. Usually such sectional dichotomies only represented deeper economic cleavages. Themes such as city versus country, farmers versus businessmen (with workers as a swing vote), human rights versus property rights, and Hamiltonianism versus Jeffersonianism pervaded the works of these writers.

Turner perceived Populism in just such sectional and, at base, economic terms. He believed that the continual advance of settlement across the American landscape established a series of frontier situations that rejuvenated American society along egalitarian lines and accounted for the continuing uniqueness of America's democratic development. For Turner, the frontier acted as a safety valve, allowing the nation to avoid unrest from the elements that had lost out in the struggle for economic independence in more developed regions. In "The Problem of the West," *Atlantic Monthly* 78 (September, 1896): 289–97, Turner interpreted Populism as the backwash of egalitarian traditions that occurred when the frontier closed and the safety valve disappeared. Populism, thus, was a product of the frontier rather than of industrialization. Because the frontier had closed, Turner forecast a tumultuous future for America, which in a sense can be considered a milder form of the Populists' own apocalyptic vision of the future. The best example of the Populists' apocalyptic view of society is Edmund Boisgilbert (Ignatius Donnelly), *Caesar's Column: A Story of the Twentieth Century* (Chicago: F. J. Schulte, 1890). Donnelly also wrote the preamble to the Omaha platform, the bible of Populism.

Progressive historians vaguely associated democracy with the western frontier and discovered a series of conflicts pitting the regenerate West against the entrenched economic privilege of the East and stretching all the way back to colonial times, thus giving depth and historical meaning to the conflicts of their own day. This produced a rough association in the minds of Progressive historians between the reform movements of the past and progressivism. Solon Buck's textbookish *Granger Movement* (Cambridge, Mass.: Harvard University Press, 1913) and *Agrarian Crusade* (New Haven, Conn.: Yale University Press,

1920), for instance, proclaimed the Populists pioneers in the field of social politics and precursors of progressivism.

For Vernon Louis Parrington, professor of American and English literature, the battle of the 1890s was between the ideals of Jeffersonian democracy and the aggressive entrepreneurship of Gilded Age capitalism. In *Main Currents in American Thought: The Beginnings of Critical Realism in America: 1860–1920* (New York: Harcourt, Brace, and World, 1930; Norman: University of Oklahoma Press, 1987), Parrington found the Populists drenched in Jeffersonian and Jacksonian sentiments, consciously seeking to create the political machinery necessary for democracy to withstand the shock of the Industrial Revolution. For Parrington, creative political thinking in the late nineteenth century was largely western and agrarian. He freely acknowledged that the movement spoke for an older America that feared rising plutocracy. Populists were idealists who drew their inspiration from the Declaration of Independence. Their great objective, according to Parrington, was to place human rights above those of property.

The Progressive historians' magnum opus on Populism came in 1931 with John D. Hicks's *The Populist Revolt: A History of the Farmers' Alliance and the People's Party* (Minneapolis: University of Minnesota Press, 1931). For Hicks, Populism was primarily interest-group politics, with have-nots demanding their fair share of the nation's bounty. Their grievances were numerous and real. Financial manipulations, deflation, high interest, mortgage foreclosures, unfair railroad practices, and a high protective tariff impoverished the farmer. Corruption accounted for their economic hardship, and replacing plutocratic rule with popular control of government was the solution.

Like Turner, his mentor, Hicks was a midwesterner and tended to overstress the role of his section. When the depression of the 1930s finally undermined the promises of New South boosters, young scholars from this section began domesticating the Progressive interpretation for their own region. C. Vann Woodward, in *Tom Watson, Agrarian Rebel* (New York: Macmillan and Co., 1938), presented the Progressive interpretation of southern Populism and laid the groundwork for his greatest work, *Origins of the New South* (Baton Rouge: Louisiana State Unversity Press, 1951). Woodward contended that the strife of the 1890s was not only sectional but also between farm and industry within the South. He found his hero of southern liberalism in Tom Watson, who resisted the racism of his era and attempted to unite blacks and poor whites in a political coalition of economic interests. For Woodward, the conflict was between the "classes" and the "masses." He presented Populists as forward-looking and rational, attempting to create a better society out of the industrialization process. For Woodward, as for the Populists, economics was the battleground, but morality was the issue. Woodward's scholarly approach, however, allowed the expression of disapproval only through the subtle medium of irony. A prime example is his recounting of the story of the defeated and disillusioned Tom Watson turning the "nigger question" on his enemies and routing them in the new century, but with disastrous consequences for southern race relations.

There are a number of usable state studies in the Progressive tradition. Roscoe C. Martin, *The People's Party in Texas* (Austin: University of Texas Press, 1933), is the effort of a political scientist who found support for the People's party strongest among whites located on poor farmland. William Dubose Sheldon, *Populism in the Old Dominion: Virginia Farm Politics, 1885–1900* (Princeton, N.J.: Princeton University Press, 1935), presented Populists as progressive egalitarians who thought of themselves as the inheritors of the "Spirit of 1776." Albert D. Kirwin, *The Revolt of the Rednecks, Mississippi Politics, 1876–1925* (Lexington: University of Kentucky Press, 1951), cast the Populist revolt in the form of class conflict. William Ivy Hair, *Bourbonism and Agrarianism* (Baton Rouge: Louisiana State University Press, 1969), showed how Bourbon elements crushed biracial agrarianism in Louisiana. William Warren Rogers, *One-Gallused Rebellion: Agrarianism in Alabama, 1865–1896* (Baton Rouge: Louisiana State University Press, 1970), presented the third-party effort as a progressive reaction to economic distress, which sought to achieve permanent benefits for poor blacks and whites.

As the nation passed through the crucible of the Great Depression and the New Deal, a spirit of reform swept through academia, even infiltrating the Northeast. The role of ideology in mobilizing the masses also seemed to gain importance in the 1930s and 1940s with the rise of Adolf Hitler. Not surprisingly, an eastern scholar found intellectual origins from his own region to the economic and political ferment of the South and West in the 1890s. Chester McArthur Destler, *American Radicalism, 1865–1901* (New London: Connecticut College Press, 1946), uncovered radical eastern urban roots to a number of supposedly western agrarian proposals and stereotypes. These included an insistence upon equal rights and an intense hostility toward monopoly, chartered corporations, banks, and the "money power." He thus portrayed Populism as the radical synthesis of an ideological intercourse between city and country, East and West, which placed great emphasis upon natural rights and social compact. In the same spirit, Donald Edgar Walters, "The Period of the Populist Party," in Royce D. Delmatier, Clarence F. McIntosh, and Earl G. Waters, eds., *The Rumble of California Politics* (New York: Wiley, 1970), revealed the strong connection between Bellamy nationalism and Populism on the West Coast. Bellamy was a native of Boston. Walters's chapter was derived from his Ph.D. dissertation, "Populism in California, 1889–1900" (University of California, Berkeley, 1952).

While the United States and the Soviet Union were allies during World War II, an interpretation of Populism emerged from the pen of American Communist party ideologist Anna Rochester. *The Populist Movement in the United States: The Growth and Decline of the People's Party—A Social and Economic Interpretation* (New York: International Publishers, 1943) generally follows Hicks's description of events but places Populism in a Leninist framework. Rochester sees the roots of certain New Deal farm programs in Populism. She also concludes that the third party failed because Populists tried to better the conditions of farmers without any perspective toward changing the system. They were reformers, she claimed, but not radicals.

While the turbulent 1930s reminded scholars of the essential divisions in America's past, World War II and the 1950s did just the opposite. With Pearl Harbor, Americans pulled together as never before. Postwar troubles with the Soviet Union kept this syndrome alive in the following decade. In times that seemed to require national unity, American scholars discovered an essential continuity in the American past. Perceived foreign threats, however, were not the only factors directing American scholarship. World War II caused the greatest redistribution of wealth in American history. Not only did full employment and massive government spending (and windfall profits taxes to keep the rich from getting too much richer) finally create a truly middle-class nation, but the spread of commerce and industry to the South and the West created a more homogeneous and integrated nation. Like Tocqueville's portrait of America, consensus or revisionist historians found America adventurous in manner but conservative in substance.

Consensus historians reduced the importance of traditional turning points in American history and emphasized the basic stability of American institutions. They either denied or trivialized as unnecessary the previous conflicts in American history. The relatively new use of psychoanalysis in social science, a practice that had its roots in wartime concerns about Adolf Hitler's behavior, helped explain conflict as irrational. Scholars of all political outlooks came to see Populism as less a realistic response to actual grievances than an irrational reaction of farmers to their declining social position in the late nineteenth century.

By far the best and most influential consensus interpretation of Populism can be found in Richard Hofstadter, *The Age of Reform: From Bryan to F. D. R.* (New York: Alfred A. Knopf, 1955). In the consensus spirit of homogenizing the American past, Hofstadter included all silverites in his definition of Populists. A liberal disenchanted with America's weak efforts at social reconstruction, Hofstadter attributed this failure to the lack of a truly radical American past. Earlier, in "Parrington and the Jeffersonian Tradition," *Journal of the History of Ideas* 2, no. 4 (October, 1941): 391–400, Hofstadter had found agrarian opposition to industrial capitalism "theoretically impotent." Populists, he contended, were not forward-looking reformers but nostalgic, backward-looking petty capitalists. Instead of pushing for real reform, he suggested, Populists exhibited provincialism, a conspiracy syndrome, and a penchant for scapegoatism that manifested itself in nativism, anti-Semitism, anti-intellectualism, and Anglophobia. According to Hofstadter, Populists were harassed country businessmen, insecure about their declining status in an industrializing America.

Revisionists' concerns about the Populists' allegedly retrograde tendencies articulated the concerns of their era. With the McCarthy scare, less careful scholars (usually not historians) produced even more severe analyses of the agrarian movement. Perhaps the most bizarre was Victor Ferkiss, "Populist Influences on American Fascism," *Western Political Quarterly* 10, no. 2 (June, 1957): 350–57. Ferkiss provided a highly questionable definition of fascism that included middle-class economic programs, Anglophobia, anti-Semitism, plebiscitary democracy, and a commitment to conspiracy theories, especially about the "money power." Ferkiss's loose application of this definition to Populism suffered from its equal applicability to previous American egalitarian figures, such as Jefferson and Jackson.

Allan Bogue, *Money At Interest: The Farm Mortgage on the Middle Border* (Lincoln: University of Nebraska Press, 1955), was one of the few well-researched efforts of the revisionist school. Bogue examined the land-credit system through sample mortgage companies and sample townships and found that interest rates were not as high as Progressive historians had assumed. He concluded that lenders did not seek to capitalize on farmer distress. The western credit situation, he claimed, had been perverted by the "hysteria of the Populist era," which was the product of misunderstanding rather than of avarice. Without the underpinning of legitimate economic grievances, the Populist Revolt appeared to be a manifestation of mass irrationality. Bogue, however, examined only the land mortgage question.

The revisionist analysis of Populism did not remain unchallenged for long. C. Vann Woodward, "The Populist and the Intellectual," *American Scholar* 28, no. 1 (Winter, 1959): 55–72, presented most of the criticisms future scholars would level against the consensus school. While acknowledging that previous historians had been too uncritical, Woodward provided evidence that the Populists' opponents were usually worse offenders and asked whether it was fair to emphasize traits not primarily associated with the movement and ignore the more egregious failings of their adversaries.

Because Hofstadter's analysis was more of a think piece than a well-researched interpretation of Populism, shooting holes in *The Age of Reform* launched several scholarly careers. Walter T. K. Nugent studied Populist attitudes in Kansas and absolved third-party advocates of irrationality in *The Tolerant Populists: Kansas Populism and Nativism* (Chicago: University of Chicago Press, 1963). Nugent found a pragmatic farmers' movement in search of rational solutions to agrarian depression. Populists emphasized their most popular issue, monetary reform. To secure their program, he contended, third-party activists were purposefully tolerant on religion and nationality in an effort to widen their appeal. He also absolved them of being anti-industry and antiurban. Instead, they opposed only the abuses that accompanied these developments.

Norman Pollack went further than Nugent, and in studying the rhetoric of western Populism, he found a coherent and radical critique of industrializing America, similar to Marxism and valid for contemporary America, in *The Populist Response to Industrial America* (New York: W. W. Norton & Co., 1962). Pollack saw Populists as social levelers seeking to reverse the widening gap between haves and have-nots, which had emerged in the late nineteenth century. He found the movement forward-looking, accepting of industrialization, and class-oriented.

While anticonsensus efforts brought considerable enlightenment to the study of the agrarian crusade in the decade after Hofstadter's *Age of Reform* appeared, the light seemed to turn to heat in the mid-1960s. This mirrored the growing convulsions in American society. In "Fear of Man: Populism, Authoritarianism and the Historian," *Agricultural History* 39, no. 2 (April, 1965): 59–67, Norman Pollack attributed the denigration of Populism to elitist historians' fear of the masses, particularly in light of the careers of Hitler and Stalin. Irwin Unger denied Pollack's charges in "Critique of Norman Pollack's 'Fear of Man,'" *Agricultural History* 39, no. 2 (April, 1965): 59–67, and emphasized Hofstadter's theme of Populists being naïve, simplistic, and essentially retrograde. H. Wayne Morgan, "Populism and the Decline of Agriculture," in H. Wayne Morgan, ed., *The Gilded Age* (Syracuse, N. Y.: Syracuse University Press, 1970), provided an economic explanation of Populism that conceded some of the negative characteristics consensus revisionists had found.

In the same edition of *Agricultural History* that contained Pollack's and Unger's tirades, J. Rogers Hollingsworth declared their debate a dead end until a better social history of the 1890s determined exactly who constituted the average Populist in "Commentary, Populism: The Problem of Rhetoric and Reality," *Agricultural History* 39, no. 2 (April, 1965): 81–85. Hollingsworth alluded to a newly developing field of research that historians Samuel P. Hays, Lee Benson, and Allan Bogue were pioneering. In "New Possibilities for American Political History: The Social Analysis of Political Life," in Samuel P. Hays, *American Political History as Social Analysis* (Knoxville: University of Tennessee Press, 1980), originally presented at the 1964 American Historical Association convention, Hays criticized the narrative approach to writing history for its preoccupation with prominent individuals, dramatic episodes, and ideological combat over national issues. He particularly denounced the Progressive historians' tendency to focus upon ritual clashes between the "people" and the "interests." Instead of focusing upon the rhetoric of leaders, Hays contended, historians should delve into structures, systems, and local relations to discover the social context in which large masses of people actually lived. To do this, election returns, legislative roll-call votes, census materials, and estate inventories became powerful tools for reconstructing the social bases of political behavior. Historical inquiry entered the age of the computer. Social-science historians began creating research designs that owed their genesis to the statistical techniques of sociology and political science. They then led their readers through the details of their assumptions and methods as they presented their findings.

In "Some Parameters of Populism," *Agricultural History* 40, no. 4 (October, 1966): 255–70, Walter T. K. Nugent examined mortgage data on county-level political leaders in central Kansas (a hotbed of Populism) and concluded that third-party leaders were less speculative than their mainstream party counterparts, a conclusion that matched Populist rhetoric. O. Gene Clanton, in *Kansas Populism: Men and Ideas* (Lawrence: University of Kansas Press, 1969), also studied the Kansas third-party leaders in detail and identified them as rural, middle-class, and highly moralistic politically. They were ethical humanists who rejected social Darwinism, viewed the gospel of wealth as a perversion of Christianity, and attacked capitalism for its selfishness. Clanton saw Populism as a constructive response to industrialization.

Stanley B. Parsons, *The Populist Context: Rural Versus Urban Power on a Great*

Plains Frontier (Westport, Conn.: Greenwood Press, 1973), brought the rural-urban theme that Robert Dykstra had pioneered in "Town-Country Conflict: A Hidden Dimension in American Social History," *Agricultural History* 38, no. 4 (October, 1964): 195–204, into full bloom. Parsons found a continuous tug-of-war between farmers and village elites for economic and political leadership in six representative Nebraska counties. According to Parsons, Populists simply wanted better entry into the existing system. He contended that most of the radical Populist rhetoric came from nationally syndicated "boilerplate" articles and seldom reflected local sentiments. Populists were small-time rural business-men reacting to economic circumstances through interest-group politics.

James Turner, in "Understanding the Populists," *Journal of American History* 67, no. 2 (September, 1980): 354–73, also contended that economic and so-cial isolation from the mainstream was a prime factor in explaining Populism in Texas. Turner chose fifteen "core" Populist counties that had returned People's party pluralities in three of the four state elections between 1892 and 1898 (each had voted Populist in 1892, 1894, and 1896) and compared them with nearby Democratic strongholds. He found that the "core" Populist counties tended toward self-sufficiency and ethnic-religious homogeneity. Populists, Tur-ner contended, were a fringe element, psychologically alienated from the main-stream. In the tradition of Richard Hofstadter, Turner explained that Populists believed themselves to be cruelly hoodwinked by more sophisticated men be-cause they did not understand the complexities of the modern world. The real significance of Texas Populism, however, was that the party grew well beyond these "core" counties in 1894 and 1896.

In *Populism to Progressivism in Alabama* (Princeton, N.J.: Princeton Univer-sity Press, 1969), Sheldon Hackney also finds a correlation between support for the People's party and geographic isolation from towns and villages. A combina-tion of geographic mobility and downward social mobility made supporters pe-ripheral to the dominant society. According to Hackney, Populists were power-rather than reform-oriented; in short, they were outsiders attempting to enter the existing system, which they accepted. Although Hackney admits that Populists were less imbued with the mythology of the New South, he contends that there was no conflict over ideology.

While Hackney deals superficially with the race question (in the form of black Republican leaders' attitudes toward fusion), other scholars have ad-dressed the subject more directly. Jack Abramowitz, in "The Negro In the Popu-list Movement," *Journal of Negro History* 38, no. 3 (July, 1953): 257–89, found C. Vann Woodward's assertion that Populists behaved well on the race question to be correct. Carl N. Degler, *The Other South: Southern Dissenters in the Nine-teenth Century* (New York: Harper & Row, 1974), portrayed Populism as the cul-mination of several earlier southern reform movements, namely antislavery, Unionism, Reconstruction Republicanism, and the Readjuster movement. The Populist Revolt was the last great dissent from the conservative and racist vision that would dominate the South in the first half of the twentieth century. At the opposite end of the spectrum, Robert Saunders, "Southern Populists and the Negro, 1893–1895," *Journal of Negro History* 54, no. 3 (July, 1969): 240–61, claimed that Democrats and Populists were essentially similar in their racial attitudes and political tactics. Gerald H. Gaither holds these earlier assessments to be simplistic. In *Blacks and the Populist Revolt: Ballots and Bigotry in the "New South"* (University: University of Alabama Press, 1977), Gaither found a meaningful biracial Populist coalition based upon self-interest, which degenerated into interracial discord as white Populists realized they would not receive a majority of black votes.

J. Morgan Kousser, *The Shaping of the Southern Politics: Suffrage Restriction and the Establishment of the One-Party South, 1880–1910* (New Haven, Conn.: Yale University Press, 1974), employed sophisticated statistical techniques to find that disfranchisement was a conservative plot designed to suppress white political dissent (Populism) in addition to eliminating blacks from the political system. In contrast, Worth Robert Miller, in "Building a Progressive Coalition in Texas: The Populist-Reform Democrat Rapprochement, 1900–1907," *Journal of Southern History* 52 no. 2 (May, 1986): 163–82, showed that Progressives led disfranchisement in Texas, which was aimed exclusively at blacks and designed to force Populists to deal with them or to have no influence at all. Peter H. Argersinger, "'A Place on the Ballot,' Fusion Politics and Antifusion Laws," *American Historical Review* 85, no. 2 (April, 1980): 287–306, presents the case for legal restrictions helping to destroy the People's party in the West. The nation's first antifusion law appeared in the Oklahoma Territory in 1895. Its repeal in 1897 did nothing to help the third-party effort of 1898 in Oklahoma.

With the cultural awakening of minority groups—blacks, Hispanics, and American Indians—in the 1960s and 1970s, it is not surprising that the sociological approach to late-nineteenth-century American history produced an ethnocultural school of thought. Paul Kleppner, *The Cross of Culture: A Social Analysis of Midwestern Politics, 1850–1900* (New York: Free Press, 1970), and Richard Jensen, *The Winning of the Midwest: Social and Political Conflict, 1888–1896* (Chicago: University of Chicago Press, 1971), contend that cultural factors, particularly ethnicity and religion, were the fundamental source of political conflict in Gilded Age America. In place of the Progressive historians' struggle between the "people" and the "interests," ethnoculturalists posited a system of political affiliation based upon "pietist" and "liturgist" religious categories. This interpretation downplays the importance of economic conflict and dramatic turning points, which are so important to the Progressive historians, while acknowledging the existence of substantial conflict in the American past, which consensus historians deny.

James Edward Wright, *The Politics of Populism: Dissent in Colorado* (New Haven, Conn.: Yale University Press, 1974), and Peter H. Argersinger, *Populism and Politics: William Alfred Peffer and the People's Party* (Lexington: University of Kentucky Press, 1974), both apply social-science techniques to their work. But they both use narrative approaches with structural analyses only as supplements, and they highly qualify the force of the ethnocultural factors in the Populist era. Wright found both ethnic and economic conflict in late-nineteenth-century Colorado. Economic conditions endemic to the state, particularly the problems of silver miners and irrigation farmers, Wright claimed, transformed the consensus politics of the 1880s into the essentially economic conflict of the Populist period.

The conclusions of historians examining Populism in other mountain states generally support Wright's findings. Thomas A. Clinch, *Urban Populism and Free Silver in Montana* (Helena: University of Montana Press, 1970), showed that the third party was almost exclusively a labor movement in Montana. Robert W. Larson, *New Mexico Populism* (Boulder: Colorado Associated University Press, 1974), presents the People's party as a pragmatic, multi-issue movement that originated in conflicts that were essentially indigenous to the territory. Each of these interpretations is consistent with the Progressive interpretation of American Populism.

In a sense, Argersinger's effort is more ambitious than Wright's. He analyzed the career of William A. Peffer within the context of both his Kansas constituency and the larger framework of the national movement. Through statistical analysis, Argersinger concluded that Populism grew out of real economic grievances. As former Republicans dropped out and former Democrats joined, however, he found the energetic reform movement of the early 1890s transformed into an ineffective adjunct of the Democratic party by middecade. Argersinger is more strident in rejecting the ethnocultural assumptions of Kleppner et al. Although he uses quantification in *Populism and Politics* (as do many other non-social-science historians) Argersinger's vociferous defense of Peffer and his ideas clearly divorces him from the consensus and social-science schools of thought.

Robert W. Cherny, *Populism, Progressivism, and the Transformation of Nebraska Politics, 1885–1912* (Lincoln: University of Nebraska Press, 1981), is another study in the tradition of Argersinger and Wright. He found cultural politics most important in the pre-Populist era, when political amateurs dominated and high turnover in office occurred. Cherny contended that partisan choice turned upon economic themes in the first half of the 1890s. During the Populist era, the GOP became the party of prosperity, while the People's party represented the underdog, and Democrats drew primarily from prosperous anti-prohibitionists. He found that Populism cut across ethnic and cultural lines in the heyday of the third-party movement but that it slowly returned to the cleavages of the 1880s as the Populist thrust abated.

While the new social history has caused historians concerned with Populism to broaden their research tools (and, frequently, to narrow the geographic scope of their studies), economic conflict has remained the primary theme in the study of the Populist movement. One problem with the use of social science techniques is the ecological fallacy. This is the use of one level of data to say something about another. For example, a strong correlation between rural poverty and Populist voting does not necessarily mean that any individual poor farmer was a Populist, or vice versa. Analyses of aggregates only reveal tendencies. One study of Populism, however, does bridge this problem to deal with individuals. John Dibbern, "Who Were the Populists?: A Study of Grass-Roots Alliancemen in Dakota," *Agricultural History* 54, no. 4 (October, 1982): 677–91, employed Farmers' Alliance roll books and census manuscripts to provide an in-depth look at those attracted to alliance activism and, by implication, to

Populism. He concluded that Alliancemen and non-Alliancemen had so much in common that conversion to Populism was largely a matter of intellectual choice. Populism, however, did have more appeal to certain types of men. Rather than attracting the most economically disadvantaged or financially overextended, Dibbern concluded, the alliance was most attractive to underfinanced family farmers threatened with the loss of their property just as they were getting started. This cycle of optimism in securing a homestead and disillusionment at the prospect of losing it, he concluded, explains a large part of the despair and sense of betrayal in Populist rhetoric.

At approximately the same time that the new social history emerged, another group of historians, whose perceptions were drawn largely from the civil-rights, War on Poverty, and anti–Vietnam War movements of the 1960s, emerged in response to the intrinsically conservative message of the consensus historians. Both of the newer groups contend that they are writing social history, or history "from the bottom up." To the behavioralists' contention that their rigorously tested hypotheses transcend the subjective limitations of humanism to offer an unbiased analysis, radical historians reply that numeric analysis may be useful for description but not for explaining why historical phenomena occur. Some factors important to historical analysis simply cannot be quantified. Scholars of this persuasion look to popular mentalities, folk rituals, and class consciousness for insights into behavior.

Radical, or New Left, historians, as they are also called, contend that social-science historians assume as the basis for their numerical comparison that people in the past acted upon assumptions equivalent to those dominating today's world. New Left scholars complain that this approach affirms the values of contemporary America, placing the past at the service of a complacent and elitist definition of society, just as consensus historians did in the 1950s. According to the consensus school, radicalism was un-American. New Left historians, therefore, have taken up the challenge of discovering a truly radical American past, which would legitimize their complaints about how America utilized its tremendous resources. Radical historians accept neither the institutions emanating from American industrialization nor the premises of the liberal state. Instead they seek to criticize the contemporary system through comparison with past arrangements in American society. In essence, they seek to reverse the deterministic consensus trend toward relegating losers in the past to historical oblivion.

Norman Pollack's *Populist Response to Industrial America* was an early effort in the New Left vein. Michael Rogin, *McCarthy and the Intellectuals: The Radical Specter* (Cambridge, Mass.: MIT Press, 1967), examined the social roots of McCarthyism, which some consensus scholars claimed were Populistic, and found them to be conservative and elitist. The People's party, Rogin contended, was a forward-looking, anticapitalist (but not anti-industrial) mass movement, essentially an American equivalent of Marxism.

To understand the meaning of past societies, the New Left claims, the social context of historical phenomena must be considered in its entirety. Robert Mc-Math, in *Populist Vanguard: A History of the Southern Farmers' Alliance* (Chapel

Hill: University of North Carolina Press, 1975), used social-science concepts of organization and social movements (as opposed to numeric analysis) to discover the dynamics involved in the proto-Populist Southern Farmers' Alliance. The alliance, McMath showed, grew best in unsettled, frontierlike conditions, which encouraged new forms of social organization. The alliance's ability to socialize its adherents made it analogous to a church, providing explanations for actions and direction to people experiencing the tensions of social and economic instability. This helped explain the development of the Populists' collective mentality and the near-religious fervor of the third-party movement.

James Youngsdale, *Populism: A Psychohistorical Perspective* (Port Washington, N.Y.: Kennikat Press, 1975), stated that Populism formed around marginal groups when large-scale industry threatened petty capitalism. He used Adlerian psychology to rescue the Populists from Hofstadter's Freudianism. Youngsdale's definition of Populism in terms that include non-People's party elements, such as Robert La Follette and the Minnesota Farmer-Labor party, however, is of questionable value. While he does not fall into Hofstadter's mistake of lumping all free-silverites with Populism, he does overstate the case for Bryanism being the antithesis of Populism.

The most ambitious product of New Left scholarship on Populism is Lawrence Goodwyn, *Democratic Promise: The Populist Moment in America* (New York: Oxford University Press, 1976). The strong connection between the Progressive historians and the New Left can be found in Goodwyn's tribute to C. Vann Woodward in the acknowledgment to the abridged edition, *The Populist Moment: A Short History of the Agrarian Movement in America* (New York: Oxford University Press, 1978). Goodwyn claimed that a mass-based "movement culture" emerged from the alliance's unsuccessful experiments in cooperative buying and selling. This failure in economic cooperation drove alliancemen into political action to obtain government cooperatives with the alliance's subtreasury plan. According to Goodwyn, the educational value of the cooperative effort turned the Populist revolt into more than simple interest-group politics. The subtreasury agitation also implied greenbackism, participatory democracy, and replacing capitalism with a cooperative commonwealth. Earlier treatments of Populism, most notably that of Hicks, found the silver issue crucial in making the Democratic party Populistic. Goodwyn defined true Populism as commitment to the subtreasury plan and contended that the collateral, but essentially alien and conservative, "shadow movement" of free silverites subverted the promising radical thrust of Populism. He drew a strong distinction between middle-of-the-roaders, who he claimed were socialized into the greenback-cooperative-subtreasury ideology, and fusionists, whom he associated with the "shadow movement." In his analysis, Goodwyn appended conspiratorial motives to fusionists to the degree that his work is best viewed as a modern-day exposition of the Texas middle-of-the-road position of 1896. Texas Populists opposed the nomination of Bryan at the third party's 1896 national convention and, seeing little difference between him and McKinley, the Republican presidential nominee, arranged an informal fusion with the GOP for state offices, which accorded most Texas Populist votes to McKinley in 1896. Goodwyn's assertion that disillusionment about the lost promise of Populism resulted in the hegemony of the elitist, Progressive alternative is perceptive and valuable.

Stanley B. Parsons, Karen Toombs Parsons, Walter Killilae, and Beverly Borgers, in "The Role of Cooperatives in the Development of the Movement Culture of Populism," *Journal of American History* 69, no. 4 (March, 1983), raised questions about a "movement culture" emerging from the economic setbacks of the alliance's cooperative experiments resulting in Populism, as Goodwyn claimed. They showed that the decline of cooperatives correlated with the rise of the People's party only in Texas. In a parting shot, they noted that the Populists did not need a "movement culture" significantly different from the inherited traditions of the Greenback, antimonopoly, and labor movements of previous decades.

Karel D. Bicha's *Western Populism: Studies in an Ambivalent Conservatism* (Lawrence, Kans.: Coronado Press, 1976) appeared in the same year as Goodwyn's *Democratic Promise* but won a decidedly less enthusiastic audience. Bicha attempted to present the evidence for the highly negative view of Populism, which Hofstadter had neglected in his poorly researched *Age of Reform*. Bicha's constant confusion of goals with tools, his hatchet-job biographies of leaders whom he identified as "untypical," and his illogical explanations of administrative and legislative dynamics betray a virulent animus toward Populism that obscures the few valuable perceptions in his work. With these, the author usually overplays his hand, comparing the third party's concern with keeping government expenses low, for instance, to using a meat axe. More important, Bicha fails to explain why Populists had these orientations. Gene Clanton, in "'Hayseed Socialism' on the Hill: Congressional Populism, 1891–1895," *Western Historical Quarterly* 15, no. 2 (April, 1984): 139–62, provided a useful antidote to Bicha's assertions about Populist conservatism in the national Congress. Hofstadter's treatment of the agrarians' shortcomings remains the superior study.

One theme that appeared in Hofstadter's *Age of Reform* has reemerged with a new vigor in recent years, although perhaps without the same implications. Hofstadter explained Populism in terms of a commitment to an archaic "agrarian myth" rooted in Jeffersonian thought. Although Hofstadter's use of agrarianism had negative connotations, earlier treatments portrayed the Populist debt to Jeffersonian ideas in a much more favorable light. Examples can be found in Vernon Louis Parrington, *Main Currents in American Thought*, Charles M. Wiltse, *The Jeffersonian Tradition in American Democracy* (New York: Hill and Wang, 1935), Chester McArthur Destler, *American Radicalism*, and Robert McCloskey, *American Conservatism in the Age of Enterprise, 1865–1910* (New York: Harper and Row, 1951). Paul W. Glad, *McKinley, Bryan and the People* (Philadelphia and New York: J. B. Lippincott Co., 1964), used the "agrarian myth" and the "myth of the self-made man" to explain the essential conservatism of the 1896 presidential candidates but found Populists more innovative and realistic than their opponents, despite their commitment to the "agrarian myth."

Bernard Bailyn, *The Ideological Origins of the American Revolution* (Cambridge, Mass.: Harvard University Press, 1967), and Gordon Wood, *The Creation of the American Republic, 1776–1787* (New York: W. W. Norton & Co.,

1969), revived and refocused the study of the founding fathers in terms of their commitment to a common republican ideology. Christopher Lasch, in *The Agony of the American Left* (New York: Vintage, 1969), placed Populism firmly within the physiocratic tradition and the democracy of Jefferson, Jackson, and Lincoln. As a Marxist, Lasch considered this orientation both promising and limiting. Gene Clanton, "Populism, Progressivism, and Equality: The Kansas Paradigm," *Agricultural History* 51, no. 3 (June, 1977): 559–81, contrasted the neorepublican, egalitarian premises of Populism with the elitist assumptions of Progressive Republicans. Progressive Democracy, he concluded, was a case of co-opted Populism. Dorothy Ross, "The Liberal Tradition Revisited and the Republican Tradition Addressed," in John Higham and Paul K. Conkin, eds., *New Directions in American Intellectual History* (Baltimore, Md.: Johns Hopkins University Press, 1977), directly addressed the emerging recognition of a dualistic intellectual tradition in the late nineteenth century, in which major portions of the population rejected the growing liberal panaceas of laissez-faire capitalism and social Darwinism.

Bruce Palmer, *"Man Over Money": The Southern Populist Critique of American Capitalism* (Chapel Hill: University of North Carolina Press, 1980), presented an exposition of the Populists' commitment to humanism and their producerist orientation, which conjures up a vision of Jefferson's mythical agrarian republic, where individuals avoid subservience to others through widespread landownership. Palmer contended that Populists believed in a simple market economy that made goods and services, but not labor, legitimate products of trade. Without being able to profit from the labor of others, Populists theorized that the gap between rich and poor would become minimal, and producers would thus avoid economic dependency. Palmer's findings are also valid for western Populism. John L. Thomas, *Alternative America: Henry George, Edward Bellamy, Henry Demarest Lloyd, and the Adversary Tradition* (Cambridge, Mass.: Harvard Unversity Press, 1983), likewise placed the political economy of these writers (Bellamy and Lloyd were Populists) within the neorepublican model. Kenneth M. Roemer, *The Obsolete Necessity: America in Utopian Writings, 1888–1900* (Kent, Ohio: Kent State University Press, 1976), showed the connection between Populism and most of the two hundred or so apocalyptic and utopian novels that appeared in this period.

Stephen Hahn, *The Roots of Southern Populism: Yeoman Farmers and the Transformation of the Georgia Upcountry, 1850–1890* (New York: Oxford University Press, 1983), presented the third-party movement as a typical peasant response to the transformation from self-sufficient yeoman farming to commercial agriculture in two northern Georgia counties. Immediately before the Populist Revolt, the republican sensibilities of yeomen engaged them in a bitter defensive struggle with the commercial world over grazing rights. Hahn claimed that the Southern Farmers' Alliance and the People's party molded this popular ideology into a humane and progressive force. He presents Populism as a revolt of small-holders (and of those recently driven into tenancy) against proletarianization. Third-party spokesmen viewed the workings of the late-nineteeth-century commercial world (indebtedness, foreclosures, tenancy, and middleman profits) as having already placed them in the position of working for others. The third party tailored the republicanism rooted in petty ownership of productive resources to the exigencies of the commercial world and commited yeomen to a producers' commonwealth with cooperative enterprise and public regulation of exchange.

Barton C. Shaw, *The Wool-Hat Boys: Georgia's Populist Party* (Baton Rouge: Louisiana State University Press, 1984), also found Populism in Georgia rooted in an earlier tradition. Shaw noted that Georgia Populism's greatest stronghold, the "terrible tenth" congressional district, had a dissenter tradition that stretched back to the antebellum Whig and Unionist movements. After the Civil War, nominal Democrats (former Whigs) Robert Toombs and Alexander Stephens carried on this anti-Bourbon, antirailroad, and antimonopoly tradition, making independent movements such as the Greenback party unnecessary until the two leaders passed from the scene in the mid-1880s. Shaw likewise pointed to the producer-oriented yeoman values of those involved in the Populist movement.

While acknowledging that the roots of Populism lay in the American past, Hahn and Shaw see the third-party movement as a progressive force in American society. In contrast to the economic explanation of Populism's decline that older Progressive historians advanced, Shaw (Hahn's study ends with 1890) agreed with Goodwyn's New Left interpretation that the Jekyll-and-Hyde nature of fusion, which compromised the moral imperatives of Populism, rather than an overdose of prosperity, brought about the demise of the People's party.

As the one hundredth anniversary of the founding of the People's party draws near, the literature on American Populism seems to be moving toward a recognition of the republican roots of the Populist critique of American capitalism. If, in fact, there were two late-nineteenth-century American minds, one liberal and the other republican, Progressive historians may not have been too far off base in seeing a dualistic society. One of the earliest major disseminators of this point of view, Vernon Louis Parrington, probably knew of what he wrote. He was active in the People's party in the 1890s, according to Richard Hofstadter in *The Progressive Historians: Turner, Beard, Parrington* (New York: Alfred A. Knopf, 1968), 368–70.

Social-science techniques show that Populist strength came largely from hinterland areas, where the newer liberal synthesis, and its accompanying materialization of standards, had not fully penetrated. Economic convulsions, in turn, even gave late-nineteenth-century neorepublican spokesmen a hearing among the disciples of the newer creed. Although these egalitarians based their critique of Gilded Age development upon preindustrial premises, most scholars see their solutions as designed to bring justice and humanity to industrial America, not to turn the clock back to some preindustrial utopia through Luddite retrogression. The validity of the Populist arguments and the efficacy of their proposed solutions can be seen in the Progressive historians' adoption of many aspects of the Populist critique of American society and in the passage into law of many of the third party's demands in the twentieth century.

Index

Abolitionists: 11, 13, 19, 96, 221n.; Vincent family, 18; Sidney Clarke, 81; Lyman Trumbull, 97

Adair, William: 47, 225n.

Agrarianism: 9, 11, 13–14, 26–27, 37, 89–90, 98, 183; *see also* labor theory of value; producerism

Agribusiness: 55, 72, 117, 182, 204, 205

Agricultural College: 46, 47, 48, 51ff., 83, 225n.

Agricultural patterns to voting: 120, 193, 203–206, 229n.; in 1892, 71–75; in 1894, 117; in 1896, 155–56; in 1898, 174; in 1900, 175–76; after 1900, 177; *see also* corn-hog cycle; wheat farmers; ranchers

Aid to destitute: 90, 186; U.S. Congress and, 30; 1890 territorial legislature and, 50

Allan, John S.: 154, 216, 218n.; on Coxey's Army, 92; on Pullman strike, 96; early life of, 99; and leadership of Populist party, 99, 120; as middle-of-the-roader, 99, 102, 141, 243n.; on wealth, 113; and silver issue, 113, 136, 137, 141; and 1894 election, 120, 122; in 1895 legislature, 125ff.; on taxes, 145; on 1896 Democratic territorial convention, 146; as alternate to 1896 Populist national convention, 147; on 1896 election strategy, 148; and 1896 congressional delegate nomination, 151; on 1897 legislature, 160; on oil inspector's office, 161; on Leo Vincent, 171; break with territorial committee, 175; and 1900 congressional delegate nomination, 175, 176; later life of, 177–78, 179; *see also Norman Peoples Voice*

Allen, James K.: 77

Allen, Miles: 236n.

Allen, William V.: 149

Alva, O.T.: 155, 164

Alva Chronicle: 141

Alva Pioneer: 96, 165

Alva Republican: 135, 166

Alva Review: 104, 178; *see also* Hudson, Clark; Towne, A. C.

American Nonconformist: 18–19, 20, 21, 31, 36, 99, 179; *see also* Vincent, Henry; Vincent, James, Sr.; Vincent, Leopold (Leo)

American Railway Union: 95, 177

Anglophobia: 217

Anoil, Robert: 217, 218n.

Antifusion law: *see* elections

Antimonopoly: *see* monopoly

Antimonopoly party (Iowa): 13, 19

Appeal to Reason (Girard, Kans.): 178, 180, 236n.

Aristocracy: 22, 37, 122; *see also* elitism; republicanism; wealth, concentration of

Arthur, Chester A.: 12

Asp, Henry E.: 64, 143

Atcheson, Topeka, and Santa Fe Railroad: *see* Santa Fe Railroad

Bailey, Fred: 100, 110

Banks and banking: 15, 21, 31, 37, 112, 183, 187; reform legislation, 57, 159, 164, 165; and panic of 1893, 84–85, 112; Baring Brothers of London, 86; and deflation, 111; *see also* deflation; free silver; gold standard; money issue

Barnes, Cassius: 115, 167

Beaumont, Ralph: 99, 178, 179, 217; and Knights of Labor, 16–17; early life of,

schemes of Oklahoma's cosmopolitan residents offended the sensibilities of family farmers and attracted them to Populism, a movement committed to leashing the forces that threatened America's classless society.

When the Oklahoma People's party fused with the Democratic party to gain legislative power, many Populists saw the move as a compromise of the party's moral imperatives and withdrew their support. The party fell into disarray, and socialism emerged as the next logical expression of America's egalitarian tradition.

Worth Robert Miller received the Ph.D. degree from the University of Oklahoma in 1984. He is an Assistant Professor of History in Southwest Missouri State University.